D1264630

U.S. NATIONAL
HEALTH POLICY

U.S. NATIONAL HEALTH POLICY

An Analysis of the Federal Role

by
Jennie Jacobs Kronenfeld
and
Marcia Lynn Whicker

PRAEGER SPECIAL STUDIES • PRAEGER SCIENTIFIC

New York • Philadelphia • Eastbourne, UK
Toronto • Hong Kong • Tokyo • Sydney

Library of Congress Cataloging in Publication Data

Kronenfeld, Jennie J.
    U.S. national health policy.

    Bibliography: p.
    Includes index.
    1. Medical policy—United States. 2. Medical care—
United States. 3. Public health—United States.
I. Whicker, Marcia Lynn. II. Title.
RA395.A3K76 1984   362.1'042   84-2169
ISBN 0-03-063609-4 (alk. paper)

Published in 1984 by Praeger Publishers
CBS Educational and Professional Publishing
a Division of CBS Inc.
521 Fifth Avenue, New York, NY 10175 USA

© 1984 by Praeger Publishers

456789 052 9876545321

Printed in the United States of America
on acid-free paper

CONTENTS

LIST OF TABLES

LIST OF FIGURES

LIST OF APPENDIXES

ACKNOWLEDGMENTS

The authors would like to acknowledge the assistance of several people who facilitated the writing of *U.S. National Health Policy: An Analysis of the Federal Role*. Our department chairs, Roger Amidon of Health Administration, School of Public Health, and Charles W. Kegley, Government and International Studies, were generally supportive, providing, at various times, aid in finding materials, graduate student assistance, xeroxing, and funds for chart preparation. University of South Carolina students in the health administration and public administration programs were helpful in responding to ideas included in the book.

In addition, Michael R. Kronenfeld provided much of the initial encouragement to undertake this project and deserves credit for insisting on the purchase of word processors, without which the book would have been less timely. The authors would like to especially acknowledge the help and understanding throughout their careers of their mothers, Bessie Jacobs and Ola Whicker, their now deceased fathers, Harry Jacobs and Gilmer Whicker, and Marcia's brother, Steve Whicker. Special appreciation goes to Jennie's husband and son, Mike and Shaun Kronenfeld, for their understanding and patience about the time constraints and demands involved in writing this book.

INTRODUCTION

Over the last 20 years, health care in the United States has grown into a multi-billion dollar industry. The number of physicians and other health care workers has increased dramatically. Modern hospitals have grown in both size and technological complexity, assuming an aura of modern temples of healing.

During the same time span, public demands on the health care system have increased even more markedly. Citizens now turn to professional healers for maladies ranging from the common cold to systemic terminal cancer. Always solid community citizens in past eras, the prestige of doctors has risen to new heights as they manipulate sophisticated technologies to bring about modern medical miracles. The public has grown to expect a steady diet of dramatic cures and solutions to our health problems.

Yet all is not rosy in the health care picture. Underlying the heightened expectations is a darker side of medical care in the United States. Costs are soaring. Citizens often evidence bewilderment at the complexities of a labyrinthian health care system. Despite an expansion of public and private health insurance, a portion of the population still has no insurance benefits. Citizens grow restless at the all-encompassing authority of the doctors in whose hands they trust their lives. Cynicism and the loss of the close personal relationship between a doctor and patient reminiscent of an earlier era have resulted in the recent growth in malpractice suits.

The role of the federal government has mushroomed over the last 20 years, enhancing the complexity of the U.S. health care system. Federal monies have supported medical research, hospital construction, and the training of physicians, nurses, and allied health professionals. Federal appropriations have extended access to health care services to the elderly and some of the poor. As the complexity of the health care system grew, a system of federally funded institutions for planning grew equivalently.

This book will examine U.S. national health policy, focusing upon the federal role. Chapter 1 will describe salient features of the U.S. health system by identifying three major characteristics: increasing reliance on technology, rising health care costs, and difficulty in evaluating health system outputs. Chapter 2 will provide an overview of three areas of national health policy: research, planning, and services, and the areas of research and planning will be discussed in depth. Chapter 3 will focus on health care services delivery, both how services are organized and delivered, and how they are financed. Chapter 4 will examine how we got where we are, including the role of political actors and the political process in the development of health-related legislative programs. Specific legislative programs and their development will be discussed in Chapter 5.

A general discussion of the characteristics of supply and demand in the health area will be the topic of Chapters 6 and 7. Especially in the 1960s, with the thrust from the war on poverty, much attention has been given to the relationship between poverty and health. But has health care policy in the United States been developed with a sensitivity to income equity and equal access? Chapter 8 will examine this issue. In Chapter 9, we envision a continuum of health care, with different points representing different stages of disease progression and health deterioration. On one end of the continuum are preventive programs aimed at keeping individuals healthy. The continuum continues with programs aimed at acute and long-term care.

Given its recent problems, some people think that the U.S. health care system itself is sick. The final chapter will discuss various proposed alternatives for health policy changes, contrasting liberal and conservative proposals. What role, if any, do each envision for the federal government?

CHAPTER ONE
ASPECTS OF THE
U.S. HEALTH CARE SYSTEM

TECHNOLOGICAL SUPREMACY

The Growth of U.S. Preeminence

Humans with mechanical hearts? Limbs that were totally severed through major accident being reattached to their owners and rejuvenated? Test-tube babies fertilized outside the womb in a laboratory culture and reinserted in a woman for gestation? These events were science fiction at the turn of the century. Today, they are but a few of the many "miracles" modern medicine has achieved for the U.S. health care system, one of the most technologically advanced in the world. When did this advanced national standing in medical technology occur in the United States? Were we always leaders in medical technology and research? In what areas do we lead? What factors and forces have contributed to our medical sophistication and preeminence?

The United States achieved preeminence in medical research and technology comparatively recently. During the nineteenth century, most U.S. medical schools were scientifically weak. They were generally located outside of universities, operated as profit-making trade schools with little emphasis on objective scientific inquiry. Students in these early schools received little clinical experience and sparse training in laboratory techniques. Only in the middle decades of the twentieth century did the United States achieve leadership status in training and technology. European countries

1

clearly dominated until the turn of the twentieth century. Britain, France, and after the U.S. Civil War, Germany provided advanced scientific training in medicine and models for clinical excellence (Stevens 1971; Starr 1982).

The Flexner Report in 1910 pointed out great deficiencies in U.S. medical education, leading to a restructuring of medical school curricula and closing of large numbers of nonuniversity-affiliated U.S. medical schools. By the 1930s, faculties in the best medical schools had become scientific investigators. Concomitant with a shift in medical school curricula was a growth in physician special-ization. Supplementing the traditional general practitioner were specialists in internal medicine, surgery, ophthalmology, and obstet-rics-gynecology, among others. Surgery was one of the fastest growing specialities. In 1931, 10 percent of physicians were in surgical specialties. By 1968, this figure had grown to 30 percent (Stevens 1971; Starr 1982).

Modern surgery requires advanced technological equipment. Heart-lung machines make open-heart surgery possible, leading to a vast growth in cardiac bypass operations, and even heart trans-plants. Surgery with the aid of a microscope has enabled advances in corrective procedures on the eye, as well as treatment of infer-tility. The advance of test-tube babies owes its creation at least in part to microsurgical techniques. Diagnostic equipment ranges in complexity from the simple and pervasive x-ray machine to modern CAT scanners. While x-rays show bones and large organs, CAT scanners enable physicians to locate diseases in the soft tissues of the body, a feat difficult and often painful to achieve with earlier diagnostic techniques (Reiser 1978).

Factors Contributing to U.S. Preeminence

Several factors have contributed to the recent preeminence of U.S. medicine. U.S. medicine has enjoyed a supportive medical infra-structure. Corporate laboratories in drugs and medical equipment companies have conducted medically-related research. Universities have undertaken medical research, generally funded by federal government and corporate contributions. Nor has all the university-based research occurred in medical schools. Since the launching of Sputnik in 1957 created a fear that the United States was falling behind in scientific inquiry, government-sponsored research in chemical, biological, and engineering fields have directly and indirectly facilitated the growth of medical technology and knowledge.

High, absolute funding levels for medical research and technology development in the United States have contributed to U.S. stature. Not only is the United States one of the largest modern industrialized countries, contributing to its ability to commit funding for medical development, but in the post-World War II period, it has been relatively prosperous as well.

Americans have long been enamored with gadgetry and technological innovations. The United States was settled by citizens who were pragmatic and often anti-intellectual, placing a value on tools and equipment over abstract knowledge. From colonial to modern times, the farmers and mechanics who were the original pioneers of the United States became known for their inventiveness. As the United States entered the industrial and electronic age, famous though not formally educated inventors such as Thomas Edison, Henry Ford, and Samuel Morse became folk heroes. This tradition, though somewhat muted, has persisted. Technological innovation has been revered as a goal worthy in its own right. Nor has the field of medicine been immune to the United States' love affair with technology, a factor contributing significantly to the development of the vast array of sophisticated equipment now available for medical purposes.

The decentralization of U.S. research and development has facilitated innovation and technological advancement in all areas, including health and medicine. With decentralization of research and development functions to a variety of institutions, ranging from universities to corporations to government agencies, ideas for technological advances were tested without reliance upon central approval. Competition among various centers enhanced the motivation to innovate. In the 1980s, decentralization will continue to be advantageous only to the extent that institutions garner adequate capital resources to enable research to progress.

Furthermore, inelastic demand for health services has contributed to a public willingness to give a carte blanche to purveyors of medical technology. Inelastic demand implies that normal constraints of supply and demand are inoperative. Normally, the quantity demanded of a service is at least partially contingent on price, so that an increase in price will result in a reduced quantity demanded. Certain products and services, including medical care, deviate from those normal marketplace constraints. Medical care is so crucial to life, especially when a patient has a life-threatening illness, that costs become unimportant compared to the primary goal of preserving life and restoring health.

RISING COSTS

U.S. National Health Expenditures

Advanced medical technologies are not cheap. U.S. attainment of preeminence in health care has been maintained at the cost of a concomitant increase in resources devoted to those activities. Despite a relatively healthy and growing economy, health expenditures have been consuming an ever greater proportion of that total economy. In 1950, national health expenditures totaled $12.7 billion, 4.4 percent of Gross National Product (GNP). By 1975, $132.7 billion were being spent on health care nationwide, constituting 8.6 percent of GNP. The escalation in health care expenditures continued to a whopping 9.4 percent of GNP, $247.2 billion in 1980 and up to 10.6 percent in 1982. In an era of economic growth, Americans have spent an ever-larger share on health and medicine (U.S. Census Bureau 1982).

The biggest jump in health expenditures when viewed as a percentage of the total economy occurred in the late 1960s. Health expenditures as a percent of GNP stabilized between 1950 and 1955 at 4.4 percent. In the five-year period between 1955 and 1960, a .9 percent increase pushed expenditures to 5.3 percent of GNP. A subsequent increase of .7 percent in the next five-year span resulted in 6.0 percent of GNP devoted to health. While previous increments across any five-year span constituted less than 1 percent of GNP, a far more dramatic increase in health care costs occurred between 1965 and 1970 when health expenditures escalated a substantial 1.5 percent of GNP, causing total national health expenditures to jump from 6.0 percent to 7.5 percent. Subsequent to this dramatic jump in health care costs, increments in health expenditures as a percentage of GNP returned to slightly smaller levels. Between 1970 and 1975, a 1.1 percent increase pushed the share of health expenditures to 8.6 percent. Between 1975 and

FIGURE 1-1
NATIONAL HEALTH EXPENDITURES: 1960 to 1980

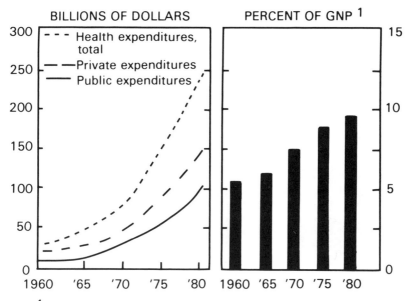

BILLIONS OF DOLLARS   PERCENT OF GNP [1]

– – – Health expenditures, total
— —Private expenditures
—— Public expenditures

[1] Gross national product.
Source: U.S. Bureau of Census, Statistical Abstract

1980, an even smaller increment of .8 percent resulted in 9.4 percent of GNP going to health.

Why did a dramatic increase in health costs occur between 1965 and 1970? The major explanation was the enactment in 1965 of the major federal programs, Medicare and Medicaid. Medicare, operating similarly to the overall Social Security system, provides federally sponsored health insurance to persons 65 years of age and older. It also provides insurance to people with disabilities or the chronic disorder of end-stage renal disease (kidney failure). Medicaid operates as part of the patchwork blanket of state and federal welfare programs. Under Medicaid, federal and state governments

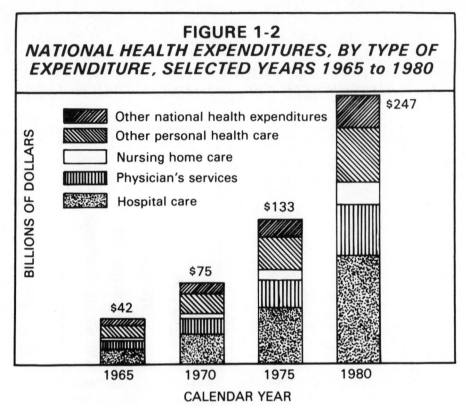

FIGURE 1-2
NATIONAL HEALTH EXPENDITURES, BY TYPE OF EXPENDITURE, SELECTED YEARS 1965 to 1980

Other national health expenditures
Other personal health care
Nursing home care
Physician's services
Hospital care

BILLIONS OF DOLLARS

$247

$133

$75

$42

1965   1970   1975   1980

CALENDAR YEAR

Source: Health Care Financing Review, September 1981

jointly pay for hospital, physician, and additional services for eligible indigent recipients.

National data demonstrate the increased role of public funds during this period. In 1950, 22 percent ($2.8 billion) of national health expenditures were derived from public sources. Public sector financing of health as a percentage of national health expenditures actually decreased slightly during the 1950s. In 1960, only 20.8 percent ($5.6 billion) of national health expenditures were derived from public sources. While the 1950s were an era of great expansion in private health insurance coverage for most Americans, public sector health expenditures did not grow equivalently. There was little change in the proportion of public-private health funding between 1960 and 1965. In 1965, 21 percent ($8.8 billion) of national health expenditures were public sector.

Due to the implementation of the Medicare and Medicaid programs in the late 1960s, 33.5 percent ($25 billion) were derived from public sources by 1970. The introduction of these and other federal programs resulted in the public sector share of total health costs increasing over 12 percent in just five years. The trend of an increased public sector share of total health costs has continued into the 1970s. By 1980, 39.2 percent ($96.9 billion) of health costs were public sector funds. A whopping trillion dollars of tax money in that year was spent on health.

Factors Affecting Rising Costs

Why have national health expenditures in the United States been rising so dramatically? Four explanations are reasonable. A general rise in inflation rates throughout the U.S. economy contributed to a price increase for most products and services, including medical care. Between 1975 and 1981, the overall consumer price index (CPI) increased at an annual rate of 9.1 percent. Health expenditures also increased markedly with only part of the rise attributable to general inflation. The medical care price index increased at an annual rate of 9.9 percent between 1975 and 1981, exceeding the annual increases in overall prices. Much but not all of rising health care costs was attributed to general inflation (U.S. Census Bureau 1982).

A more detailed analysis of trend data point to 1978 as a breakpoint in the relationship between the growth of the CPI and the medical care price index. With few exceptions, prior to 1978 the growth in medical costs was greater than the growth in general prices. The two indexes converged in 1978. In the period between 1978 and 1981, medical care prices grew at a lesser rate than general prices. Part of the post-1978 decline in medical care price increases relative to general price increases was caused by a very high general inflation rate, rather than a decline in medical care price inflation (Health Care Financing Administration 1982).

Why were national health expenditures consuming an ever-larger share of the total economy during the 1978 to 1981 period when medical care prices were not growing faster than the CPI? This growth exceeded that explained by population growth as well as price growth and is attributable to an increase in the rate of uses of services per capita, and in the intensity of services provided (Gibson and Waldo 1981).

Three additional factors beyond inflation have contributed to increased per capita use of health services and a more intense individual usage of available health care. Favorable attitudes toward the increased usage of sophisticated and costly medical technology exists among all parties in the medical system — patients, hospitals, and physicians.

Under the traditional medical financing and reimbursement structure employed in most of the United States, some economic incentives encouraged hospitals to buy and use new and more technologically advanced equipment. An expensive piece of medical equipment represented a high fixed cost to the purchasing hospital or institution. Increasing the number of patients receiving treatment on expensive equipment spread the fixed costs over a larger number of service units (patients).

Although hospitals and institutions have made decisions about buying advanced equipment, doctors have made decisions about the use of equipment for an individual patient. Physicians have absorbed the pervasive cultural belief that more technology is better. Fear of malpractice suits also influences physicians to use more technology. A confluence of general citizen, patient, physician, and hospital orientations has contributed to increased intensity of U.S. medical care and rising national health care costs.

Second, the nature of disease and morbidity among Americans has gradually changed. At the beginning of the twentieth century, infectious diseases were predominant and their treatment was a short-term phenomenon. Medical science produced both advances in cures and vaccinations to prevent major infectious diseases. Subsequently, chronic illnesses such as heart disease, kidney disease, and cancer superseded infectious diseases as leading causes of death.

Compared to curing disease, medical treatment of chronic diseases has involved controlling the spread of the disease and further deterioration of the patient. Often persons suffering chronic diseases have undergone treatment for the remainder of their lives. Both the long-term duration and high capital intensiveness of treatment of chronic disease contribute to escalating medical costs. These technologies are known as "half-way" for their inability to affect a cure and their focus upon disease control and abatement (Fuchs 1974).

An example of half-way technology involves treatment of kidney failure. A patient with end-stage renal disease has kidneys incapable of maintaining a volume, composition, and distribution of body fluids necessary for healthy life. These patients can be treated through kidney transplant, but donors are often unavailable and many patients cannot be candidates for transplants due to advanced age or coexistence of other diseases. A second and more widely used treatment of end-stage renal disease is kidney dialysis, which circulates the patient's blood through an artificial kidney outside the body, removing toxic wastes and excess fluids. Usually, a patient is hooked to the machine for several hours at a time, frequently three times a week. The cost per patient of dialysis treatment was about $12,000 in 1979 (Lowrie and Hampers 1981). Since 1973, when patients with this disease became eligible for Medicare coverage, 80 percent of the cost of kidney dialysis has been paid by the federal government. In December of 1980, there were 63,000 kidney patients receiving Medicare payments. The annual cost of this treatment to the federal government was $1.5 billion (Kutner 1982).

Another example of chronic disease at the stage of costly half-way medical technology is heart disease. Although medical knowledge about ways to prevent heart disease and preventive efforts have increased greatly, many people who are still living developed heart disease before knowledge about prevention was as developed or as widely disseminated as today. Improvements in prevention have only partially eliminated the need for more expensive treatments and therapies such as the aortocoronary-bypass operation, a procedure generally used for patients with angina pain and frequently performed after myocardial infarctions (heart attacks). The costs of bypass surgery were estimated to be between $10,000 and $20,000 per patient in the mid- to late 1970s, depending upon the severity of the patient's condition and the geographic location of the operation (Mundth and Austin 1975; Kronenfeld et al. 1979). In the early 1980s, approximately 100,000 heart-bypass operations were performed in the United States.

If half-way medical technologies are so costly, why are they so widely used? The most common answer is that half-way technologies are the state of the medical art in chronic disease treatment. Even when an alternative technology which more closely approximates a cure is technically possible, as in the case of kidney transplants, appropriate donors may not be available in sufficient numbers to make it a feasible alternative. Many alternative treatments are only suitable for patients whose general health, aside from the specific chronic disease, is good. The value of improvements in the patient's condition relative to the high cost of half-way medical technologies used to treat chronic illnesses varies by viewpoint. Even marginal improvements for high costs are often valued by severely ill patients, whereas healthy people and less severely ill patients may regard those same procedures as too expensive.

A third additional factor contributing to escalating health care costs and the rise in the percent of national income spent on health is increased availability of health insurance. The number of Americans protected by private health insurance or by government programs had increased from only 7 percent of the population in 1940 to almost 90 percent by 1980. By 1976, almost 13 percent had public coverage for health care services. Another 14 percent had combined public and private coverage, and 63 percent had private health insurance (U.S. Census Bureau 1982). Unlike many other Western industrialized countries, U.S. health care coverage is not yet universal, although the large expansion in the numbers of people covered by some type of insurance has made care more accessible to most population segments. People with health care coverage are more likely to use health care services, contributing to increased total expenditures.

Before widespread health care coverage, physicians and hospitals sometimes provided free medical care to patients unable to pay from personal resources. This practice has diminished. Free medical services previously excluded from health care cost data are now included as expenditures of health insurance companies and government programs, contributing to the visible increase in total national health expenditures.

Not only do more people have health insurance, but the average health insurance coverage is more extensive. In earlier decades, most health insurance policies covered only hospital and surgical expenses. While still the most common type of coverage, many people now have some protection for ambulatory care, psychiatric care, medications and drugs, and home health care services. Some policies also cover dental services, although less than a third of the population under 65 had coverage for dental care in 1979.

Health care expenditures have risen in recent years from these four factors. General inflation, especially prior to 1978, resulted in rising costs of most products and services, including medical care. Supportive attitudes toward technological solutions have led to the development and dissemination of expensive capital-intensive medical equipment. The leading causes of morbidity and mortality have changed from infectious to chronic disorders. Treatment patterns are characterized by expensive half-way medical technologies. Health care coverage has increased dramatically both in numbers of people covered and comprehensiveness. Each of these factors has escalated national health expenditures to a larger share of GNP. No one knows when this escalation will end.

THE EVALUATION CONUNDRUM

A third feature of the health care system in the United States concerns the measurement of the system output. All systems have inputs and outputs. In economic systems, inputs include labor, materials, and supplies. Outputs are the end products and services generated by the productive process. Ideally, the costs of both inputs and outputs can be established in monetary terms to facilitate comparisons and to compute efficiency. Efficient systems either minimize input costs for a given amount of output, or maximize outputs for a given amount of inputs.

The health care system in the United States is not easily amenable to evaluation in the above sense. Inputs for the health care system can be readily ascertained and measured. For example, health system inputs include the total number of physicians, other health care workers, hospitals, other health care institutions, and medical equipment, supplies, and drugs. For each of these inputs, monetary values can usually be determined, so that total input costs for the system, as well as costs for any subcategory of inputs can be calculated.

Health care system outputs, however, present an evaluation conundrum, making overall assessment of the system difficult and, at times, impossible. While there is some agreement among policy analysts examining the U.S. health care system on the appropriate way to measure system inputs, no consensus exists about an appropriate output measure. No single measure has been developed for health system output, reflecting the fact that analysts, policy makers, and health providers do not hold a single view on what the health care system should achieve.

One important output measure is the accessibility of services. Data are more readily available on this facet of health system output than on other equally important but less measurable facets. There are two different types of accessibility – physical or geographic, and financial. Ways to measure geographic accessibility include the computation of provider to population ratios and patient average travel time. Frequently employed measures of financial accessibility include the percentage of people covered by private medical insurance or some type of government health program, and the details of the degree of comprehensiveness of that coverage.

The next level of output measures are data on the actual usage of available services, including statistics on inpatient hospital utilization, physician utilization, and dental visits. Data on the usage of institutional-based services (for example, inpatient and outpatient hospital utilization) are more readily available than noninstitutional-based services since most hospitals routinely collect such information for reporting and billing. Most other types of utilization data require special surveys, either of patients or of special care settings, such as physician offices. The central collection of nonhospital-based utilization data that does occur is generally organized by the federal National Center for Health Statistics.

Complicating the measurement of health system outputs is a lack of consensus about a definition of health. A broader output of the health system than merely measuring geographic and financial accessibility would be the extent to which the overall health of the population and quality of life is improved by the system. Measuring improvements in the health status of the general population requires some agreement about what constitutes health. At least two definitions of health have been employed by health system analysts and observers.

A traditional way to define health is the absence of disease or illness. The major criticism of this negative definition of health is its limited nature, with almost exclusive focus on physical health. The definition gives little attention to mental health and ignores social health. To meet these criticisms, in the 1950s the World Health Organization (WHO) adopted a broadened definition of health, including not only the negative aspects of absence of disease, but also a stress on nonphysical aspects of the quality of life. The WHO definition of health was a tripartite conceptualization of an individual's total ability to function in his or her relevant environment, including physical, mental, and social dimensions (World Health Organization 1958).

Conceptualizing and defining health continues to plague health analysts and researchers. Some researchers have focused on the concept of functional limitations and have broken this dimension of health into categories such as physical activities, self-care activities, social role activities, and mobility (Haber 1966; Reynolds et al. 1974; Patrick et al. 1973). A different way of conceptualizing health is Schlenger's two-dimensional model. One dimension is the traditional absence of disease; the second emphasizes the affective or feeling aspect of health. A person with terminal cancer has very poor health on the absence of disease dimension; however, some cancer patients could rank high on the affective dimension by having accepted the reality of their situation and having dealt positively with it (Schlenger 1976).

Even if health analysts and providers could agree on how to define health, the data collection required under many of these definitions would be difficult if not impossible. Many studies have tried to develop readily employable measurement instruments where health data could be easily obtained. Most of these attempts used population and community surveys to avoid sole reliance on physician-collected data. Yet, agreement on a particular definition of health has rarely produced subsequent agreement on which survey instrument best implements that definition (Patrick et al. 1973; Renne 1974; Reynolds et al. 1974; Williams et al. 1976).

In addition to definition and measurement difficulties, establishing causal linkages between the activities and services of the U.S. health system and general population health has proved elusive (McKinley and McKinley 1977; McKeown 1979). Health system analysts have not been able to definitively demonstrate that overall improvements in health are the direct result of health services. The greater the specificity of the analysis, the more analysts have been able to show the effectiveness of health and medical services. For instance, data on polio incidence (number of new cases) clearly show the major impact of the introduction of Salk polio vaccine in the early 1950s. New drugs and treatments for tuberculosis have resulted in previously hospitalized TB patients continuing to work and live normally. Beyond examining specific diseases and effectiveness of their respective treatments, the difficulty of assessing the impact of the health system on overall citizen health and well-being remains.

Many factors other than medical care services play a role in how well people feel and live. Sorting out the relative impacts of these other factors versus that of the health care system on overall health has proved difficult. Levels of nutrition, sanitation, and other related environmental factors, as well as social factors such as income and housing all affect health, often in major ways. Inadequate nutrition, poor sanitation, and poverty significantly contribute to the lowered health status of the populations of Third World countries. While these conditions are less prevalent in the better fed, more sanitary, and relatively wealthier United States, variability within the United States causes these factors to impact on overall health. During the Great Depression of the 1930s and prior to the implementation of more extensive government programs such as food stamps, poorer regions of the United States, especially the South, experienced higher incidences of nutrition-related diseases, lowering overall health.

SUMMARY

Not only do the three salient features of U.S. health care — technological supremacy, rising costs, and the conundrum of evaluation — affect the overall system, they also interact with each other and permeate specific sectors within the system. Technology and evaluation difficulties have accentuated the trend of rising national health expenditures. The purchase of capital-intensive medical technology has directly fueled rising health care costs. An inability to assess when and if different components of the health system are effective makes citizens willing to allow ever-larger shares of the national economy to be spent on health-related activities. Each of these three factors has affected the health care system sectors of research, planning, and services. Exactly how and in which ways is what will be discussed next.

CHAPTER TWO
AREAS OF NATIONAL HEALTH POLICY: RESEARCH AND PLANNING

National health policy mirrors the structure of the health care system in the United States. The system itself can be divided into the three areas of research, planning, and services. To a greater or lesser extent, national health care policies have been developed in each of these areas. Health research, not always visible to the average consumer of health care services, has received considerable congressional attention. Health research is broad in scope, including inquiry into ways to control and cure major killers such as heart disease, stroke, and cancer. Other research foci include the examination of new technology and new drugs to combat diseases, as well as health services research to ascertain optimal or at least better ways to organize the health care delivery system. An additional facet explores the role of environmental factors such as air pollution, water pollution, or specific toxic substances on health.

Sometimes the term "planning" has been used narrowly to imply special federally mandated area planning agencies, such as Health Systems Agencies (HSAs). We will use the term planning here more broadly to encompass policy formulation — ascertaining system goals, considering alternative approaches to goal achievement, and allocating resources in a rational way to achieve desired policy objectives. Planning also includes regulatory procedures to facilitate the implementation of resource allocation decisions, and evaluation to assess whether those decisions have been effective and should be continued. In addition to specially defined planning agencies at federal, state, and local levels, regulation and control activities occur in state and local health departments, in agencies dealing with environmental issues, and in some licensing bureaus.

Health care services include all situations in which consumers visit a health care provider, such as physicians, dentists, podiatrists, chiropractors, and optometrists. Surgery, both for inpatients and outpatients; laboratory tests, such as Pap smears to detect cervical cancer; x-rays to determine the presence of illnesses or injuries ranging from tuberculosis to broken bones; and stress tests to ascertain the overall fitness of the cardiovascular system are further examples of common health services. An army of institutions ranging from the average physician's office to new free-standing emergency care centers, to traditional acute care hospitals, and to nursing homes provide health services for the consumer.

Each area of national health policy will now be discussed in greater detail. The areas of research and planning are covered in this chapter. Each of these areas is important, but has received less national attention and funding than the area of health services. Health care services will be covered in Chapter 3.

HEALTH RESEARCH

The reality of health research in the United States is that it is essentially a post-World War II phenomenon. In 1897 a Hygienic Laboratory which focused on microbiology research was created as part of the Marine and Hospital Service. Called the National Institute of Health after 1930, it remained focused on microbiology rather than a full range of diseases. The National Cancer Institute, created in 1937, complemented the National Institute of Health (NIH). The 1935 Social Security Act included a health research component and authorized expenditures of up to $2 million annually for the investigation of diseases and problems of sanitation (Strickland 1972; Strickland 1978; Shyrock 1947). While the $2 million authorized in the Social Security Act was a large expenditure at the time, the overall percentage of federal dollars in the pre-World War II period was small by comparison with today.

World War II escalated health research activities and expenditures. The wartime Office of Scientific Research and Development, an executive branch bureau, created the Committee on Medical Research (CMR). Representatives from the Army, Navy, Public

Health Service, and nongovernmental scientific and health care delivery institutions served on the CMR. Established to reduce the effects of disease and injuries incurred in military theaters, or related to national defense, the CMR mobilized medical and scientific personnel to establish a major program of research. Between 1941 and 1947, the CMR spent $25 million in six medical research areas — medicine, surgery, aviation medicine, physiology, chemistry, and malaria (Strickland 1972).

Medical research successes in this period were heady, generating enthusiasm for the potential of medical sciences and the role of the federal government in research activities. One success was the development of penicillin, the most commonly used antibiotic even to the current day. The discovery of gamma globulin to treat hepatitis and help control measles was federally funded. Also cortisone, which alleviated symptoms of arthritis and has since been used to treat a variety of disorders and injuries, resulted from federally funded wartime medical research activity.

A second war-related impetus for federally funded health research came from concern over the fitness of potential soldiers. Military induction exams screening potential recruits revealed an alarmingly large number of draft-age Americans physically or mentally unfit for military service. Approximately one-third of all men examined were rejected for health-related reasons. Senator Claude Pepper's Subcommittee on Wartime Health and Education held hearings in 1944 highlighting these distressing figures, alerting the public to the problem, and suggesting increased public funds to aid medical research (Strickland 1972). Rather than phasing out the wartime medical research effort, over 50 projects were transferred from the Office of Scientific Research and Development to the Public Health Service.

Out of World War II emerged an enlarged and predominantly disease-based federal role in health and medical research. In 1946, the National Institute of Mental Health was created, followed in 1948 by the creation of the National Heart Institute. In 1950, Congress passed the Omnibus Medical Research Act, which established the Institutes of Neurological Diseases and Blindness, and of Arthritis and Metabolic Diseases. NIH became the National Institutes of Health, part of the Public Health Service, with the surgeon general having the authority to establish additional institutes (Strickland 1978).

NIH was not the only federal medical research agency. After great controversy over its purpose and scope, the National Science Foundation (NSF) was established in 1950 with one division concerned with biological and medical sciences. Hospitals under the Veterans Administration (VA) performed little research between the two world wars. After World War II, many VA hospitals became affiliated with medical schools and actively participated in research. Armed services hospitals continued their research activities begun during the Second World War.

The federal health research budget is now divided among a large number of agencies, although the majority of funds are under the major federal health agency (the Department of Health and Human Services, DHHS). In 1978, roughly 2.56 billion of the 3.5 billion federal research dollars for health were in DHHS (previously called the Department of Health, Education, and Welfare). Over 12 other government departments or independent agencies spend some money on health research issues. As part of the broadening of the concept of health, the Environmental Protection Agency (EPA) has conducted research focusing on environmental problems which impact on health.

A long list of other agencies not ordinarily considered to be health-related agencies nonetheless spend money for health research. These include the departments of Defense, Interior, and Commerce, and the National Aeronautics and Space Administration (NASA). If chemical contaminants pass into the food chain through water, severe health hazards develop for the exposed population. The Department of Interior examines these geochemical problems and conducts water-related research. Fire safety, radiation standards, and sanitation systems are studied by the National Bureau of Standards in the Commerce Department. The Department of Defense researches combat casualty care and the spreading of infectious diseases – a problem during war. Many NASA studies examine the response of the human body to stressful and unusual living conditions. Other NASA studies on miniaturization and communication systems to accomodate space travel have been applied in medical technology development.

Within DHSS, many agencies spend funds on health research, but the vast majority of health research monies are for the National Institutes of Health. In 1978, 88 percent (2.255 billion of 2.561 billion dollars) of health research funds in DHHS were allocated to NIH. The remaining 12 percent was dispersed to the Food and Drug Administration (FDA), the Centers for Disease Control (CDC), the National Center for Health Services Research (NCHSR), and other smaller agencies (Strickland 1978). The FDA conducts research on the safety of new drugs and various food additives, including controversial studies on the cancer-causing effects of red dyes and sugar substitutes. By contrast, the CDC has focused mainly upon infectious diseases. In the recent past, Toxic Shock Syndrome and AIDS (Acquired Immune Deficiency Syndrome) created public panic and were studied with epidemiological techniques by CDC. Another area of health care research examines why, and under what conditions, citizens use health services. This line of inquiry, along with other research on how the health care system is organized, including the application of computer technology to medical records and hospital information systems, occurs in NCHSR.

With the expansion of NIH after World War II, allocations of federal funds for health research were made predominantly for studying specific diseases. The structure of NIH reflects this disease-specific focus. Various institutes have been created for individual diseases – allergy, arthritis, metabolic and digestive diseases, cancer, dental disease, eye disease, heart disease, lung disease, blood diseases, neurological disorders, and stroke. Exceptions to this disease focus among the NIH institutes include the National Institutes on Aging (created in 1975), Child Health and Human Development (1964), Environmental Health Sciences (1970), and General Medical Studies (1966) (National Institutes of Health 1981).

Despite the recent creation of nonspecific-disease institutes in NIH, the bulk of the funding continues to flow to disease-specific institutes, especially the two major institutes for cancer; and heart, lung, and blood disease. In 1980, 29 percent of the total NIH funding ($999,869,000 out of $3,425,685,000) was allocated to the National Cancer Institute. An additional 15 percent ($527,488,000) of NIH funding in that same year went to the National Institute of Heart, Lung, and Blood Diseases. These two disease-specific institutes alone consumed almost 45 percent of total NIH funding (National Institutes of Health 1981).

Not all of the huge expenditure of federal dollars for research is spent in government laboratories on the NIH campus in Bethesda, Maryland, nor is it paid directly to scientists employed by the U.S. government. One of the major mechanisms for spending federal research funds is through grants to universities, medical schools, or other specialized research institutes. Grants are largely competitive among scientists at major universities. Approximately three times each year, groups of nonfederal scientists submit applications for research monies. In universities and nongovernmental research institutes, receiving a large federal research grant is regarded as a significant career achievement, and can be instrumental in determining the career success and status of a scientist. In 1980, 69 percent ($2,356,062,000) of NIH funding was allocated to grants for research, fellowships, training, and health research facilities. Over two-thirds of federal monies for health research and training are spent by nonfederal institutions (National Institutes of Health 1981).

The disease focus for research funding becomes self-reinforcing through interest-group politics. Often interest groups, comprised of grieving relatives and friends of patients stricken with a particular disease, form with the primary mission of finding and disseminating cures and treatments. Specific disease-oriented institutes in NIH provide a focus for interest-group activities. The interest group becomes a primary advocate for increased funding. The clout of interest groups has often been exercised through Congress. In the recent past, Congress has approved funding levels exceeding those requested by the executive branch, often conducting elaborate public hearings with many witnesses in the process. For example, hearings by a house subcommittee dealing with the NIH budget in 1976 took up over 2,000 pages when printed (Strickland 1978).

In addition to the disease focus of federal funding for health care research, the role of that funding has increased. Before 1940, private sector funds dominated the health research effort in the United States. Part of the private funds came from industry, especially chemical and drug companies and some manufacturing companies. Private foundations provide the bulk of the research support to individual scientists.

Expenditure data illustrate graphically the enhanced role of federal funds in health research. Federal funds for biomedical research in 1947 shortly after World War II were $28 million, 32 percent of the national total in that year. In 1960, federal funds ($448 million) constituted 50.7 percent of total health Research and Development (R&D). This percentage steadily increased throughout the 1960s, reaching as high as 62.3 percent in 1966 ($1,459 million). The role of federal funds in total health R&D subsequently has hovered around 60 percent of total funds. This trend has continued into the recent past. In 1980, federal health-related R&D had risen to $4,726 million out of a total of $7,894 million, 59.9 percent of research funds that year (National Institutes of Health 1981).

The increase in the federal role in health research is even more dramatic when contrasted with the role of federal funding in all research and development. Since 1965, the percentage of federal funds for total R&D has steadily declined. In 1965, federal dollars were 62.9 percent of total monies spent for basic and applied research in the United States. By 1980, the federal figure had dropped to 54.8 percent. When total R&D funds are examined instead of just basic and applied research monies, the decline in the federal role is even more apparent. In 1965, federal funds constituted 64.9 percent of the total, while in 1980 that figure had fallen to 47.9 percent (National Institutes of Health 1981; U.S. Census Bureau 1982).

The increase in the federal role in funding health research directly contrasts with the decline of the federal role in funding general research. The effect has been to increase federally funded health research as a percentage of total federal R&D monies. In 1960, federal funds for health research were only 5.9 percent of total federal R&D expenditures. The significance of health as a component of federally funded research rose throughout the 1960s and early 1970s, peaking in 1974 at 15.8 percent of the total federal research effort. Since then, health research has constituted 14 to 15 percent of total federal research funds (National Institutes of Health 1981; U.S. Census Bureau 1982).

Despite the increased federal role, private funds in health research remain significant. Private funding from pharmaceutical companies has remained important throughout the shift to increased federal health funding overall, with greatest emphasis on the development of new drugs and marketable medical devices. Funding from private foundations, however, has changed greatly over the last 40 years. As the role of the federal government increased in the 1950s and 1960s, many of the pioneering foundations in the support of health research shifted their emphases. Some, such as the Commonwealth Fund, continued their interest in health, but rather than funding biomedical research, focused on education in medicine and other health professions. Others, such as Carnegie and Markle, left the health area entirely.

Criticisms about federal health research funds abound, with two major strains. The first focuses on the organizational arrangements for the federal funding of health research. The categorical disease-oriented nature of most of the NIH research institutes leaves some scientific areas uncovered, underfunded, and uncoordinated. Broad areas of inquiry (for example, nutrition and epidemiology) spanning many diseases are rarely considered as a whole in the allocation of health funds. Interdisciplinary health research, whether linking biological and chemical subspecialties, sociocultural and physiological fields, or organizational and financial concerns, is not easily promoted under the current categorical approach. Even when institutional arrangements exist to allow research which is more broadly focused, such as environmental health research or health services research, the dominance of a disease focus prevents these broader areas from receiving much attention or funds (Strickland 1978).

The second type of criticism concerning federal health research applies to many policy areas within the government. Senior policy makers in health as in other policy areas often become captured by the specific interests within their immediate responsibility, failing to consider linkages of their area to other areas and to overall national goals. Policy makers in NIH, DHHS, and Congress do not always consider the relationship between health research policies and programs; the interrelationship between those areas and programs dealing with health professions, health services, and public education; nor the relationship of all of these to overall national health needs and problems. No single set of policy makers has responsibility for overseeing national health research or for evaluating whether federally funded health research is effective.

HEALTH PLANNING

Health planning is the second major area of national policy. Health planning is a broad function, encompassing many seemingly disparate activities, such as setting policy goals, assessing methods of goal attainment, formulating specific policy objectives to implement goals, allocating resources, and monitoring the degree of policy effectiveness and goal attainment through regulation. Binding all these activities together is the common theme of making resource allocations to achieve health system objectives.

Planning activities within the health care system include the determination of whether additional hospital beds are needed in a geographic area, and assessing whether hospitals should purchase more expensive equipment. Planning functions also include a determination of whether a particular area has an adequate supply of health personnel, such as physicians or nurses. From these assessments of available health personnel, decisions about expansion of educational and training programs arise.

Regulation is intimately related to planning in two ways. Information generated in the regulatory process may be instrumental in effecting planning for future resource allocations. By compelling institutions and individuals to carry out a plan, regulation implements planning and is the embodiment of the plan "made flesh." In health regulation, licensing of nursing homes and other health care institutions occurs mainly at the state level. Licensing requires data on the type of care, current and potential shortages, and medical services, which are used in determining future resource allocations and needs assessment.

An interactive exchange exists between the regulating authority and the regulatees which generates new information for future planning. For example, when the Medicare law was passed in 1965, federal and state administrators quickly discovered that a large number of hospitals and nursing homes could not meet the standards strictly applied to achieve Medicare eligibility. Through negotiation between regulators and regulatees, a concept of "substantial compliance" was created, in which institutions would be certified for Medicare participation, even if they failed to meet statutory requirements so long as they demonstrated their actual condition was somewhat close to the original standards, and that they intended to improve (Vladeck 1980).

Health services planning began in the United States as a voluntary activity. Planning as a comprehensive activity oriented toward affecting subsequent resource allocations in a major way were manifested first in private hospitals, which began to incorporate goal delineation, objective specification, and evaluation of performance into financial allocation decisions to meet patient needs. Planning efforts by state health departments were rudimentary, with initial activities focused on preventive and environmental health issues, and later on planning service delivery for the poor. Broad based health planning with a comprehensive focus potentially affecting all segments of the population was rare in most state health departments.

New York City was the first major metropolitan area to attempt voluntary areawide planning to organize hospitals through the formation of the Hospital Council of Greater New York in 1938. The economic depression of the 1930s created severe overcrowding in municipal hospitals providing free services, and led to a decline in the number of paying patients in voluntary hospitals. Through the newly formed Hospital Council functioning outside of government and supported by philanthropic donations, financially strapped voluntary hospitals coalesced to collect data and to discuss potential solutions to common problems. The governing board members were prominent local citizens whose major interests were estimating the numbers of hospital beds needed in different neighborhoods. As the idea of a hospital council spread, equivalent councils sprung up in Rochester, Buffalo, Detroit, Chicago, Kansas City, Los Angeles, and Pittsburgh within a few years (Pearson 1976; Bice 1980; Raffel 1980).

From the experience with hospital councils, two facets of health planning emerged. First, organized foundations became the standard mechanism for engaging in health planning. The tradition of using private, specially organized boards with volunteer input continued in much of the subsequent health planning legislation of the 1960s and 1970s. Second, the concept of planning on a metropolitan or regional basis was adopted from the Dawson Report in England which argued for regional principles for reorganizing health care services in Great Britain, and from a report by the Committee on the Cost of Medical Care in the United States. Composed of multidisciplinary researchers from the social sciences and public health, and some lay leaders with funding from a number of philanthropic foundations, the committee studied the use, organization, and financing of health services. One recommendation was the establishment of local and state agencies to conduct research and to devise plans to coordinate health services (Pearson 1976).

Planning of health services remained a nongovernmental activity until after the Second World War. By the mid-1940s, politicians recognized an imbalance in the location of hospitals and areas of population growth. Many facilities were delapidated and deteriorating, due to the Great Depression in the 1930s, and the halt of major hospital construction during World War II in the 1940s. No substantial nondefense-related construction, including hospitals, had occurred in the United States since the 1920s.

To deal with the shortage of adequate hospital facilities, Congress enacted the Hospital Survey and Construction Act, better known as the Hill-Burton Act, in 1946. This legislation required that each state develop a plan for health facility construction, to be updated annually, that would serve as a basis for the allocation of federal construction grants in that state. Hill-Burton represented the first real federal governmental role in health planning, and was continued in later decades through the Comprehensive Health Planning Program and later the Health Systems Agencies.

A ten-year federal planning effort dealing with heart disease, cancer, and stroke was initiated in 1965. Its focus shifted across that period from a disease-specific orientation to the promotion of comprehensive health services. The Regional Medical Programs Act (RMP) created an organizational structure which allowed medical schools and teaching hospitals to obtain federal monies for a variety of projects deemed worthy by the recipient institutions. The original planning focus of the RMP became lost over time as the act became an omnibus funding device for recipient institutions' priority projects (Bice 1980).

In an attempt to bring order to the statewide health planning process, and to make the process more comprehensive, Congress in 1966 passed the Comprehensive Health Planning Act (PL 89-749). States established statewide and areawide (substate) agencies to devise and implement more comprehensive health plans. Each planning agency had an advisory council composed of a majority of health services consumers. The legislation specified that planning was to be accomplished without interfering with the prevailing patterns of medical practice. This, along with the absence of any regulatory authority over health services institutions, crippled any efforts to implement plans.

In 1974, the National Health Planning and Resources Development Act (PL 93-641) was passed to create a slightly revised version of health planning. This law established Health Systems Agencies (HSA) to write area and statewide plans. In contrast to earlier legislation, some regulatory powers were included. With the rise of an increased role for states under Reagan's New Federalism proposals, the amount of federal funding provided for this system of health planning has declined, and states have more flexibility in determining the structure of their health planning systems.

Regulatory policy is the enforcement of health planning at its best, and obstructionist "red tape" at its worst. Americans remain, as they have been throughout their history, ambivalent to an almost schizophrenic degree about the need for regulation. On the one hand, regulation represents an intervention by the government into "free markets." On the other hand, the goals of regulatory policy are often cost containment, efficiency increases, and improvements in the quality of health care, objectives to which most Americans also subscribe. Compounding this ambivalence is that regulatory policy is usually not regarded as a viable alternative until free markets and other approaches have failed. Confronted with crises and malfunctioning markets, Americans then turn to regulatory policy as a necessary if undesirable evil.

Four types of regulatory mechanisms affecting both individuals and institutions are subsidies, entry controls, rate or price controls, and quality controls (Bice 1980; Weidenbaum 1978). Subsidies are more common than alternative regulatory approaches, and because of their real and visible benefits, are more accepted by citizens than entry controls, rate or price controls, and quality controls which have less visible benefits. Subsidies for individuals include training grants, Medicare, Medicaid, and tax exemptions for health expenditures and insurance, subsidies for institutions include construction grants and loans, institutional training grants for health service professionals, and tax credits to employers for employer-provided health insurance. Some health programs serve the dual functions of providing regulatory subsidies and health services.

Examples of training subsidies are forgiveness clauses in educational grants for individuals (for example, not requiring a loan payback if a doctor or nurse provides a specified number of years of service in rural or inner-city areas), plus federal subsidies to medical schools and other health professional programs based upon enrollments. In the case of individual educational grants, recipients were motivated through the regulatory "carrot" of federal funds to provide health services in geographic areas lacking an adequate number of physicians and other health professionals. In the case of institutional training grants, to receive federal funds the medical and health professional schools had to comply with federal guidelines regarding the size of entering classes and the appropriate mix of medical specialties. The Hill-Burton Act contained the "carrot" of federal funds to get institutional recipients to meet federal planning objectives. In exchange for federal grants, hospitals had to provide a formula-determined amount of "free care" to indigents in the community, facilitating one federal objective of disseminating health care services among the poor.

Entry controls, the second regulatory mechanism, restrict the ability of institutions or individuals to offer goods and services in a particular area. The restriction may be total, or may screen out as providers, individuals and institutions not meeting some minimum competence criterion. Both licensing and certification are examples of entry controls. Licensing is the most formal and limiting of the two types of entry controls. Failure to obtain a required license prevents practice of the given profession. Certification, by contrast, is less stringent. Certification in a particular specialty or field may not be necessary to practice a profession, but obtaining certification indicates to potential patients and clients, as well as to health professional colleagues the demonstration of a desired level of expertise.

Federal use of entry controls as a regulatory device has been almost nonexistent. Most personnel and facilities licensing laws occur at the state level. Each state sets its own requirements for licensing. State-facility licensing has focused on physical plant requirements, such as fire safety, heating, space allocation, and sanitation. Most certification systems are implemented and maintained by professional associations, such as the various specialty boards in medicine.

Hospital accreditation is one major type of facilities certification which occurs in health care. The Joint Commission on Accreditation of Hospitals (JCAH) conducts hospital accreditation in the United States. The JCAH, as the name implies, is a joint effort of a number of professional associations: the American College of Physicians, the American Hospital Association, the American Medical Association, and the American College of Surgeons. Hospital accreditation is an example of certification by nongovernmental, nonprofit professional organizations and is a voluntary process not mandated directly by any state law. Often, however, accreditation is a requirement to receive federal and state funds and private insurance reimbursements.

Rate and price controls are a third regulatory mechanism used in market economies when markets are less than perfect, and when competition is restricted. Without competition, prices and rates would rise to high levels not reflective of costs of production. In the health area, two situations often result in restricted competition and consequently a need for rate or price controls: monopsony where government is the predominant purchaser of the product or service, and oligopsony where only a few firms are producing a needed medical product.

Rate and price controls may be applied to health services delivered by individual providers as well as by institutional providers. The major use of rate controls for individual providers occurs with state-established Medicaid fee schedules. In most states, reimbursement rates for participating physicians have been set below the prevailing market price, and often below reimbursement levels permitted by private insurance companies. One consequence of this rate fixing, in addition to the intended effect of holding down total outlays for government Medicaid expenditures, has been to dampen enthusiasm for participation in Medicaid among many physicians.

Medicare and Medicaid both have reimbursement limits for various hospital and nursing home services. With hospital services, a complex set of federal regulations has determined the appropriate reimbursement on an individual hospital basis. A similar type of negotiation process between the receiving institution and government officials has been used for nursing homes. Medicare is a federal program and the regulations to facilitate its implementation have been homogenous across states. By contrast, Medicaid is a joint federal-state program and considerable heterogeneity in implementation regulations has existed across states. Most payments to nursing homes occur through Medicaid, rather than Medicare, therefore leading to state-by-state variability in rate setting for reimbursement schedules. Payments to hospitals come from both Medicare and Medicaid. Generally, states have applied the Medicare regulations and reimbursement limits to hospital payments under Medicaid.

State rate-setting commissions also set reimbursement levels for hospitals. At least 28 states have experimented with some form of prospective rate setting. Most of these experimental programs have been voluntary efforts involving private health insurance payers, such as Blue Cross and rate-establishing committees of state hospital associations. Only a few states have required nonvoluntary rate-setting commissions which regulate prices for hospital services ("State Rate Controls" 1978). Maryland has implemented a required prospective reimbursement system for all hospitals in the state. Traditionally, decisions about reimbursements have been made after the services were provided on a per service unit basis. Hospitals could unilaterally raise their prices and expect reimbursement, as long as the price increase could be justified, leading some to describe traditional reimbursement schemes as "cost-plus" arrangements. Under the prospective system established by Maryland, the state negotiates in advance for many services. The total amount to be received by the hospital is based on previous patterns of usage.

New Jersey has implemented a diagnostic-related grouping (DRG) reimbursement system. Unlike current reimbursement schedules, the DRG plan standardizes service unit payments across institutions. The New Jersey rate commission has applied an elaborate typology of types of services, with many diagnostic subcategories which become the basis for standardized payments. For example, under obstetrical services the diagnostic subcategories would include uncomplicated vaginal delivery, various types of complicated vaginal deliveries, uncomplicated Caesarean deliveries, and various types of complicated Caesarean deliveries. Instead of being paid for each patient day of hospitalization, for each specialized service, and for each item of supplies used, under the New Jersey DRG plan all similar hospitals receive the same lump sum payment for a hospital stay with a particular diagnosis.

A fourth regulatory mechanism is quality controls. Elements of quality control are manifested in other regulatory mechanisms, especially entry controls. At the individual level, the Professional Standards Review Organization (PSRO) program regulates the quality of care reimbursed by Medicaid and Medicare as provided by physicians in hospital settings. At the institutional level, the Food and Drug Administration (FDA) reviews the safety and efficacy of new pharmaceutical products, employs quality standards, and regulates the production of drugs to ensure quality in the production process (Bice 1980; Weidenbaum 1978).

Americans often lump all government regulation into the category of needless red tape. Yet increasing public dissatisfaction over rising costs of health care services dictates rationally developed plans to determine efficient allocations of funds and resources, and when plans are enforced, regulation occurs. In the post-World War II era, all modern nations have increasingly relied on planning and regulation for all economic and social development, including and especially government functions (Lindblom 1977). The increased reliance on planning and regulation is particularly evident in the health services systems of modern industrialized nations (Blanpain et al. 1978). Yet, U.S. public attitude remains schizophrenic. Survey data show disapproval of planning and regulatory tools, but approval of the overall goals of governmental planning and regulation.

CHAPTER THREE
AREAS OF
NATIONAL HEALTH POLICY:
SERVICES

TYPES OF HEALTH SERVICES DELIVERY SYSTEMS

A popular critique of health services delivery in the United States is that no comprehensive system for providing care exists (Health PAC 1971). Health services delivery in the United States is pluralistic, characterized by a variety of subsystems, each specialized in location and type of clientele. Torrens (1978) identifies four health delivery systems: middle-class, middle-income individuals and families (the private practice fee-for-service system); poor, inner-city minority citizens (the local government health care system); active-duty military personnel and their dependents (the military health care system); and veterans of the U.S. military services (the Veterans Administration health care system).

The health services system oriented toward middle-class, middle-income families is the predominant image of health services delivery in the United States. In any of the popular media, ranging from journalistic treatments of services delivery to soap operas, the private practice fee-for-service system is most frequently depicted. This delivery mechanism is loosely and informally organized. Each individual or family structures its own set of services and facilities, within financial constraints. The primary exception to this pattern is families using group practice Health Maintenance Organizations (HMO), where a preset package of health care services are available for a standardized prepaid fee.

For the majority of Americans, the private practice physician is the center of the individual and family-based delivery system. The private practice family physician is sometimes the first contact with the health care delivery system. Other families begin contact with an array of specialist physicians: a pediatrician for the children, an obstetrician-gynecologist for the mother, and perhaps an internist for the father. As specific problems arise, family members may also contact, either through referral from a physician or by direct patient initiation, a dermatologist; an otolaryngologist (ear, nose, and throat specialist); a cardiologist (heart specialist); or an array of other specialists. If middle-class families need hospital services, they are usually provided in a local community hospital and arranged by one of the family's personal physicians. In addition to physician specialists, families may include nonphysician health care providers, such as podiatrists, chiropractors, dentists, and optometrists in their family-based system of health care.

The middle-class health services delivery system is predominantly financed from personal nongovernmental funds, whether paid directly out-of-pocket by the consumer or indirectly through a private health insurance plan. While physician, dental, and optometric services are primarily financed out-of-pocket, hospital services are more likely to be covered by private insurance. A major exception to the overall trend of private financing for middle-class, middle-income patients is Medicare. When most people reach age 65, they become eligible for federally sponsored and supervised health insurance through Medicare. These senior citizens can still use or receive their health services from the providers they customarily used before reaching age 65, with part of their bill now paid by federal funds.

The middle-class health care system maximizes control by the patient. The patient is free to choose a physician, and often influences the site of hospitalization. Many employers also offer competing alternative private health insurance plans, further increasing consumer choice. Nor are consumers under this system locked into initial choices. Patients disgruntled with the care they are receiving from a particular private physician are free to switch physicians. In the extreme, this has led to "physician shopping" where patients wander from doctor to doctor, looking for an acceptable diagnosis and plan of treatment. Less consumer flexibility and patient choices exist under the other three health care systems.

The health care system for poor, inner-city persons lacks the degree of coordination found in the middle-class system. Most services, unlike the middle-class system, are provided through government rather than private funding. Local government agencies such as municipal and county hospitals and local health departments are major service providers in the poor, inner-city system. Through the mid-1960s, health services for the poor were usually provided without charge to the patient. Frequently local health departments did not charge for vaccinations for infants, blood tests for syphilis, Pap smears for women, and other preventive services often made available to indigent patients. Nor did municipal and county hospitals charge the poor for hospitalization for major illnesses.

Since the introduction of Medicaid — the major federal program to provide health care services to eligible poor — some low-income people have had greater options concerning providers. Previously restricted to institutional health care providers, under Medicaid as originally enacted, low-income patients could choose private physicians willing to accept Medicaid fees as payment for services rendered. The increased choice created by the introduction of federal funding through Medicaid, however, was often greater in theory than in practice. Many private physicians were reluctant to accept Medicaid payment due to the comparatively low rate of reimbursement, the large amount of paperwork involved, and in many states, the delay in receiving payments. Similarly, not all hospitals were willing to accept Medicaid payments for the same reasons. With the recent growth of proprietary (for-profit) hospitals, the number of hospitals unwilling to accept Medicaid patients has increased.

Recent changes in federal laws now allow states to restrict the freedom of choice of Medicaid recipients. Some states are planning to require all Medicaid recipients to use only officially approved hospitals and physicians. In an effort to control total Medicaid expenditures, states are contracting with hospitals that can provide services at lower costs to eligible Medicaid patients. This reduced flexibility for Medicaid patients, coupled with the fact that only 50 percent of the poor qualify for Medicaid, leaves the average low-income consumer of health services in the United States with considerably less choice and control than that available to the average middle-income consumer.

The third health care delivery system services active members of the various branches of the military. A well-organized system of reasonably high-quality care is available free of direct charge to all active-duty personnel. Most military employees have an encounter with the system as soon as they enlist for routine vaccinations, shots, and a general physical exam. When compared with the previous two systems oriented toward middle-income and poor, inner-city Americans, the military health care system has a greater emphasis upon prevention. This includes an orientation to keeping people well and to preventing illnesses and absences, as well as a more general preventive health program that includes vaccinations, regular physical examinations, various tests, and accident prevention strategies. Beyond personal health services provided by medics and doctors, traditional public health services that are delivered by a local government agency in most communities are usually offered by special military public health and safety officers.

The core personnel for delivery of both preventive and first-line sickness services is most typically a medical corpsman, trained within the military in extensive first-aid procedures, immunizations, and other types of simple medical practices. The medic is trained to start the diagnostic procedure, and to provide routine preventive and ambulatory services, with supervision by nurses and doctors. More complicated services are provided by physicians trained in standard medical schools or the special interservice military medical school whose graduating students then select active-duty assignments from all service branches. Depending on the size of the base, a large array of specialized services and hospital facilities comparable to a university hospital or large community teaching hospital may be available. On smaller bases, personnel requiring more complicated or nonroutine treatments would be referred to facilities on a large base. Large base medical facilities become regional centers of military health care, serving personnel from smaller bases throughout the region.

The military health care system differs dramatically from the previous two systems serving middle-income and poor, inner-city Americans in several ways. The military system is much more tightly organized and highly integrated than the loose, almost haphazard collection of delivery mechanisms and services comprising the other two systems. However, turnover in both providers and patients, coupled with the structure of a system which emphasizes the medic as the first line of service, does not assure a patient of seeing the same provider even at the same facility and prevents the development of the personalized physician-patient relationship more prevalent in the middle-income health care system and sometimes present in the poor, inner-city health care system. Great continuity of care, though, exists in the sense of an integrated and comprehensive record system. A complete record on each military patient is constructed upon enlistment and is maintained throughout the person's career. The record moves constantly with the serviceman or woman although providers of care change as personnel move from base to base.

An additional major difference between the military and middle-income health care system is the reimbursement structure for personnel employed within the system. In the middle-income system, physicians are reimbursed on a fee-for-service basis, although most other health care workers (nurses, aides, technicians) are salaried. In the military system, all health care workers are salaried, including physicians. Physician incomes are lower within the military than outside, contributing to a high turnover of military doctors. To partially counter this turnover and attract doctors into active duty, a subsidy program paying for the medical education of prospective doctors in return for a commitment to a specified number of years of active-duty service has been established. The integration of the military medical system not only includes directly controlling personnel, but also owning and operating the hospitals and health care facilities.

From the patient's viewpoint, choice is considerably less in the military system. The service employee does not choose who provides care. Nor, if the employee is disgruntled, does he or she have the option of easily switching providers. Compared with the middle-class system, this lack of patient control generates complaints about military health care independent of the quality of particular treatments and services. The lack of patient control experienced by active-duty personnel only partially affects their dependents. Dependents and families of active-duty military personnel are covered by a special health insurance plan — the Civilian Health and Medical Program of the Uniformed Services (CHAMPUS). This plan is financed by the military and allows the family to receive care from private medical practitioners and local community nonmilitary hospitals if similar services cannot be provided at a military installation within a reasonable distance. Families of military personnel effectively participate within two health care systems — both the military system for active-duty personnel, and the middle-class, insurance-based private practice system.

The military system also differs from other health care delivery systems in the United States in the type of patient care provided as well as the degree of patient control over that care. Unlike the middle-income and V.A. systems, the military does not provide long-term care services, such as nursing home care. If an active-duty military employee develops a severe medical problem that is long-term in nature, that person is generally discharged from the service. If long-term care is needed, the newly discharged veteran would be referred to the Veterans Administration system. Depending on the financial resources of the recent veteran, he or she may opt instead to purchase private health insurance and to rely upon care within the middle-class private practice system. Retirees are eligible to continue using the military system.

The Veterans Administration health care system is available to retired, disabled, and otherwise deserving veterans of previous military service. Unlike the military system where families and dependents of active-duty military personnel have access to that system, the VA system does not service families and dependents of former military personnel. The VA system has traditionally been hospital and long-term care oriented, although it also provides outpatient care for immediate problems. It is a very large system, operating over 170 hospitals, over 200 outpatient clinics, and serving as a primary source of inpatient hospital care for over 1 million veterans.

A patient profile for the VA system reveals a different average consumer of health care. Currently, the VA patient is likely to be almost exclusively male, older, and to have either physical or mental chronic illnesses. The VA system is often said to be the largest single provider of long-term care services in the United States. A larger amount of long-term care is provided in acute short-term general VA hospitals than is true in general community hospitals. The VA also operates nursing home facilities and domiciliary facilities. Recently, due to shortages of nursing home beds within the system, the VA system has also paid for care for their clients in community nursing homes.

Access to the VA health care system is part of an overall system of benefits for veterans of U.S. military service, including not only health care, but also disability compensation, educational assistance, and home loans. The VA health system has a unique relationship with organized interest groups. Many veterans are members of local and national veterans clubs and associations, such as the American Legion, the Veterans of Foreign Wars, and Amvets. These groups have been potent lobbying forces and have succeeded in getting congressional legislation favorable to ex-military personnel, including health benefits.

A similarity between the military and VA health care systems is the self-contained nature of each. Each employs salaries as the method of payment for all personnel, including physicians, and lacks patient control over entry into the system or receipt of services. Originally designed to serve veterans with service-connected disabilities, the VA system offers services to other veterans if they are unable to obtain those services elsewhere, and if room is available in VA facilities. Eligibility for VA health services as a consequence remains unclear, and subject to local variation in availability and interpretation. Unlike the military health care system, eligibility criteria are decentralized to the regional and even local levels. Like the military system, the patient has little control over which provider he sees and little power to change providers if personally dissatisfied.

HEALTH SERVICES EXPENDITURE TRENDS

Regardless of the categorization scheme employed for distinguishing service delivery systems, the trend for service expenditures over the last 20 years is clear: aggregate health expenditures for services have been escalating dramatically. In 1960, total national expenditures for health services and supplies were $25.2 billion. In 1980, $235.6 billion were spent nationally for health services and supplies, a 834 percent increase across two decades (U.S. Census Bureau 1982).

Included in the 1980 health services total were $217.9 billion for personal health care (92.5 percent), $10.4 billion for health insurance prepayment and administration (4.4 percent), and $7.3 billion (3.1 percent) for government public health activities. The preponderance of total health services expenditures is used for personal health care, such as hospital care, physicians' services, dentists' services, other professional services, drugs and sundries, eyeglasses and appliances, and nursing home care (U.S. Census Bureau 1982).

Another illustration of this increase is the concomitant rise in per capita expenditures for personal health care services. In 1977, $663 was spent for every man, woman, and child in the United States on personal health care. In one year, that figure rose to $736, an 11 percent increase. By 1980, the per capita expenditures for personal health care were $941. In 1981, $1,043 was spent per person, a 57 percent increase in merely four years (Health Care Financing Administration 1982).

Hospital care expenditures ($99.6 billion) in 1980 were 45 percent of total personal health care expenditures (see Table 3-1). This constituted the largest share of outlays for personal health care. Hospital care has increased in the share of total personal health expenditures. In 1960, hospital costs were 38.4 percent of total personal health care expenditures. By 1970, hospital outlays had risen to a 42.7 percent of total personal health care expenditures (U.S. Census Bureau 1982).

The trend of rising hospital care costs relative to personal health care has continued in the recent past. In 1981, 47.9 percent of personal health outlays were consumed by hospital care. In 1977, per capita figure for hospital care outlays were $302. In 1980, that figure had risen to $430. In 1981, an average of $481 for each person in the country was spent on hospital care (Health Care Financing Administration 1982).

The increase in the share of personal health care costs spent for hospital care has resulted from both increases in the use of hospital services and price inflation. Over 70 percent of the growth in expenditures for hospital care can be attributed to inflation. To measure price inflation, the Health Care Financing Administration has developed the Hospital Input Price Index, or alternatively, the Hospital Market Basket, which reflects the prices of goods and services used by hospitals to provide hospital services.

The Hospital Input Price Index rose 11.9 percent in 1980, a more rapid increase than overall inflation. Two factors contributing significantly to the dramatic jump in this index between 1979 and 1980 were energy prices and an average 11 percent increase in hospital wage rates (Gibson and Waldo 1981). Rapidly escalating price inflation in hospital care services continued in the period from 1980 to 1981 when the index leaped upward 13.6 percent.

Relief in the dramatic increases was forthcoming the following year. The general economic recession and decline in the economy

TABLE 3-1
PERSONS COVERED BY PRIVATE HEALTH INSURANCE: 1967 to 1979

TYPE OF CARE	PERCENT UNDER 65 YEARS						PERCENT 65 AND OVER					
	1967	1970	1975	1977	1978	1979	1967	1970	1975	1977	1978	1979
Hospital care	77.0	78.6	78.1	79.2	79.2	79.5	45.0	51.4	62.7	67.3	66.4	64.1
Physician's services												
Surgical services	75.2	76.9	77.9	78.1	78.5	79.3	44.1	46.7	55.0	49.7	42.4	42.8
In-hospital visits	65.5	75.1	79.6	78.3	79.2	80.4	31.1	41.1	42.8	42.1	44.0	44.0
X-ray and laboratory exams	50.0	73.8	78.2	71.6	73.6	80.0	18.7	37.4	37.1	37.2	37.4	42.†
Office and home visits	(NA)	35.2	63.9	61.2	66.7	65.1	(NA)	17.3	28.6	28.5	28.4	26.5
Dental care	2.6	6.5	15.5	22.6	27.0	30.2	.4	.6	2.4	4.8	6.6	6.1
Prescribed drugs (out-of-hospital)	39.0	53.5	76.1	66.2	66.2	65.2	9.7	15.9	21.8	18.2	18.8	17.5
Private duty nursing	41.5	53.1	74.3	65.8	67.5	63.4	11.7	15.8	21.7	15.7	14.2	14.1
Visiting nurse service	44.6	56.4	71.8	65.7	69.1	78.4	13.0	18.8	24.1	18.2	26.8	33.7
Nursing home care	8.9	15.4	34.6	29.7	39.3	44.0	15.2	24.7	19.6	23.3	35.1	47.8

NA Not available

Source: U.S. Health Care Financing Administration, *Health Care Financing Review* Fall 1981. Data for 1967-1975 published by U.S. Social Security Administration in *Social Security Bulletin,* September.1978, and earlier issues.

mitigated the rapid increase in hospital price inflation between 1981 and 1982. Largely due to moderately reduced growth of unit labor costs and sharper reductions in growth of capital and other non-labor items, the index increased at the slower rate of 8.5 percent. The decline in the rate of price inflation for hospital care was consistent with the decline in the rate of price inflation for the overall economy ("Hospital Expenses Continue Decline" 1983).

During the 1979 to 1980 period, one-fifth of the increase in hospital care costs can be attributed to increased usage. Inpatient days in community hospitals rose 3.6 percent, the highest annual increase since the implementation of Medicare and Medicaid in 1966, three-fourths of which was attributable to increased usage of hospital services by senior citizens over the age of 65. Consequently, hospital occupancy rates rose slightly from 74 percent in 1978 to 76 percent in 1980 (Gibson and Waldo 1981).

A moderating trend in hospital usage, also attributable to the general economic recession, began in 1981. Overall admissions declined 1.4 percent compared to the previous years admissions. This decline in usage was manifested for both citizens under age 65, and for senior citizens 65 years of age or older. The decline in hospital usage continued into 1982 only for citizens under age 65. High unemployment levels resulting in the loss of health insurance benefits precipitated the decrease in hospital utilization rates ("Hospital Expenses Continue Decline" 1983).

The long-term 30-year trend in hospital care has been a growth in nonfederal short-term general hospitals. Between 1950 and 1979, short-term general hospitals doubled their share of hospital expenses from 40 percent to 80 percent of total hospital care costs, and the share of inpatient days for short-term general hospitals also doubled up to 70 percent simultaneously with a decline in nonfederal psychiatric hospitals. The share of inpatient days of care in psychiatric hospitals fell from almost one-half to less than one-fifth. Reflective of the deinstitutionalization trend in mental health care, the decline in inpatient days in psychiatric hospitals was made possible by the development of new drugs for treating the mentally ill (Gibson and Waldo 1981).

The second largest category of expenditure for personal health care is consumed by physicians' services. Expenditures for physicians' services include the costs of all services and supplies provided in physicians' offices; the costs for services of private practitioners in hospitals, nursing homes, and other institutions; and physician-ordered diagnostic laboratory work from independent clinical laboratories. In 1960, $5.7 billion (24 percent of personal health expenditures) was spent on physicians' services. By 1980, physicians' services outlays were $46.6 billion, 21.5 percent of total health expenditures in that year (U.S. Census Bureau 1982). In 1977, per capita expenditures for physicians' services were $142. This figure rose to $201 in 1980, and $224 in 1981 (Health Care Financing Administration 1982).

The actual impact of physicians on personal health expenditures greatly exceeds direct outlays for their services. Physicians influence many other types of personal health care spending, by determining whether a patient will use hospital services and how much care the patient will use (Fuchs 1975). Physicians also determine the use of prescription drugs. By one estimate, physicians influence over 70 percent of personal health care spending (Blumberg 1979).

The third largest category of expenditures for personal health care is spent for nursing homes. Nursing home expenditures include services provided in skilled nursing facilities, intermediate care facilities, and in personal care homes which provide nursing care. Only $0.5 billion were expended for nursing home care in 1960, 2.1 percent of total personal health expenditures in that year. In 1980, $20.7 billion of total personal health expenditures or 9.5 percent of 1980 personal health care outlays were spent on nursing home services, an astounding 4,040 percent increase in 20 years (U.S. Census Bureau 1982).

Why has the growth in nursing home outlays been so astounding? The answer lies in increased federal funding for nursing home care primarily through Medicaid. Other factors contributing to growth in nursing home expenditures include increased longevity, and changing lifestyles which increased the acceptability among many U.S. families of placing elderly members in nursing home facilities. Nor did the growth in nursing home utilization slow in the recent past. Nursing home days-of-care increased on average at a rate slightly greater than 3 percent annually between 1975 to 1980. During the same five-year period, the U.S. population aged 65 and over increased at the somewhat lower average annual rate of 2.7 percent (Gibson and Waldo 1981). By 1980, the rapid growth in nursing home utilization was abating. In that year, the growth in the number of days of care provided (about 3 percent) was lower than the preceding five-year average.

Drugs and sundries represented the fourth largest expenditure category for personal health care services. In 1980, drugs and sundries constituted 8.8 percent ($19.2 billion) of total personal health care services expenditures. This category includes spending for prescription drugs, over-the-counter drugs, and medical sundries dispensed through retail channels and excludes drugs purchased or dispensed by hospitals, nursing homes, other institutions, physicians, or dentists. The expenditures for drugs in those settings are included in the dollar totals for those respective categories.

Drugs are a major treatment regimen in U.S. medicine. Of all physician consultations, 59 percent result in at least one prescription for medication. Around 57 percent of all dollars in the drugs and sundries category are spent on prescription drugs. Another 31 percent is spent on over-the-counter medication (Gibson and Waldo 1981).

Spending for drugs has increased at a 9.1 percent annual rate between 1965 and 1980. Despite rapid growth, this rate of increase is significantly below the growth in spending for other major health care services, causing the share of total personal health care expenditures spent on drugs and related items to drop. In 1960, 15.6 percent of total personal health care dollars were used for drugs. Equivalent share figures for drugs fell to 14.5 percent in 1965, 12.3 percent in 1970, and 10.2 percent in 1975. Despite this constant decline in share of personal health care dollars, a substantial $3.7 billion was spent on drugs in 1960, $5.2 billion in 1965, $8 billion in 1970, and $11.9 billion in 1975.

Dental care consumed $15.9 billion (7.3 percent of total dollars for personal health care) in 1980, the fifth largest category of expense. This category includes spending for the services of dentists, dental specialists, and dental laboratories. Trend data show a very slight decline in the share of spending for dental care. The share of spending for dental care was 8.4 percent in 1960, 7.8 percent in 1965, 7.2 percent in 1970, and 7.0 percent in 1975. After 1975, very slight annual increases occurred to the present.

The proportion of dental health care expenditures paid by health insurance has increased from 2 percent to 21 percent between 1965 and 1980 (Gibson and Waldo 1981). This change in the financing of personal dental care from almost universal out-of-pocket outlays to increased use of third-party payments has influenced patterns of dental care usage. Traditionally, the use of dental care services has been very sensitive to business cycles and the state of the economy, declining during recessions and rebounding during business cycle peaks. More recently, however, increased dental insurance and third-party payments for dental care have mitigated these cyclical swings in dental care expenditures. For example, in 1980 the general U.S. economy was in a major slump, but dental care expenditures as a share of total personal health care dollars did not swing downward.

Spending for all other types of personal health care goods and services was $15.9 billion (7.2 percent) in 1980. This included dollars spent for eyeglasses and appliances such as hearing aids, orthopedic appliances, artificial limbs, and wheelchairs. Also included were the professional services of private duty nurses, including home health nurses, podiatrists, clinical psychologists, chiropractors, physical therapists, occupational therapists, and other types of practitioners. This category has declined as a proportion of personal health care across the past two decades. In 1960, other types of health care were 11.8 percent of total health care, and 8.6 percent in 1970.

One specialized category of interest is mental health. National expenditure data typically do not break down into a separate category spending for mental health. In the data presented above, several of the areas of expenditures include dollars for mental health. Some hospital expenditures, including mental hospitals and alcohol and drug treatment institutions, are for mental health care. Similarly, physicians' services include psychiatric services. The category of drugs and sundries includes spending for medication for mental health purposes, while the other types of professional services include psychologists and mental health counselors.

FINANCING OF HEALTH SERVICES

There are three principal methods of paying physicians who deliver health care services: fee-for-service rendered, capitation, and salaries. The dominant physician reimbursement scheme for health services financing overall in the United States, and especially in the middle-class health care delivery system, has been the fee-for-service method of payment. Through Medicaid, fee-for-service payments are also increasingly common in the poor, inner-city delivery system. It is less common in the military and VA delivery systems, although it is a part of the dependent coverage within the military system.

The fee-for-service reimbursement method provides a payment for each procedure or service performed by a physician. A service could be a small discrete service unit, such as a follow-up visit, reading of an EKG (electrocardiogram), or the reading of an x-ray. Alternatively, a service could involve very substantial procedures such as major surgery, or a series of services, such as care during pregnancy where one fee generally covers all prenatal office visits, the delivery itself, and postnatal care both in the hospital and later in the physician's office.

The fee-for-service payment method is consistent with the strong ideological bias toward individualism and economic bias toward capitalism prevalent in the United States. Under free enterprise, impersonal laws of supply and demand guided by profits and controlled by competition, rather than a central decision-making authority such as government, determine both the price and quantity of goods to be produced.

Health economists engage in vigorous debate about whether health services exhibit the marketplace characteristics assumed in capitalist theory. Critics of the fee-for-service payment method point out that competition among physicians does not occur. Physicians do not advertise the nature, quality, or the prices of their services, whereas in true market economies, the consumer is assumed to be aware of both service quality and service price through advertising, and sensitive to both. In the case of physicians' services, third-party payments have made this an increasingly unrealistic assumption, especially for complex and expensive services. Consumers do not regard physician and health care as a typical commodity. Since health care may involve issues of life and death, normal consumer price sensitivity does not prevail. Lastly, the patient rarely makes direct purchasing decisions as would occur in a true economic marketplace. While the consumer makes the initial decision about whether or not to enter the health care system by visiting a physician, once at the physician's office, the doctor rather than the patient decides what type and intensity of services are purchased.

Physicians strongly favor the fee-for-service payment method, despite the fact that physician and health services delivery in many ways bears little resemblance to a true economic market. Fee-for-service payment represents the profit aspect of markets — a facet which has been retained in physician financing. Under this method, the amount a physician earns is directly related to the amount of care he or she provides, just as corporate profits in other areas of the private sector economy are at least partially related to the amount of goods and services produced. The economics of this reimbursement scheme provide a direct incentive for the physician who wishes to raise his or her income level to deliver more services, especially complex expensive technical procedures which on average are reimbursed at a higher rate. Under fee-for-service payment, the physician's income from practicing medicine is a function of both the number of patients and the nature and quantity of the services he or she provides to each.

The second method for reimbursing physicians is capitation — paying the physician a fixed amount per patient served without regard to the volume and quantity of services provided. A physician agrees to provide services for a group of patients, often called a panel, for a fixed period of time (for example, a month or a year). The physician's income from medical practice is dependent on the number of patients in the panel, not the services provided to each. A few health maintenance organizations (HMOs) in the United States utilize this payment method for physicians. The National Health Service in Great Britain also uses this payment method for primary care physicians.

The third method for physician payment is salary, essentially payment per unit of time. Generally, when physicians are paid salaries, they work for some type of institution or organization. Many U.S. health maintenance organizations pay physicians by salary, as does the military and the Veterans Administration. Hospitals hire some physicians as well on a salary basis.

Most nonphysician health care providers emulate the success of physicians in developing and retaining fee-for-service as their predominant payment method. Dentists, optometrists, chiropractors, podiatrists, and clinical psychologists are among health care providers who use a fee-for-service payment scheme. In some states price advertising for services rendered does occur for some types of nonphysician health services such as optometrists and dental services. This manifestation of competitive market conditions, however, remains controversial, despite the fact that the manifestation of profits and the fee-for-service payment method is not.

In addition to fee-for-service payment schedules for physicians, health services financing in the United States is characterized by third-party payments for personal health care. Third parties in health financing are groups other than the consumer or provider of services which collect funds from the potential consumer of health care services, pool both the dollars collected and the risks for major health expenditures for any single consumer, and then pay providers making legitimate claims on the funding pool. Usually the third party retains a fee or percentage of collected fees in compensation for administering the health insurance plan. Examples of companies that administer third-party plans include Blue Cross/Blue Shield and private insurance companies.

In the late nineteenth and early twentieth centuries, the insurance industry did not believe that health care, especially for illness, was an insurable risk. While accidents, fires, other catastrophes, and sometimes burials were considered insurable, illness-related health care expenditures were not. One factor causing this common perception that insurance was not appropriate for health care outlays was the relatively low cost of personal health care in that time period. Health care was not technologically oriented, and hospital stays were uncommon. Even major illnesses were typically treated in the home. By the late 1920s, the hospital had become the perceived appropriate setting for the treatment of serious illness, and personal health care costs began to rise substantially.

The financial hardships of the Great Depression in the 1930s compounded the burden of rising personal health care costs. Families with a hospitalized member were often unable to pay their medical bills. Community hospitals faced major financial problems as increasing numbers of patients were unable to pay for hospital services. With the support of local hospital associations and the American Hospital Association, Blue Cross plans to provide coverage for hospital care were created during the 1930s. Special legislation was passed in most states to enable Blue Cross plans to operate on a nonprofit tax-exempt basis. Started a few years after Blue Cross plans, Blue Shield plans to cover physician expenses were organized originally by doctors, and grew more slowly during the 1930s and 1940s.

Blue Cross/Blue Shield plans originally employed a community-rating scheme to establish premium levels, under which everyone covered by the plan in a geographic area such as a city was charged identical rates, regardless of whether the person was young and healthy or older and at greater risk of illness. Traditional insurance used experience ratings where estimates of expected claims were established for different age and occupational groups. Different premium levels were charged these various groups, based on the expected claims calculated.

Blue Cross/Blue Shield plans were initially marketed to individuals. During the 1940s, health insurance became an important fringe benefit in the work place, especially since wartime wage controls prevented companies from competing by offering higher wages and salaries. Companies competed by offering different fringe benefit packages. Health insurance coverage offered by the employer was declared a negotiable item exempt from wage controls.

When Blue Cross plans first developed coverage for employee groups in the 1940s, they continued their earlier approach to setting premiums of community ratings. Commercial insurance companies were able to underprice Blue Cross plans in many companies, especially those with low-expected claims, by using experience ratings. As the share of the total health market covered by private insurance grew, Blue Cross plans were increasingly left with groups with high-expected claims and poorer health records, a trend which would have left Blue Cross covering the high-cost poor and elderly, while private insurance companies covered lower cost groups. This prospect prompted Blue Cross/Blue Shield plans to shift work-related group settings from community ratings for premiums to experience ratings to remain competitive with private insurance companies (Law 1976).

Each state currently has at least one Blue Cross/Blue Shield plan, with some larger states having more than one of each plan. Although there are great similarities in operating rules and marketing strategies across plans, each plan is independently incorporated in its own state. The plans are joined together nationally by a federated structure, sharing a common name, public relations, research staff, and contracting capacity for Medicare.

Across time, the differences between Blue Cross/Blue Shield plans and private insurance plans have diminished. Initially, Blue Cross/Blue Shield plans differed from private insurance plans on both rate setting and payment structures. Over time, both rate-setting differences and payment structure differences between the two have largely disappeared. Originally, Blue Cross/Blue Shield plans paid benefits on a service basis to the actual care provider. Private insurance plans paid retroactively on an indemnity basis to the patient receiving services. Now both Blue Cross/Blue Shield and private insurance plans use both payment methods.

Insurance payment structures vary greatly and can range from small amounts of indemnity coverage, such as $100 per day of hospitalization up to paid-in-full service benefits for inpatient and outpatient services with very few exclusions. Historically, the development of health insurance began with hospital coverage, then expanded to surgical benefits and other inpatient physician benefits. More recently, coverage for a wide range of medical services, sometimes including outpatient physician services, drugs, appliances, and even dental and vision care, is available.

Typical insurance protection would be basic coverage for inpatient hospitalization and physician services. Increasingly, many basic plans also cover outpatient surgery, such as vasectomies, tubal ligations, dilation and curatage procedures, and some types of eye surgery. Generally, this basic protection covers the entire hospital bill, although another common variant is the requirement of a small copayment for at least the early days of hospitalization. Copayments have been adopted by some insurance plans in an attempt to discourage unnecessary hospitalization.

Beginning in the 1950s, major medical policies were often added to basic coverage. These policies were first offered by private insurance companies, and subsequently by Blue Cross/Blue Shield plans. Major medical benefits can be paid toward all kinds of health care prescribed by a physician. Although there is great variability in covered services from plan to plan, commonly covered services might include sickness or injury-related outpatient physician visits, x-rays, special nursing care, medical appliances, drugs, and ambulatory psychiatric care.

Major medical insurance operates through the use of deductibles, coinsurance, and with payment ceilings per individual. A deductible is an amount which must be paid by the individual patient before coverage occurs. Common deductible limits are in the $100 to $200 range aggregated across all covered services for a given year. Once the deductible limit has been reached, the insurance covers a portion of the bill with the individual responsible for another portion. The part of the bill above the deductible limit covered by the individual is called coinsurance or copayment. The most common coinsurance provision is 20 percent covered by the individual, with the remaining 80 percent covered by the plan up to some maximum amount. The maximum amount paid by the major medical insurance plan may range from $100,000 to $500,000.

Coverage for special types of health problems, such as psychiatric care, alcoholism, or dental care, often vary more than coverage for typical physical health problems. Psychiatric benefits often include a specific limitation on the number of outpatient visits, or a dollar ceiling, such as $1,000, which does not apply to other types of services. Coinsurance provisions for psychiatric and alcoholism treatments are often much higher, sometimes up to 50 percent. If dental coverage is provided, it is usually a separate policy from basic or major medical coverage. Dental plans vary enormously in what is covered, and are often structured differently from medical coverage. A limited number of preventive visits are often paid in full. Coinsurance portions for covered services are often higher, typically around 50 percent, although great variability exists. Very high-cost services, such as orthodontics, may be excluded from coverage. Another variant of dental coverage is to specify a maximum amount of payments for each patient each year.

Coverage for all types of health insurance has been increasing in recent decades. Third-party coverage for health costs is largely a phenomenon of the last 40 years. In 1940, less than 10 percent of the population had coverage for inpatient care, and an even smaller percentage had coverage for any other type of health care. By 1967, 77 percent of people under 65 had coverage for hospital care, and 45 percent of people 65 and over had private health insurance hospital coverage. For those people 65 and over, this coverage supplemented Medicare (see Table 3-2).

Coverage for physician services in hospitals was also fairly high by 1967, with 75 percent of people under 65 having coverage for surgical services, and 66 percent having coverage for other inhospital physician services. Of those people 65 or over, equivalent percentages were 44 percent and 31 percent, somewhat lower than for the non-elderly. Coverage for prescription drugs was less common in 1967 than coverage for hospital or physician services. Thirty-nine percent of people under 65 and 10 percent of people 65 and over had such coverage. A rarely covered service in 1967 was dental care. Less than 3 percent of people under 65 and almost no one over 65 had dental coverage.

TABLE 3-2
NATURE OF HEALTH EXPENDITURES FOR
PERSONAL HEALTH CARE, 1980, BY TYPE OF CARE

TYPES	% OF TOTAL HEALTH EXPENDITURES
Hospitals	45.7
Physicians	21.5
Nursing Homes	9.5
Dental	7.3
Other Personal Health*[1]	7.2

[1] Includes eyeglasses,appliances,home health services
chiropractry, and products etc.
Source: United States Bureau of the Census

The large spurt in growth in health insurance coverage occurred in the decade between 1965 and 1975. Most of this growth occurred for services other than hospitalization. By 1975, 78 percent of the nonelderly and 63 percent of the elderly had hospital coverage. Coverage for physician services in the hospital, both surgical and nonsurgical, was also 78 percent for the nonelderly and about 50 percent for the elderly. In 1975, coverage for x-rays and laboratory tests for the nonelderly was 78 percent, whereas only 50 percent of this age group were covered in 1967. A similar dramatic jump occurred in coverage for office and home visits by physicians. In 1970, only 35 percent of people under 65 had such coverage. By 1975, the extent of coverage had almost doubled to include 64 percent of this cohort. While other categories of coverage have leveled off, dental care coverage is still expanding. Dental coverage doubled from 15 percent of the nonelderly covered in 1975 up to 30 percent in 1979.

The period between 1965 and the present has also included an expanded role for the federal government in services delivery. The most dramatic examples of expanded federal coverage are the Medicare and Medicaid programs. Federal funding for health care services, along with the expansion of third-party private insurance payments, has been a factor in rising health care costs. While 50 years ago, most people paid for all of their health care services directly through out-of-pocket expenditures, most people today have many health costs paid for through third-party coverage or government programs. Critics of the U.S. health system argue that the consumer of services is less sensitive to the actual price of services if a health insurance company pays all or 80 percent of the charges. While achieving the desirable goal of expanding access to health care for a large part of the population, third-party payments have simultaneously contributed to health care price inflation and rising costs.

CHAPTER FOUR
POLITICS AND THE
HEALTH POLICY PROCESS

A nation's health policy is a part of its general overall social policy. As such, health policy formulation is influenced by the variety and array of social and economic factors that impact on social policy development. The nature and history of existing institutions, the general climate of opinion, ritualized methods for dealing with social conflict, attitudes and behavioral characteristics of key political actors, and the general goals and values of a society all play a role in the formulation of social policy (Fein 1980). Influencing all these factors which, in turn, shape social policy formulation, is the underlying ideology to which citizens adhere. A nation's basic ideology is critical to the perception of what social policies are legitimate and fair.

The basic ideology of the United States for two centuries has been liberalism. Liberalism, as developed in Europe in the eighteenth century and nurtured in the United States when transplanted, emphasizes individualism — both individual rights and freedoms. Individuals were the basis and justification for governments and their policies. In order to prevent government from imposing arbitrary choices upon citizens, government and governmental policies were to remain small in scale, so that individuals could attain maximum choice.

Most things affecting individual well-being, including responsibility for personal health care, were to be both the choice and the responsibility of the individual. Only in the twentieth century did liberals begin to see government and governmental policies as a counter to other powerful forces within society which impinged on individual freedom. While the attitude toward the role of government shifted somewhat, to regard big government and government policies as a sometimes necessary evil to counter other forces, particularly economic, the supreme emphasis on the individual remained. The open frontier and large expanse of resources in the United States throughout its first 200 years of development permitted and even accentuated the comparatively extreme focus on individual freedoms and rights.

Closely related to political liberalism is its economic philosophical twin: capitalism, which also has significantly influenced the development of policy in the United States. Capitalism was also initially articulated in a coherent fashion in the eighteenth century with Adam Smith's ground-breaking book, *The Wealth of Nations* in 1776, the same year as the American Revolution (Samuelson 1973). The simultaneous timing of the births of capitalism as an economic theory and the United States as a country make it understandable that the new nation would adopt the new philosophy (Macridis 1983; Burns et al. 1981).

Capitalism represented a significant departure from the prevailing Christian philosophy, especially Catholicism, which dominated thinking to that point. Christianity maintained that society was better off as a whole if each individual within it eschewed individual gain and adhered to norms of self-denial. Poverty was an esteemed value at the time, especially among some religious orders. By contrast, the brash new capitalistic theory contended the reverse: society was to be better off as a whole if each individual within it vigorously pursued his or her own welfare to the greatest extent possible. While traditional Christian philosophy glorified individual denial, capitalism and some of the growing Protestant religions glorified individual gain (Weber 1958).

Capitalism operated through private markets in which individuals were free to choose jobs, investments, and consumption patterns. The driving force of capitalism was competition, where no single unit of production controlled either the total quantity or price of a product or service. Profits were the difference between total revenues from the sale of goods and services and total costs from the purchase of supplies and labor. Profits were the guiding force which efficiently, without central government control, moved labor and equipment from an oversupplied industry to an undersupplied one

(Samuelson 1973). Government intervention, under capitalistic theory, was neutral at best and usually malevolent (Friedman 1962). Government intervention resulted in monopolies and impeded the competition so necessary to an effective functioning of capitalism. Only in the late 1800s and early 1900s was government intervention perceived as necessary to regulate and enforce competition in the private marketplace through antitrust legislation. At that point, government became a referee among powerful private corporations and magnates anxious to build financial empires (Burns et al. 1981).

In the twentieth century, a further shift in attitude toward government intervention in the private economy occurred. Government began to be regarded as the provider of public goods — services needed for overall well-being, but which, for various reasons, were not being provided within the private marketplace (Musgrave and Musgrave 1976; Downs 1967). Despite the recent recognition of the legitimacy of the role of government as a provider of public goods through social policy formulation and execution, the ideological bias in the United States toward capitalism and private markets as the preferred service delivery mechanism remains strong.

Given the strong ideological biases in the United States toward the twin philosophies of liberalism and capitalism, and the extensive consensus that those philosophies are appropriate, Americans appear nonideological in their attitudes toward government and national policies when compared with European countries (Campbell et al. 1960). Part of the U.S. nonideological bias comes from a pragmatic orientation. U.S. political structures further reinforce the nonideological bias, in contrast to the way conservative, labor, and socialist political parties operate in many European countries. Positions deviating from capitalistic and liberal philosophy remain outside of the mainstream of the two major political parties because such little support for extreme positions exists in the population. Americans are also nonideological in their attitudes toward national social policy including the role of government in health services delivery, in part, because their ideology is covert and homogeneous.

THE POLICY FORMULATION PROCESS

The policy formulation process has been dominated by three major actors in the political process: interest groups concerned about and affected by a particular policy area, the bureau or agency in the executive branch which administers the policy area, and the committees and subcommittees within Congress responsible for legislation and appropriations in that area. These three major actors have often been called the "Iron Triangle," a name which reflects both their numbers and their lock on policy development (Peters 1982). Each becomes an advocate for the continuation of programs in that policy area and the development of new programs. Each, for different reasons, typically favors policy expansion and increased funding in the given policy area.

The relationships among the three actors has been a symbiotic one of mutual dependence. Interest groups need access to Congress to get legislation passed favorable to their group's members, and to relevant administrative agencies to influence the rules and regulations created in the executive branch. Congressional committees need access to the administrative agency to perform their oversight function of policy implementation and to determine what policy development would be desirable. Members of Congress and administrative agencies use interest groups for information and to mobilize support for particular programs.

In the United States, separate and equal branches of government theoretically have primary responsibility for a particular phase of the policy process. Constitutionally, Congress is given the responsibility for policy formulation by the mandate of making laws. The president, as head of the executive branch, is mandated to faithfully execute the laws. The judicial branch is required to interpret the laws as disputes arise and are litigated. In reality, each of the three branches performs most of the policy functions of formulation, implementation, and interpretation. In addition to making laws, Congress is involved in policy administration via its oversight function (Dodd and Schott 1979). The executive branch often writes and develops legislation which a supportive member of Congress will subsequently introduce. Executive agencies further engage in policy formulation by developing more detailed rules and regulations which provide the detailed framework for a particular piece of legislation (Warren 1982). Executive regulatory agencies and commissions fill a judicial role by ascertaining the legitimacy of specific interpretations. Increasingly, the courts make policy by the establishment of common law and court orders.

THE ROLE OF CONGRESS

Congress, unlike some other national legislatures, has additional legislative roles beyond policy formulation which compete with the policy formulation role for institutional resources and time of members of Congress. Three typical legislative roles are often assumed by national assemblies: a law-making role, a representative role, and a constituency service role. The U.S. Congress assumes all three roles (Ripley 1983). By contrast, national legislatures in developing countries often abdicate the policy formulation role to a strong executive, leaving legislators primarily as ombudsmen who interface with constituents and a comparatively developed and potent bureaucracy. In many parliamentary systems, the ombudsman role has been formally institutionalized separately from the law-making and representative roles. In these systems, a formal institution distinct from the national legislature called the ombudsman has been created to carry out constituent service. In the United States, these three sometimes conflicting roles are all the responsibility of members of Congress.

The two major operating mechanisms within Congress are the seniority system and the committee structure (Keefe and Ogul 1977). Seniority within the House or Senate is a major criterion in making committee assignments. On individual committees and subcommittees, seniority among the ranks of the membership of the dominant party usually determines committee and subcommittee chairmanships (Dodd and Oppenheimer 1977). When Congress is active in policy formulation, the activity occurs within committees and subcommittees. New legislation that deals with a particular problem would originate in the relevant subcommittee. Major committees dealing with health include subcommittees on the finance and appropriations committees in each house and authorizing committees, including the subcommittees on aging, alcoholism and drug abuse, and health and scientific research of the Senate Committee on Health and Human Resources, and the House Committee on Education and Labor.

The emphasis on committees evolved in reaction to the dictatorial reign of House Speaker Joe Cannon during the first decade of the 20th century (Dodd and Schott 1979). Committees allowed congressmen to specialize in areas of particular relevance to their constituencies, enhancing their re-election potential. Dodd and Schott trace a further devolution of policy formulation from committees to subcommittees, as both the complexity of economic and social issues addressed by government and the scope of the government in policy formulation grew.

Policy formulation in Congress is a lengthy process, filled with numerous veto points where interest groups can either influence the shape of legislation or stop its progress entirely. All authorizing legislation must be approved by both houses of Congress. For legislation first introduced in the House of Representatives, new legislation can be delayed by the chairperson of the House substantive subcommittee, the House substantive committee, the House Rules Committee, the House, the chairperson of the Senate subcommittee, the Senate committee, the majority of the Senate, 41 members of the Senate in the case of a filibuster, the House-Senate conference committee if the chambers disagree, and the president (Burns et al. 1981).

FUNDING PROGRAMS THROUGH THE CONGRESSIONAL BUDGET PROCESS

After the authorizing legislation is passed, separate and similar hurdles in the budgetary process must be overcome to secure funding. All revenue and appropriations bills must originate in the House (Schick 1981). In 1974, with the passage of the Congressional Budget and Impoundment Control Act, the budget process was reformed to coordinate congressional budgetary actions and to restore power to Congress vis-à-vis the executive branch. Before the 1974 reforms, only the president with the assistance of the Office of Management and Budget, formulated a national budget (Lynch 1979).

In the absence of an alternative congressional budget, any overall coherence in budget formulation resulted from the framework provided by the president's budget. Appropriations bills in each specific policy area were passed sequentially through both houses. At no point was the budget debated in entirety. Explicit trade-offs between increased funding in one area and equivalent decreased funding in another area were eschewed. Deference was given to the positions of subcommittee members, who were usually advocates for increased funding in their areas of expertise (Fenno 1973).

Symptoms of the difficulties with this decentralized and uncoordinated process were rising annual deficits, an increasingly overheated and inflated economy, and a growing willingness by presidents, especially Nixon, to use impoundments as a tool to thwart the will of Congress in budgetary decisions. The 1974 Budget Act created budget committees within each house to hold hearings on the macroeconomic policy decisions, as well as to set targets within 16 (now 19) broadly defined functional areas, one of which was health. The Budget and Appropriations Committees were aided in their tasks by the analyses and staff of the newly created Congressional Budget Office, the congressional equivalent to the executive branch's Office of Management and Budget.

The act set up a budgetary calendar. After holding hearings in the fall on fiscal policy needs, and in the early spring on new program requests, the budget committees simultaneously present a first concurrent budget resolution to their respective houses in April for a prescribed number of hours of debate. Passage of the first budget resolution establishing target spending levels within each of the functional areas must occur by May 15. During the summer months, the appropriations subcommittees and committees perform their usual tasks of passing bills within their specialized areas, now guided by the overall functional spending targets established in the first concurrent budget resolution. By September 15, Congress reevaluates macroeconomic needs and makes needed changes in a second concurrent budget resolution. Discrepancies between the overall and functional totals in the second concurrent budget resolution and the actual totals passed in the various appropriations bill are addressed in the reconciliation process.

The thrust of the 1974 Budget Act was to invert the decision process in congressional budget decisions from a bottom-up to a top-down decision structure. Before the act, initial decisions were micro-level spending decisions at the program level. Budget totals and functional area subtotals were the result of these micro-level decisions and were not the primary consideration. The intent of the act was to make decisions about overall and functional totals supersede and bind subsequent decisions about specific program spending. One unintended impact limited the influence of interest groups by rationalizing the process and forcing more stringent justifications and five-year projections of costs for proposed programs.

Has the Congressional Budget and Impoundment Control Act of 1974 been successful in reforming congressional budgetary politics and decision processes? The results have been mixed, with some successes and some failures. The Congressional Budget Office has provided an additional source of expertise and estimates, improving the quality of budgetary information available to congressional decision makers. The CBO, as a congressional agency, does not exhibit the bias toward presidential policies in estimates and information that often occurs in OMB documents. A third success is sensitizing most members of Congress to budget considerations and constraints. The first and second concurrent budget resolutions must be debated on the floor of each house, focusing attention on both the fiscal ramifications of program level funding decisions, and the priorities and implicit trade-offs encompassed in the budget (Boskin and Wildavsky 1982).

Conservatives initially supported the 1974 budget reforms as a means to control the rate of government growth and spending. The budget reforms have not, however, significantly altered either rate. Nor have the 1974 reforms dealt effectively with the issue of backdoor spending. Across the years, a large amount of total federal outlays (about 75 percent of each year's budget) have been removed from annual decision making through a backdoor spending process. Backdoor spending devices include contract authority where government officials can obligate the government to spend monies in future years through legal contracts; borrowing authority such as legal obligations occurred in financing the national debt, earmarked revenues such as funds from a specific source (for example, the gasoline tax) which can be legally expended for only selected activities (for example, highways and mass transit); loan guarantees where the government promises to refund lenders in the event of default by debtors (for example, some student and housing loans); and entitlement programs (Lynch, 1979; Boskin and Wildavsky 1982).

With entitlement programs, benefits are guaranteed at a legislated level to all eligible recipients. Once benefit levels are legislated, total spending levels are a function of the number of eligible recipients claiming their entitlement. The federal government is obligated to make entitlement payments to eligible recipients, even if initially insufficient funds were allocated in the budget. The federal budget includes approximately 70 entitlement programs which constitute more than 50 percent of total federal expenditures, including major health and welfare programs such as Medicaid, Aid to Families with Dependent Children (AFDC), and food stamps; Social Security Trust Funds including Medicare; and veteran's benefits including medical care (Schick 1981).

A third problem with the 1974 budget reforms was in the reconciliation phase, intended to modify the appropriations bills to make spending totals conform to the desired amounts specified in the second concurrent budget resolution. In the original act, only ten days were scheduled between the adoption of the second concurrent budget resolution and final passage of a reconciliation bill – an inadequate time frame preventing the use of the reconciliation process. Originally conceived as a device to force changes in appropriations enacted during the current budget cycle, the reconciliation process was moved in 1980 from the end of the deliberation on the budget to the beginning (Schick 1981). The shift allowed the reconciliation bill to instruct authorizing committees to change legislation enacted in previous years. The impact of reconciliation at the beginning of the budget cycle has been to enhance the adjustment of budgetary outcomes to political sentiment. Indirectly, this restores some power in the budgetary process to the president and the executive branch by providing a mechanism to force trade-offs among funding for different functions. Without such a trade-off mechanism, interest groups could continue to demand increased funding for their specialized areas without forcing reductions in funding for other levels. The shift in reconciliation provided a device for the administration to limit these demands by institutionalizing a process for more forcefully expressing administration priorities.

THE ROLE OF THE EXECUTIVE BRANCH
AND ADMINISTRATION

The role of administrative agencies in establishing policy has always been considerable in the U.S. system. Textbook separations of the functions of government into legislative branch policy formulation, executive branch policy execution, and judicial branch policy interpretation are analytic but not realistic distinctions. In reality, all branches of government to a greater or lesser degree engage in each phase of the policy process. Over time, the mixture of policy phases handled by each governmental branch has become richer and more varied, rather than leaner and more homogeneous. The role of the executive branch and administrative agencies in policy formulation has likewise increased dramatically in recent years.

One important activity of administrative agencies is rule making. Rules are the mechanism by which agencies provide detailed restrictions, regulations, and guidelines to congressional statutes stated in terms of broad, less-defined goals. The interpretation of the intent and nature of the statute by the administrative agency through the administrative rules that the agency establishes both gives the statutory law life and determines the extent and scope of impact (Warren 1982). In the case of complicated legislation, such as Medicaid, the administratively developed regulations are vast in length compared to the considerably shorter length of the enabling legislation. Each time an amendment affecting the basic legislation is passed by Congress, such as the Omnibus Reconciliation Act of 1981 which affected Medicaid, new rules and regulations are issued by the appropriate administrative agency.

While not all laws are so vague as to require an accompanying array of administrative rules, the tendency of Congress in recent years has been to increase the number of laws devoid of elaborate detail and worded in more vague general terms. The courts have recognized the tendency of Congress to delegate its constitutional authority to develop policy via the law-making process to administrative agencies, but have declined to force Congress to be more specific in establishing details through statutory law, as opposed to administrative rules.

Through a series of court cases which collectively have established the delegation doctrine and have become incorporated into common law, the authority of the Congress to delegate policy formulation to administrative agencies has been upheld by the U.S. Supreme Court. Beginning with the case, *United States* v. *Curtis-Wright Export Co.*, 299 U.S. 304 (1936), the courts have consistently supported the right of Congress to delegate rule-making authority to administrative agencies, as long as Congress set some meaningful standards to guide government administrators in their efforts to formulate detailed policies. In *United States* v. *Cable Co.*, 392 U.S. 157 (1968), the courts expanded rule-making authority even further by vaguely interpreting "standards" required in congressional law to direct administrators as anything mandating administration in a manner which is consistent with law as "public convenience, intent, or necessity requires" (Warren 1982).

Congressional legislation granting wholesale discretionary power to agencies to formulate rules has often included a "legislative veto." Through legislative veto, both houses, one house, or even a single committee retains the right to overrule policy developed by administrative agencies through rules. After a period of rapid growth, the legislative veto was declared unconstitutional in 1983.

The role of administrative agencies in policy formulation has typically been that of advocate for increased funding for the policy area in which the agency has jurisdiction. As one of the three parts of the "Iron Triangle" of policy formulation, administrative agencies have generally also argued for increased benefits for major client groups (Wildavsky 1979). Bureaucrats have been more liberal than Congress in supporting increases in social programs, for such programs are accompanied by an expanded role of the administrator, as well as greater administrative power, authority, and prestige. Conservative proposals typically emphasize cutbacks, cost-saving measures, and reduced administrative authority and prestige.

The advocacy role of the agency in policy formulation often contrasts with the role of the department in which the agency is organizationally located. While department officials may be overall advocates for the entire department, that position may require a cutback position for any specific agency. The advocacy role of department officials is further tempered by the official positions and policy thrusts of the particular president whom they are serving. The Office of Management and Budget is likewise more sensitive to overall presidential policy goals and may be either an advocate for increased funding or a supporter of reduced funding, depending upon presidential initiatives.

Presidential initiatives in shaping the orientation of administrative agencies in policy formulation are often thwarted. While the president remains both the titular and actual head of the executive branch, including all administrative agencies except for independent regulatory commissions, bureaucratic agencies have become so independently powerful in policy formulation that some scholars regard them as the "fourth branch of government." The power of administrative agencies to circumvent the policy intent of the president to whom they are organizationally accountable stems from several sources (Rourke 1976; Fesler 1980).

Administrators, as part of the federal civil service established originally by the 1883 Pendleton Act, have some degree of job security. As part of a career civil service, most bureaucrats work for their agencies for many years. By contrast, the term of any president is limited to a maximum of eight years by the Twenty-second Amendment to the Constitution. Political appointees in any given administration frequently serve an even briefer time span, returning to the private sector and to nongovernmental careers. Bureaucrats can simply outlast superiors with whose policy goals they disagree. Only a small proportion of all agency employees are political appointees whose main allegiance is to the president who appointed them. The bulk of agency personnel are permanent civil servants.

Of at least equal if not greater importance in establishing the independence of administrative agencies in policy formulation, even vis-à-vis the president, is the expertise of higher-level career civil servants. Bureaucrats become functional specialists in their particular policy area, or at higher levels within the agency, are hired because of prior policy expertise. Their detailed expertise provides a power base with which other actors in the policy process, including the president and his political appointees, must cope. Specialized knowledge and expertise are especially important in health policy formulation. The areas of health policy and health programs have become both very complex and very technical, leaving political appointees without substantive health knowledge and expertise at a particular policy disadvantage.

THE ROLE OF INTEREST GROUPS

The third leg of the iron triangle is composed of health interest groups. In addition to congressional committees and subcommittees, which constitute the first leg, and agency bureaucrats and political appointees, who make up the second leg, interest groups play a significant role in developing national health policy. While interest groups have no formal government position or power base, they have nevertheless been coopted into the policy process (Chelf 1981). Like bureaucrats, interest groups provide specialized knowledge and expertise in different areas of health policy.

In addition to providing accurate but often biased and partial information to policy makers, interest groups take stands on health-related issues. They monitor the progress of health-related legislation through the congressional labyrinth of subcommittee hearings, committee hearings, floor debates, and amendments. Interest groups alert their membership to upcoming crucial votes, often focusing on mobilizing group members to affect vote outcomes.

Often, the role of interest groups in policy formulation moves beyond passive monitoring of proposed legislation to active initiation of new policies. Given the specialized expertise and knowledge of interest groups, they sometimes propose innovative solutions to health-related problems, which become the basis for coalition-building in the bureaucracy and in Congress. Yet another role of interest groups is an educational one: informing both their membership and sometimes the general public about the need for health policy changes. In this role, interest groups facilitate general consensus-building for various health policy initiatives they support.

The clout of interest groups is enhanced in health policy formulation by relatively unorganized and inchoate citizen attitudes toward health. Typically, citizens think about the health care system and services delivery infrequently, unless they are personally involved through employment in the system, temporarily in need of health care, or personally have a chronic illness or have a family member with one. The absence of citizen concern enhances the role of health-related interest groups in policy formulation, as does conflicting citizen opinions on health issues. For example, while many citizens agree that health care costs should be contained, they also believe in fee-for-service reimbursement for physicians, without understanding the connection between payment methods and costs.

Interest groups influence policy by forming political action committees (PACs) to raise funds for candidates or political parties for elections. PACs have been used by labor groups since the 1930s. Their numbers and impact mushroomed in the 1970s with changes in campaign laws. In 1974, sweeping federal legislation was passed forming the Federal Election Commission, and establishing federal election campaign contribution limits of $1,000 for individuals donating to a candidate in a primary or general election, and $5,000 for an organization, including a PAC (Burns et al. 1981).

The goal of the 1974 legislation was to limit the impact of PACs and interest groups on election outcomes. This goal was undercut by 1979 amendments which allowed interest groups to distinguish between "hard money" and "soft money." While stringent federal limits applied to hard money, soft money expenditures used for party-building and opinion development are controlled only by state laws (Drew 1982a and 1982b). Through the less restricted category of soft money, the role of PACs in election outcomes and the role of the interest groups they represent has increased dramatically.

During 1977 and 1978, approximately 112 health PACs provided funds to candidates for federal and state offices. Both national and state AMA-related health PACs were large contributors to favored candidates, together providing $5.6 million for candidates for the Ninety-sixth Congress. These groups were the largest contributors of the various health PACs. Other health-related contributors in the 1978 congressional races who donated significant amounts were dental-related PACs representing both state dental associations and the American Dental Association. Together these groups contributed $1.7 million. In the same year, for congressional races, PACs representing nurses donated nationally $100,000; podiatrists, $258,000; optometrists, $112,000; and nursing homes, $123,000 (Feldstein and Melnick 1982).

In addition to affecting election outcomes, PACs have a second motivation in donating campaign contributions to political candidates. Often PACs view their contribution as the price of access to politicians in the interim between elections. This motive is reflected in a typical campaign donation strategy of giving small amounts to candidates having ideologies similar to the interests of the health PAC members. In such cases, the PAC contribution may be too small to influence the election outcome to any major degree, but may generate good will on the part of the candidate toward the PAC.

The tact taken by a PAC in developing a donation strategy may depend at least in part on the size of the PAC treasury. With a large budget, as with the AMA-related health PACs, contributions may be directed to candidates in races with no incumbent, or challengers. For example, MEDPAC, the group of PACs which are tied to the AMA, gave large contributions both in absolute dollars and in relation to the candidate's overall receipts in 1978 to challengers or incumbents in close elections. This strategy was designed to influence election outcomes. By contrast, small PACs develop "support your friend" contribution strategies designed to generate good will. A version of the "support your friend" strategy employed by health PACs are contributions to members of Congress on health-related committees.

Not all health-related interest groups function alike in the health policy formulation process. Supply-oriented interest groups may differ from demand-oriented interest groups on the goals of policy formulation as well as strategies for PACs and other tactics. Supply-oriented interest groups include doctors, hospitals, dentists, nurses, nursing homes, chiropractors, and other professions and institutions which provide health care to client groups.

Demand-oriented interest groups include clients of health services. These groups are usually organized on a disease basis, such as the Heart Association, the Cancer Society, and the Lung Association. Specialized interest groups for less common diseases, such as muscular dystrophy, spina-bifada, and multiple sclerosis also attempt to influence health policy. Although demand-oriented interest groups have large numbers of lay members, physicians, nurses, and researchers are also active participants. Consequently, demand-oriented interest groups often have a concern about research frequently lacking in the policy goals of supply-oriented groups.

Generally, supply-oriented groups focus less on legislation relating to health research than do demand-oriented groups. Supply groups focus primarily upon legislation which might affect the organization of the health care delivery system in general, and particularly upon pending statutes which would alter the procedures and practices of their particular profession. For example, physicians as an interest group were among the most active opponents of Medicare legislation prior to its passage, because they perceived the legislation as altering the relationship which physicians had to the government in their practice of medicine. Since Medicare legislation has been passed, the AMA has been active politically on any proposed changes that affect funding levels and reimbursement payments for physicians. Supply groups may differ with each other, since the various interest groups represent different interests and may, at times, be competitive with each other in their attempts to shape national health policy.

By contrast, demand groups focus on increased funding for their particular diseases. Demand groups not only disagree with supply groups about the ranking of research funding in health policy priorities, but they also disagree among themselves about which diseases have the greatest need for increased funding and national attention. While in the areas of funding for services, supply groups favor programs and appropriations which benefit their member providers, demand groups favor increased funding for services received by patients with their particular disease.

Supply and demand groups often differ in tactics they employ to affect policy formulation, as well as in priorities and policy goals. Both groups use traditional lobbying tactics of providing accurate but biased and partial information to key members of Congress. Supply groups, more than demand groups, also rely upon the traditional technique of influencing policy formulation through campaign contributions to favored candidates. By contrast, demand groups often arouse public opinion and organize emotional appeals to Congress. One common demand group strategy is to arrange the testimony of victims of a particular disease and their relatives at congressional hearings where programs and funding requests are being explored.

While policy process observers agree that supply and demand groups differ in strategies employed to generate health legislation, no consensus prevails that one has been more important overall than the other in the policy process. Both supply and demand interest groups have played, at different times, sometimes with different foci, major roles in shaping health policy goals and implementing legislation. Nor do observers agree that one of the three major policy process actors — congress, administrative agencies, and interest groups — exceeds the others in its importance in shaping the federal role in health. The iron triangle remains potent and intact.

CHAPTER FIVE
POLICY PROCESS OUTCOMES: MAJOR FEDERAL HEALTH LEGISLATION

Numerous pieces of legislation implementing national health policy have been passed in the last 50 years. Federal involvement in health issues, however, began in 1798 with the passage of a law that provided for health services for sick and disabled U.S. seamen. Within a year, the first marine hospital was established to implement the 1798 act. Shortly thereafter, arrangements were made to care for seamen in most major coastal seaports. In 1832, hospitals were also built at ports along major lakes and rivers. Other federal legislation as early as 1799 authorized federal officers to cooperate with state and local officials in enforcing quarantine laws. Very little additional federal involvement in health issues occurred until after the Civil War.

Federal involvement in health through statutory legislation, as in any area of federal policy, must be bolstered by authorization in the U.S. Constitution. Federal powers in the U.S. Constitution were delegated, while remaining powers not specifically given to the federal government were reserved for the states. Specific clauses must be used to justify federal involvement in health.

Constitutional authority for the early legislation just described and subsequent pieces of federal legislation come from three different sources in the U.S. Constitution. One authorization – the power to raise and support armies, to provide and maintain a navy, and to pass laws "necessary and proper" to carry out those powers – is the original authority for marine hospitals. Today it justifies the expenditure of funds for the military health system and the VA health system. A second authorization is derived from the constitutional power of the federal government to regulate foreign and interstate commerce. The original mandate for federal officials to work with quarantines comes from this source. Much of the federal regulatory activity in areas such as control of food and drugs, product and occupational safety, and some areas of environmental health are justified by the interstate commerce clause. The third and major clause for federal involvement in national health policy is the general welfare clause, the most commonly used justification for federal involvement in health today. It is used as authorization for medical research, major service delivery programs such as Medicare and Medicaid, and health manpower and training programs.

Often health legislation emerging from the policy formulation process is multifaceted, encompassing research, planning and regulation, and service objectives in the same statute. Basic pieces of health legislation have frequently been omnibus bills, including several national health policy goals. Nor are pieces of health legislation congruent with the structure of bureaus and agencies charged with administering them. As legislation is amended repeatedly across time, responsibility for implementing one piece of legislation may be allocated to several different agencies, especially agencies within the Department of Health and Human Services.

DHHS health-related agencies include the National Institutes of Health, the Centers for Disease Control, the Food and Drug Administration, the Alcohol Drug Abuse and Mental Health Administration, the Health Resources and Services Administration, and the Office of the Assistant Secretary for Health. While the major governmental unit responsible for administering health legislation is the DHHS, other government units such as the Environmental Protection Agency, the Federal Trade Commission, and the Veterans Administration are located outside DHHS and also play a role in health policy implementation.

Two charts display the organizational structure of health-related agencies and bureaus. In Figure 5-1, the relationships between major governmental units which deal with health are shown, specifically, the Department of Health and Human Services, the Environmental Protection Agency, the Occupational Safety and Health Administration, the Veterans Administration, and the Federal Trade Commission. In Figure 5-2, greater detail on the health-related agencies within the Department of Health and Human Services is displayed.

FIGURE 5-1
HEALTH RELATED FEDERAL ORGANIZATIONS

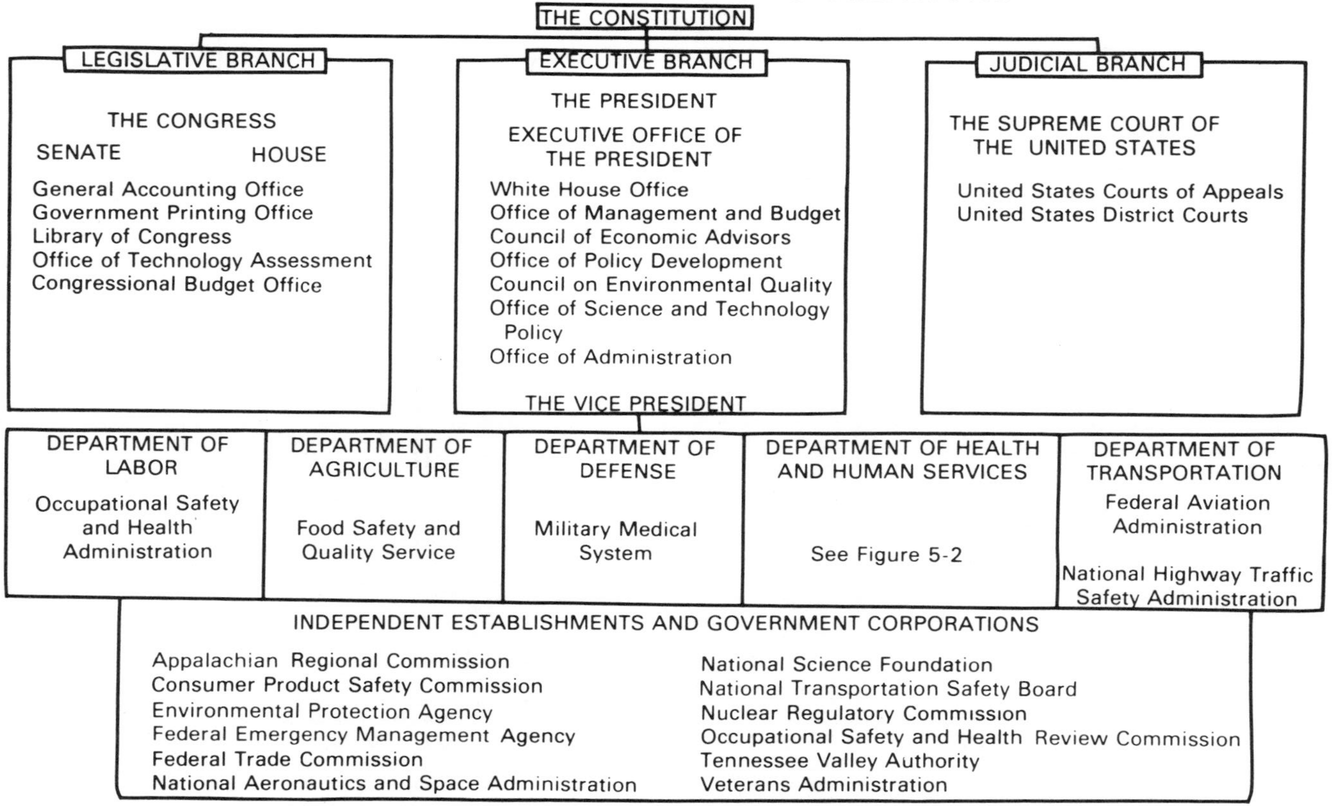

THE CONSTITUTION

LEGISLATIVE BRANCH

THE CONGRESS

SENATE   HOUSE

General Accounting Office
Government Printing Office
Library of Congress
Office of Technology Assessment
Congressional Budget Office

EXECUTIVE BRANCH

THE PRESIDENT

EXECUTIVE OFFICE OF
THE PRESIDENT

White House Office
Office of Management and Budget
Council of Economic Advisors
Office of Policy Development
Council on Environmental Quality
Office of Science and Technology
Policy
Office of Administration

THE VICE PRESIDENT

JUDICIAL BRANCH

THE SUPREME COURT OF
THE UNITED STATES

United States Courts of Appeals
United States District Courts

**DEPARTMENT OF
LABOR**

Occupational Safety
and Health
Administration

**DEPARTMENT OF
AGRICULTURE**

Food Safety and
Quality Service

**DEPARTMENT OF
DEFENSE**

Military Medical
System

**DEPARTMENT OF HEALTH
AND HUMAN SERVICES**

See Figure 5-2

**DEPARTMENT OF
TRANSPORTATION**

Federal Aviation
Administration

National Highway Traffic
Safety Administration

INDEPENDENT ESTABLISHMENTS AND GOVERNMENT CORPORATIONS

Appalachian Regional Commission
Consumer Product Safety Commission
Environmental Protection Agency
Federal Emergency Management Agency
Federal Trade Commission
National Aeronautics and Space Administration

National Science Foundation
National Transportation Safety Board
Nuclear Regulatory Commission
Occupational Safety and Health Review Commission
Tennessee Valley Authority
Veterans Administration

71

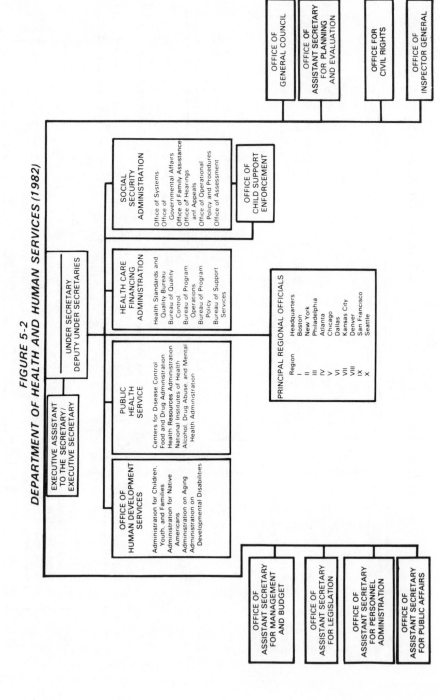

FIGURE 5-2
DEPARTMENT OF HEALTH AND HUMAN SERVICES (1982)

Appendixes 1 through 3 break federal health legislation into the three subcategories of research, planning and regulation, and services. While all major health legislation described in the Appendixes have been characterized as falling into at least one of these three categories, some federal legislation may be included in more than one category.

THE PUBLIC HEALTH SERVICE ACT
AND RELATED LEGISLATION

Legislation Leading to the Public Health Service Act

One major piece of federal health legislation, the Public Health Service (PHS) Act of 1944, consolidated previously existing health legislation. Many early federal health statutes were later incorporated in the PHS Act, including the Merchant Marine Seaman Act of 1799. The thrust of federal efforts in the merchant marine area started a trend of providing services to clearly defined and selected groups. This trend may be contrasted with universal coverage, and has continued into the twentieth century with coverage for the elderly and the poor.

There were several reasons for federal provision of health care services to merchant seamen. A strong and healthy merchant marine was crucial to both the economic development of the nation and to national defense. The mobility of merchant seamen precluded them from easily fitting within the existing system of health care in port cities and specific states, creating a need filled by federal marine hospitals. The Merchant Marine Act also met a federal objective of preventing epidemics, since merchant marines were transient and often carried diseases to new locations.

The Marine Hospital Service, formally organized in 1870, was followed by the establishment of the Commissioned Corps in 1899. Under the Commissioned Corps, physicians were commissioned by the federal government to engage in public health activities, in much the same way the federal government commissioned military doctors to handle health care services for members of the armed services. In 1930, the Commissioned Corps was expanded to permit the hiring of engineers and dentists. The Commissioned Corps, through its public health functions, served both federal objectives of preventing epidemics and maintaining a healthy merchant marine.

An expansion of the federal role to combat epidemics and infectious diseases occurred with the Federal Quarantine Act of 1878. The Marine Hospital Service was given the authority to centralize quarantine laws and to provide such laws for ports that lacked either state or local regulations. This role was further expanded in 1893 when the Marine Hospital Service was given full responsibility for foreign and interstate quarantine.

Advancements in medicine at this time were based on the developing fields of microbiology and bacteriology, including new techniques of vaccination and the discovery of the tuberculosis and cholera bacilli by Robert Koch. The Marine Hospital Services established the Hygienic Laboratory in 1887 at the Staten Island hospital. Four years later, the laboratory had proved its worth and was moved to Service headquarters in Wahington, D.C. The functions were expanded into the four areas of pathology, chemistry, pharmacology, and zoology. This laboratory became one of the foundations for the National Institutes of Health in 1930 (Raffel 1980; Strickland 1972).

In 1902, a separate health act was passed, clarifying federal health functions and recognizing the expansion of the activities of the Marine Hospitals Service by renaming it the Public Health and Marine Service of the United States. This act legitimized the dominant role of the federal government in public health by specifying a system of communications among state and territorial health officers. The surgeon general, the administrative head of the Public Health Service, was authorized to convene an annual meeting of state and territorial health officers to discuss major health policy initiatives and disease campaigns to control trachoma (an eye disease), typhoid fever (a highly infectious disease transmitted by contaminated food or water), and pellagra (a nutritional-deficiency disease caused by lack of niacine). Also in 1902, the Biologics Control Act was passed which gave the Public Health Service (PHS) responsibility for licensing and regulating the production and sale of biologically derived health products, such as vaccines and serums.

A different type of thrust in health legislation started with the Maternal and Infancy Act of 1921, better known as the Sheppard-Towner Act. This act provided grants to the states to develop health services for mothers and children and was the first federal grant-in-aid program for direct health services. This act proved to be quite controversial, generating criticism and opposition from conservative groups and from medical groups such as the AMA who openly called the Sheppard-Towner Act "an imported socialistic scheme." Adding to the controversy of the act was a requirement that services provided under its aegis be available for all residents of a state, regardless of race. Massachusetts was so upset that it unsuccessfully initiated court action to have the act declared unconstitutional. The act was allowed to lapse in 1929 (Wallace et al. 1982). Many of the functions of this act were resumed with the passage of the Social Security Act in 1935, to be discussed later.

A major separate federal involvement in the direct provision of health care services involves veterans. Although some limited efforts to provide services to seriously disabled veterans had begun at the end of World War I, the Veterans Act of 1924 codified and extended the role of the federal government in the provision of health care services to veterans. That act extended medical care to veterans not only for treatment of disabilities associated with military service, but also for other conditions requiring hospitalization. Preference was given to veterans who could not afford private care. In 1930, the Veterans Administration (VA) was created as an independent U.S. government agency to handle medical care services in VA hospitals, the facilities for disabled soldiers, and other veterans matters such as pensions.

The next major legislative developments were originally passed as Title V and VI to the Social Security Act of 1935, but were incorporated into the Public Health Service Act in 1944. Title V provided grants to the states for maternal and child welfare functions, including grants to crippled children. This Social Security Act title was broader than the previously abolished Sheppard-Towner Act and doubled the appropriations in the latter. The program for crippled children represented a new thrust in federal legislation. Included were demonstration monies which became the foundation of experience for innovative project grant amendments in later legislation. The program had both comprehensive and preventive aspects, paying for all related medical care for crippled children or children threatened with crippling conditions.

Title VI authorized annual federal grants to states for the investigation of disease and problems of sanitation, reinforcing the dominance of the federal government in its partnership with state and local governments on health-related issues. By the close of the 1936 fiscal year, approximately 175 new local health departments were created as a result of this federal funding. During the next year, states were able to turn to the PHS for consulting services in the areas of nutrition, dental hygiene, laboratory methods, and accounting (Raffel 1980; Strickland 1972).

The health research functions of the federal government had begun with the creation of the Hygienic Laboratory and were expanded by two acts passed in the 1930s. In 1930, the Ransdell Act created the National Institute of Health (NIH) incorporating the already operative Hygienic Laboratory. This act, along with the ongoing activities of the lab, marked a departure from the originally constricted federal role of providing services to merchant seamen or directly combating epidemics. With this act, the federal government edged into general health activities and began a minuscule role in manpower training. The act provided money for additional buildings to house health research activities, created a system of health fellowships, and authorized the federal acceptance of donations for research on the cause, prevention, and cure of diseases (Strickland 1972).

The second act expanding the federal role in health research established the National Cancer Institute (NCI) in 1937. NCI was authorized to award grants to nongovernment scientists and institutions, to provide fellowships for the training of scientists and clinicians, and to fund direct government cancer research. Representing a break with tradition, federal funds for nongovernmental institutions and scientists became a pattern for all federal support of biomedical research.

In 1938, a Federal Food, Drug, and Cosmetic Act adding coverage for therapeutic devices and cosmetics was passed to replace the Wiley Act of 1906, significantly strengthening federal laws on food and drug safety. An important provision required that new drugs be approved for safety before being marketed in the United States.

The Venereal Disease Control Act of 1938 returned to the federal role of combating specific diseases, like earlier federal efforts to combat typhoid fever and pellegra. Unlike previous federal efforts, which were not specifically authorized in legislation, this act mandated the PHS to launch a national control program against syphilis and gonorrhea. Over the next 40 years, as other diseases became publically prominent, additional pieces of disease-specific legislation were passed as amendments to the basic Public Health Service

Act of 1944, such as the Heart Disease, Cancer, and Stroke Amendments of 1965; the National Sickle Cell Anemia Control Act of 1972; the National Cooley's Anemia Control Act of 1972; and the Sudden Infant Death Syndrome Act of 1974.

The Roosevelt administration was interested in the consolidation of federal health functions as part of an overall administrative reorganization of the federal bureaucracy. In a 1939 reorganization, the PHS became a component of the Federal Security Agency (FSA). The FSA became the umbrella for many domestic social programs, including the Food and Drug Administration in 1940. Under the Eisenhower administration in 1953, reflecting the growth in the size and number of domestic social programs, the Federal Security Agency was renamed and given department status as the Department of Health, Education, and Welfare. During the Carter administration in the late 1970s, a separate Department of Education was created, leaving federal health and welfare functions in the renamed Department of Health and Human Services.

A number of specialized emergency health and sanitation functions became the responsibility of the PHS during World War II. Most of these functions were of short duration and did not have a lasting impact on the federal role in health policy. During the later war years, Congress and the Roosevelt administration saw a need to centralize health-related legislation and functions, resulting in the Public Health Service Act of 1944.

THE PUBLIC HEALTH SERVICE ACT
OF 1944 – ORIGINAL STRUCTURE

The scope of the 1944 Public Health Service Act was mammoth. The act revised and compiled previously existing legislation about the Public Health Service, including Title V and VI of the Social Security Act, into one statute. The legislation included five titles (subsections). The first title defined crucial terms. The second title specified the administrative structure of the PHS. The Service was to be administered by the surgeon general, originally under the direction of the head of the Federal Security Administration and after 1953, under the secretary of the Department of Health, Education, and Welfare.

There were four bureaus in the original PHS: the Office of the Surgeon General, the National Institute of Health, the Bureau of

Medical Services, and the Bureau of State Services. This title also specified grades, ranks, and titles of the Commissioned Corps personnel. Under this law, commissioned officers included not only physicians and surgeons, but also dentists, sanitary engineers, pharmacists, nurses, and other related scientific specialties in public health.

Title III set forth the general powers and duties of the PHS. One duty was research and investigation into selected diseases and health problems, including the use and misuse of narcotic drugs. A second duty was working with state and local health agencies, especially for the purpose of preventing and controlling communicable diseases. Specific activities mandated included an annual conference of state health authorities, provision for the collection and compilation of vital statistics (birth records, death records, etc.), grants to the states to assist in venereal disease control and tuberculosis control, and grants for the establishment and maintenance of adequate local and state health departments.

A third PHS duty specified in Title III was the continued maintenance of the marine hospitals and the provision of services to merchant seamen and other eligible groups. The PHS was also to provide medical services to penal and correctional institutions, to federal employees for work-related illness or injury, and to provide medical examinations to aliens. Care for persons with leprosy and narcotics addicts were added PHS responsibilities. This title also specified two additional nonservice functions to PHS: the regulation of the manufacture, labeling, and sale of biological products related to the prevention or cure of diseases or injuries (an incorporation of the earlier Biologics Control Act); and the authority to conduct inspections, quarantines, and other procedures needed to prevent the transmission and spread of communicable diseases.

Earlier legislation before the PHS Act had created the National Cancer Institute. Title IV of the PHS Act relocated the NCI to within the PHS, where it remained for the subsequent 40 years up to the present. The NCI became a part of a newly created subdivision of PHS called the National Institute of Health. While no other institutes in research areas other than cancer existed at that time, this organizational shift created a bureaucratic framework to later add additional institutes, such as the Heart Institute in 1946. Title V dealt with miscellaneous regulations (Wilson and Neuhauser 1982; Strickland 1972). Over time the original act has been amended greatly, with both revisions of the original title and with the creation of additional titles.

The Organizational Structure of the Public Health Service

The Public Health Service has undergone reorganization a number of times since its inception in 1944. In 1967, an organizational structure with five bureaus was created; the National Institutes of Health, the Bureau of Disease Prevention and Environmental Control, the National Institute of Mental Health, the Bureau of Health Services, and the Bureau of Health Manpower. PHS structure reflected areas of concern within public health at that time: disease-specific orientations toward prevention and cure, a growing concern with the impact of the environment upon health, another growing concern with mental health, a traditional focus on service delivery and coordination of state public health activities, and an increasing focus upon health service personnel.

Constant shifting and changing of the organizational structure and location of the PHS has continued since 1967 to the present day, reflecting crisis development of health policy in the United States. A typical response to a problem, either new or newly articulated, is to create a new bureau, restructure a bureau, or move a bureau around. Restructuring is further driven by the turnover of presidential administrations and political appointees in the bureaucracy. Each new administration enters the foray of Washington bureaucratic politics with fresh ideas about how to organize the bureaucracy in a rational manner. The result of perceived or real crises and the considerable turnover in administrations and political appointees has been the creation of a bureaucratic merry-go-round where bureaus are constantly reorganized and relocated. Often newly printed and published organizational charts indicating the latest reorganization barely have dry ink before they are out-of-date.

The 12 years between 1967 and 1979 saw 8 major reorganizations of traditional functions of the PHS and of related federal health activities. In 1968, line responsibility for public health programs was taken away from the surgeon general, the head of PHS, and was given to the HEW assistant secretary for Health and Scientific Affairs. Agencies, such as the Food and Drug Administration (FDA) and the National Library of Medicine, were incorporated into the

PHS and the five bureaus of 1967 were consolidated into three agencies. That same year, one of the three agencies was drastically reorganized by the addition of some new programs, and the pulling of programs from one of the other agencies (Raffel 1980).

Ten years later, in 1983, the PHS had seven major divisions. The FDA, the first major PHS division, had four basic program areas: foods, drugs and medical devices, radiological products, and the National Center for Toxicological Research. The Indian Health Service, the second major PHS division, provided services for native Americans on reservations. The Centers for Disease Control (CDC) was the third major PHS division. Two CDC sections included programs for venereal disease control and immunizations. Another major section of CDC dealt with infectious diseases, including research on diagnosis and prevention. The CDC section on Chronic and Environmental Disease Protection was concerned with lowering risk factors in environmental hazards and chronic diseases. This section has examined problems of radiation, toxic substances, birth defects, and diabetes, among others. Another major section was the National Institute for Occupational Safety and Health, which in 1983 was the only federal agency with a specified mission of conducting research on work-related hazards. The last major section of CDC in the 1983 PHS organizational structure was the Epidemic Services which conducts work in rapid detection and response, diagnosis, and surveillance of a wide range of disease programs.

The fourth of the seven major divisions in the PHS in 1983 was the National Institutes of Health (NIH). There were 11 separate institutes under the overall direction of NIH and 2 specialized components, The John E. Fogarty International Center and the National Library of Medicine. The 11 institutes were: (1) Cancer; (2) Heart, Lung, and Blood; (3) Dental Research; (4) Arthritis, Diabetes, Digestive, and Kidney Diseases; (5) Neurological and Communicative Disorders and Stroke; (6) Allergy and Infectious Diseases; (7) General Medical Sciences; (8) Child Health and Human Development; (9) Eye; (10) Environmental Health Sciences; and (11) Aging.

The Alcohol Drug Abuse and Mental Health Administration was the fifth major PHS division. Its three major components were the National Institute of Mental Health, the National Institute on Drug Abuse, and the National Institute on Alcohol Abuse and Alcoholism, all of which funded both research and training. The National Institute of Mental Health also funded demonstrations.

The last two divisions of PHS were quite complicated. The Office of the Assistant Secretary for Health administered both the general management of the PHS as well as a number of special programs of particular interest, including the National Center for Health Statistics, the National Center for Health Services Research, the Office of Health Promotion, and the Adolescent Family Life Program.

The Health Resources and Services Administration of PHS (HRSA) was created in 1983 from two previously separate agencies, the Health Resources Administration and the Health Services Administration. Most of the health professions training money and loan money fell under HRSA, as did the reduced amounts of funds available for health planning and health maintenance organizations. The remaining federal effort under PHS in the direct provision of services, such as monies for the treatment of Hansen's Disease (leprosy), also fell under the polyglot HRSA.

Since its beginning, the PHS has been characterized by constant reorganization and organizational shifts. The structural reorganizations have accelerated in pace and number during the last 20 years. These reorganizations, designed to enhance rationality and policy implementation, in many ways have impeded both. Working within PHS agencies in Washington has been very chaotic. PHS personnel have been faced with constant uncertainty about the programs they will be implementing and the personnel with whom they will work.

Rationality is further undercut in federal bureaucratic relations with state and local health officials. Constant restructuring and reorganizing at the federal level have impeded the development of smooth-working relationships between the levels of government. Often, state and local officials in specific program areas could not locate the appropriate federal officials or agencies after an administrative change.

The division of PHS least affected by organizational relocation and structural turmoil has been the National Institutes of Health. Most of the changes which have occurred in NIH over the last 40 years have been the addition of new functions and new institutes in additional research areas. While the creation of each new institute has involved the movement of some grants and research areas away from older institutes, reorganizational shifts have been minimized within NIH. Instead, new institutes have expanded the roles and breadth of NIH research. By contrast, other divisions in PHS have experienced a constant reshuffling of existing responsibilities. While the reshuffling of existing functions and organizational structures experienced by non-NIH divisions within PHS creates considerable chaos and uncertainty, the addition of new functions and responsibilities is less unsettling to agency personnel and to interagency and intergovernmental working relationships. Not totally coincidentally, research promulgated and funded by the NIH has been regarded as one of the more successful areas of national health policy.

The Hill-Burton Amendment to the PHS Act

The Hospital Survey and Construction Act of 1946 (more commonly known as the Hill-Burton Act) was the first major amendment to the original PHS legislation, and the first of many post-World War II federally funded health programs. Very little hospital construction in the United States occurred during the Great Depression and World War II, setting the stage for federal legislation funding the building of hospitals. The Hill-Burton Act provided grants to assist states to inventory their existing hospitals and health centers, and to survey the need for the construction of additional facilities. After state surveys were completed, grants for hospital construction were available. Funds for surveys and planning were allocated to states on the basis of total state populations. Federal funding covered up to one-third of the total costs. Funds for construction were allocated through a formula based on population and per capita income, and again covered up to one-third of the total costs.

States had to meet several conditions to be eligible to receive funds. The law required state advisory councils which included representatives of nongovernmental and state agencies concerned with hospitals, as well as representatives of consumers of hospital services (an innovative expansion at the time of representation on an advisory council). States had to submit a plan conforming to the regulations disseminated by the surgeon general for the construction of facilities, based on their statewide survey of need. One regulation which had little immediate impact but did establish a precedent for federal limits on health facilities construction with federal funds was a ceiling on the bed-to-population ratio.

The immediate impact of the Hill-Burton Act was considerable. Hill-Burton was the first federal statute to pump large amounts of federal money in a visible fashion into local communities. By 1949, three years after the adoption of the Hill-Burton legislation, all states and territories had approved state plans. Also as a result of the incentives in the act, most states had adopted licensing laws applicable to all hospitals in the state by the same year. Generally, state health departments became the administering agencies for the law.

Many amendments to the Hill-Burton Act were passed in subsequent years, extending federal financing for both hospitals and for medically-related nonhospital institutions. The Hospital Survey and Construction Amendments of 1949 increased the funding and upped the federal share of cost of hospital construction to a maximum of two-thirds. The act also authorized funding for research and demonstrations relating to the development, utilization, and coordination of hospital services. The Medical Facilities Survey and Construction Act of 1954 provided for grants for surveys and construction of diagnostic and treatment centers such as hospital outpatient departments, rehabilitation centers, and nursing homes. Although chronic disease hospitals were already eligible for Hill-Burton funding, the 1954 amendment specifically named chronic disease hospitals as potential recipients of federal funds.

The Community Health Services and Facilities Act of 1961 was a separate statute but included amendments to the Hill-Burton program increasing the amount of funds available for nursing home construction and extending the research and demonstration grant program to other medical facilities. The Hospital and Medical Facilities Amendment of 1964 specifically designated funds for modernization of hospitals, and gave greater priority for such funds to urban areas. Increased planning monies were also part of this amendment. The Medical Facilities Construction and Modernization Amendments of 1970 extended preexisting aspects of the program, and added loan guarantees for construction and modernization. A new area of program grants for emergency rooms, communications networks, and transportation systems was also created. The Hill-Burton Amendment to the PHS Act, along with its own amendments, were subsequently revised and incorporated into a new Title XVI of the Public Health Service Act in 1974.

The Comprehensive Health Planning and Public Health Service Amendments of 1966

This act also amended the PHS Act and became known among both professionals and lay persons as the Partnership for Health. The Comprehensive Health Planning Act (CHP) represented a departure from the way most federal support for health had been provided. Prior to this amendment, categorical grants of designated funds for specific purposes, such as cancer, dental disease, tuberculosis, and venereal disease, were the major federal funding mechanism. The CHP Act authorized block grants for public health programs, and also included provisions for the development of state and local planning for health services. Block grants were broader in focus than categorical grants, were less bound to specific categories, and gave state and local health departments greater flexibility in how federal funds would be spent within their jurisdictions.

The CHP Amendments were a complete revision of Section 314, Title III, of the original Public Health Service Act. There were five major provisions under Section 314 after the CHP Amendments. To qualify for funds, states were required to submit a plan for comprehensive state health planning. Each state had to designate a state "A agency," a reference to this section of the CHP Section 314 amendments, to be responsible for health planning functions. States also had to establish a state health planning council, including representatives of governmental and nongovernmental organizations and consumers of health services. This council, which was required to have a majority of consumer representatives, was to advise the state A agency. Section B provided grants to public or nonprofit organizations to develop comprehensive regional, metropolitan, or other local area planning agencies, known as "B agencies." While A agencies were statewide, B agencies were local in focus.

The other sections of the CHP 314 amendments provided grants for public health services, health services development, and training and demonstration. Included were monies available to any organization to study health planning. Monies for states to provide public health services including training of personnel required state-matching funds and specified that 15 percent of a state's allotment had to be used for mental health services. Grants were also authorized to public or nonprofit agencies for services to meet geographically localized specialized health needs. Seed monies offered for a limited time period were available to stimulate and initially support new health services.

Amendments to CHP were passed in 1967 and 1970 which extended CHP planning. Local governments were required to be represented in the areawide planning agencies. State plans needed to assist health institutions to consider capital expenditures and to try to develop new expenditures consistent with the overall facilities needs of the state were required. Both state and areawide plans were now mandated to include home health services. This legislation was completely revised and renamed in 1974 under Title XV of the Public Health Service Act.

National Health Planning and Resources Development Act of 1974

This act amended the Public Health Service Act by adding titles dealing with national health planning and development, and with health resources development. It also superseded and greatly modified the CHP legislation, Hill-Burton, and Regional Medical Programs. The Regional Medical Programs, formally the Heart Disease, Cancer, and Stroke Amendments of 1965, established regional cooperative programs among medical schools, hospitals, and research institutions. This act provided programs of research, training, continuing education, and demonstrations of patient care in heart disease, cancer, stroke, and related diseases.

The first title of the National Health Planning and Resources Development Act of 1974 required the secretary of Health, Education, and Welfare (now Health and Human Services) to issue national health-policy-planning guidelines. These guidelines were to be implemented through the establishment of health service areas and health systems agencies, known as HSAs throughout the United States. Governors designated health service areas in accordance with federal guidelines. HSAs were to have a population between 500,000 and 3 million, and except in special cases, were not to separate Standard Metropolitan Statistical Areas (SMSAs).

An HSA could be a unit of local government, a public regional planning body, or a special nonprofit corporation. Agencies had to form governing bodies with majority consumer representation. Responsibilities of the agencies were to collect and analyze data, to establish a health systems plan (known as HSPs), and to develop an annual implementation plan. They were given the authority to review and approve or disapprove the use of federal funds within their area for health services or resource development. Periodic reviews of the appropriateness of institutional health services and yearly recommendations for modernization, construction, and conversion of medical facilities were part of their responsibilities. HSAs were funded through federal grants on a per capita basis.

Governors of each state were to designate a state health planning and development agency (SHPDA), and a statewide health coordinating council (SHCC). The SHPDA coordinated health planning for the state, prepared an annual state plan, periodically reviewed all institutional services in the state with regard to appropriateness, and administered a state certificate-of-need program. If hospitals or other health care institutions wanted to add new facilities, expand old facilities, or purchase new major pieces of medical equipment, both the local HSA and the state SHPDA had to approve the change and grant the necessary certificate of need. The state SHPDA planning agency could receive up to 75 percent of its costs from federal monies.

The second title of the National Health Planning and Resources Development Act of 1974 provided assistance for modernization for medical facilities, for construction for new outpatient facilities, and for construction of new inpatient facilities in areas of rapid population growth. Additional facets were assistance for the conversion of facilities to provide new health services. Monies were also in the act to allow institutions to eliminate safety hazards, and to avoid noncompliance with licensing or accreditation standards. The state SHPDA had to develop a state medical facilities plan separate from but consistent with the overall state health plan.

While amendments to the National Health Planning and Resources Development Act of 1974 were passed in several years, creating relatively minor changes in the original program, major changes were implemented through amendments appended to the 1981 Omnibus Reconciliation Act. HSAs received a reduced level of federal funding, and were allowed to accept contributions from health insurance companies. If a governor wished, he or she could request the elimination of federal designation and funding in that state. In such a case, all health planning functions would be carried out by the SHPDA and the SHCC. The time limit for state compliance with certificate-of-need requirements was extended. A number of required functions, such as conducting appropriations reviews, review of proposed use of federal funds, and the collection of data on hospital costs could be waived under the 1981 amendments.

The 1981 amendments greatly weakened the role of the HSAs, undermining their original function of areawide health planning. As of 1983, some states had eliminated local HSAs and had devolved those functions to SHPDAs and SHCCs. Even in states where local HSAs remained, the level of funding and staffing were cut substantially, and their aggressive role in health planning was undercut.

The major focus of the Comprehensive Health Planning Act was to interject national planning and some coherence into a relatively haphazard and often barely existent planning system. It was revised and strengthened by the National Health Planning and Resources Development Act of 1974. The overall intent of the 1974 legislation was to move the United States toward a comprehensive national health policy supported by an organizational planning structure, building from local to state levels of government. Over time, the HSA system became a major vehicle to control rising health care costs and expenditures for new facilities.

In accordance with Reagan's conservative philosophy that governmental regulations should be reduced, the Reagan administration greatly weakened but was not able to totally abolish the HSA system. In fiscal year 1981, the entire health planning program was funded at $126.5 million. By fiscal year 1983, the funding level had been reduced to $58.3 million, a 54 percent decrease. For fiscal years 1982 and 1983, the presidential budget had requested the complete elimination of health planning programs. However, Congress continued health planning programs at a low level of funding. Reagan repeated his request for the total elimination of federal aid to health planning in the 1984 budget.

Health Manpower Legislation

The federal role in funding training and development of health professions grew from a minuscule one to a substantially greater effort by the late 1970s. Expansion of the federal role ended and substantial retrenchment began during the Reagan administration. In addition to the compatibility of retrenchment with the Reagan administration's attitude toward social spending, a reduced federal role in health manpower also was congruent with the perception of many health policy analysts that earlier health professional shortages had been successfully combated. In the early 1980s, many policy analysts even predicted an overabundance of physicians by the 1990s.

Except for temporary programs during World War II, the Health Amendments Act of 1956 was the first federal legislation that specifically addressed the issue of health manpower outside of the federal system. This act authorized traineeships for public health personnel and for advanced training of nurses. Formula grants to schools of public health were authorized in 1958. The Health Professions Education Assistance Act of 1963 provided construction grants for teaching facilities. Federal funding for training was expanded beyond public health and nursing to include physicians, dentists, pharmacists, and podiatrists. Student loan funds were made available to schools of medicine, osteopathy, and dentistry, and were later expanded through numerous amendments to include other health areas, such as optometry, veterinary medicine, and medical technology. Special acts dealing with nursing and allied health were passed in 1964 and 1966. Modifications to these programs were included in amendments in the late 1960s.

Since the 1950s, federal involvement in health manpower has consisted of grants to students and institutions. A deviation from this pattern was the Emergency Health Personnel Act of 1970 which authorized assignment of Commissioned Corps and other health personnel to areas in critical need of health manpower, and provided the statutory basis for the National Health Service Corps (NHSC). The NHSC sent physicians and other health personnel to geographic areas experiencing doctor shortages in exchange for loan forgiveness, enabling students from less affluent economic backgrounds to acquire medical training.

The Comprehensive Health Manpower Training Act of 1971 expanded the federal role in training health professionals. Construction grants were extended, and special project grants and authorizations to health professional schools in financial distress were created. A new system of capitation grants was created for most health professional schools. To be eligible for these funds, schools had to increase first-year enrollments. Another extension of the federal role also aimed at increasing the supply of health manpower was start-up assistance to new schools of medicine, osteopathy, and dentistry. Loan provisions were broadened so that students who practiced for three years in health-shortage areas could have up to 85 percent of their loans canceled. Scholarships for needy students were increased and special programs were created for geographic areas with physician shortages and for family medicine. Similar nursing programs were created by the Nurse Training Act of 1971.

The last major expansionary federal legislation in the health manpower area was the 1976 Health Professions Educational Assistance Act. Capitation grants and special project grants were extended to include schools of public health and graduate programs in health administration. Start-up grants, grants for schools in financial distress, and monies for special cooperative interdisciplinary programs were expanded. Medical schools continuing to receive capitation funds had to maintain previous levels of first-year enrollments, and by 1980, had to have 50 percent of their residency programs in primary care areas (internal medicine, family medicine, or pediatrics). Restrictions were placed on the entry to the United States of foreign physicians. With this legislation, the federal role in physician training shifted from global expansion of numbers of physicians to targeting of selected high-priority areas of physician specialization.

As in other areas of national health policy, the Reagan administration retrenched the role of the federal government in manpower planning and training. The administration drastically cut funding for new scholarships provided through the National Health Service Corps. Capitation grants to health professional schools were either totally eliminated or cut back severely. In 1981, capitation grants for schools of nursing were eliminated. By 1982, capitation grants for medical schools were also eliminated. Capitation funds for schools of public health and health administration were sharply reduced. The student loan program was cut from $13.4 million in fiscal year 1982 to $6.6 million in fiscal year 1983, a 51 percent reduction. All nurse training funds were cut 26 percent from $65.9 million in fiscal year 1981 to $48.5 million in fiscal year 1983.

The Mental Retardation Facilities and Community Mental Health Centers Construction Act of 1963

Federal activity in the area of mental health has also been inserted as major amendments to the Public Health Service Act, although mental health problems were not included in the original statute. Congressional interest in mental health problems began with the Mental Health Act of 1946. That act included mental health problems in the grant programs of the PHS and established the National Institute of Mental Health. The Mental Health Study Act of 1955 provided grants for research in resources and methods for caring for the mentally ill. An amendment in 1956 authorized special project grants dealing with the problems of state mental hospitals.

These previous legislative efforts were precursors to the Mental Retardation Facilities and Community Mental Health Centers Construction Act of 1963. Part of this amendment to the PHS Act added mental retardation to the list of health problems addressed by the federal government. Much of the funds provided through this act were for construction for research or treatment facilities for the mentally retarded. While most states had some facilities to treat the mentally retarded, this statute initiated federal involvement.

A second part of this 1963 landmark legislation provided monies to construct community mental health centers. Few states had previously funded such centers, instead focusing their efforts on large inpatient mental hospitals often known in the vernacular as "insane asylums." The 1963 act not only represented the initiation of federal effort in the previously ignored area of community mental health, but also created a whole new emphasis on deinstitutionalization of the mentally ill. Two years later, the act was amended to include grants (a 35 to 70 percent federal match, depending upon state income) to assist in meeting the initial cost of technical and professional personnel to staff the centers, recognizing that facilities without proper staffing were useless.

A number of amendments to the 1963 act were passed through 1980 which extended the types of problems and people covered. In 1968, monies for facilities and personnel to treat alcoholism and narcotic addiction were added. In 1970, incentives to develop community mental health centers in rural or urban poverty areas were passed, as were monies to stimulate the development of mental health services for children. The scope of drug treatment services was expanded beyond narcotics to include drug abuse and drug dependence from any substance.

Mental retardation services were enlarged to include other neurologically handicapping conditions by the Developmental Disabilities Services and Facilities Construction Amendments of

1970. Initially, federally funded community mental health centers were required to offer five basic services: inpatient, outpatient, partial hospitalization including day care, 24-hour emergency, and consultation and education services. Subsequently, the requirement was expanded from 5 to 12 service categories. A new emphasis on mental health services for the elderly was created.

The Omnibus Budget Reconciliation Act of 1981 superseded all of the earlier community mental health legislation. The Reconciliation Act created two block grants to the states – one for mental health and a second for alcohol and drug abuse. As with all the categorical programs which were converted to block grants by the Reagan administration, the amount of funds provided to states through the block-grant mechanism was reduced by 25 percent from their previous level under the categorical format.

Other Amendments to the Public Health Service Act

In addition to the major areas of health planning, construction, and manpower, the Public Health Service Act has been a device for much other federal health legislation in the post-World War II era. As a catchall piece of legislation containing many unrelated statutes passed at different points in time, the PHS Act and particularly its amendments have illustrated the expansion of health programs on a categorical noncomprehensive basis. The addition, subtraction, and merger of numerous specific programs have contributed to a frequent lack of overall coordination and coherence in health policy.

Amendments to the PHS Act have frequently created special programs for targeted groups or targeted health problems. In 1962, a special program of grants for family clinics and other health services for migrant workers was created. In 1970, a categorical grant program was reestablished for control of communicable diseases, including tuberculosis, venereal diseases, rubella, and diphtheria. Also in 1970, the family planning services and population research amendments established an office of population affairs and authorized project training and research grants for all family planning services except abortion. The family planning programs became the major provider of health screening for low-income women and adolescents in the United States during the 1970s. In 1972, a special program of grants for screening, treatment, counseling, research, and educational services was passed for sickle cell anemia and Cooley's anemia. This program was expanded in 1976 to include Tay-Sachs and other genetic diseases. An amendment in 1973 created emergency medical systems by establishing a program of grants and contracts to states and local areas.

In addition to consolidation, the block grants were used to cut federal funds. The Reagan administration argued that consolidation would lead to administrative savings, so that cost reductions could be incurred without substantially decreasing service levels. The funds under block grants represented an initial cut of 25 percent from the funding levels for the preceding categorical programs. However, most states did not experience large administrative savings. The real impact of the block grant consolidation and funding cuts was a reduction in monies available for delivering services. The Omnibus Budget Reconciliation Act of 1981 also eliminated traditional services provided by the PHS. The entitlement of merchant seamen to care provided by the PHS was eliminated, by the closure or transfer from federal control of all PHS hospitals.

Another example of a very specific amendment was the Health Maintenance Organization Act of 1973. This act established a program of financial assistance for the development or expansion of health maintenance organizations (HMOs). HMOs have several organizational structures. All forms have the common characteristic of collecting a prepaid monthly or yearly fee from consumers of services which guarantees that consumer unlimited access to a range of specified services. This amendment represented the first active federal involvement in HMOs. The expansion of HMOs was advanced in this and subsequent amendments to the PHS Act through the provision of federal monies for feasibility studies, planning projects, and loan guarantees. The legislation established basic requirements that a HMO had to meet to be eligible for federal funds, such as provision of certain basic medical services, evidence of fiscal responsibility, and a policy board that included at least one-third of enrolled members.

Another way the growth of HMOs was enhanced was a requirement that every employer of 25 or more persons had to include an HMO option available in the geographic area along with traditional health insurance. Federal legislation nullified state statutes and regulations inhibiting the growth of HMOs, such as prohibitions of solicitation of members through advertising and requirements that all physicians in a geographic area be permitted to participate in the provision of any services offered by an HMO. State requirements for universal physician participation had been particularly prevalent in southern and midwestern states and effectively eliminated any possibility for closed-panel HMO growth in those areas. Under the closed-panel model of HMOs, a specified group of physicians offer medical services and HMO participants must obtain all general care only from a participating physician. Universal physician participation requirements were directly contrary and undercut the intent and organizational structure of closed-panel HMOs.

Under the Reagan administration, federal funds for HMOs were eliminated. All new HMO funds were cut out of the federal budget in fiscal year 1982. HMOs were initially embraced by all parties — Republicans, Democrats, and health policy experts — as an organizational device which would hold down rising health care costs and shift the focus of care to a greater emphasis upon prevention of illness. Paradoxically, Reagan voiced support of the HMO concept, even while eliminating HMO federal funds. HMOs were a part of a Reagan administration orientation toward greater competition, since multiple HMOs in the same geographic area would be competing for customers. The stance of the administration, however, was that federal funds were unnecessary to stimulate this competition, and that private market forces were sufficient to facilitate HMO growth.

The Omnibus Budget Reconciliation Act of 1981 included extensive budget reductions and program revisions for the Public Health Service. One major change was a movement away from specific categorical grants dealing with special programs and diseases to the consolidation of these programs under block grants. Eight programs dealing with rodent control, water fluoridation, health education, home health agencies, hypertension, emergency medical services, and rape crisis centers were consolidated under a preventive health services block grant. Similar consolidations occurred for mental health, alcohol abuse, and drug abuse programs, and for primary care programs.

The amendments to the PHS Act again illustrate the turmoil and rapid changes which occur in both health legislation and health agency structure. Instability has undercut the development of a coherent and chronologically consistent federal policy. Each presidential administration has changed the role of the federal government vis-à-vis states, local governments, and private health-related organizations. The federal government, in a relatively short time span, has moved from being supportive of HMOs through financial and organizational assistance to assuming a neutral role. While the federal categorical grant programs encouraged local health departments to develop a multitude of specialized and separately organized programs, often independent of the state health department, the block-grant procedure forced local health departments to work through their state units and encouraged consolidation rather than separation of program functions. These federally required rapid shifts in program focus and in state-local relationships have been deleterious to ongoing continuity in agencies and to smooth administrative functioning. Chaotic federal changes have lead to a public perception that state and local health officials are ineffective managers. In reality, the atmosphere of chaotic changes and crisis development of policy is federal in origin.

THE SOCIAL SECURITY ACT

The Social Security Act of 1935 was part of the voluminous amount of New Deal legislation passed in the throes of the Great Depression. The best-known thrust of this significant statute was to establish a retirement fund for eligible workers. Originally sold to the U.S. public as a concept emulating a private pension plan, the act, even originally, also included significant welfare features. This act was the first major statute involving the U.S. government in social insurance, and it represented a major increase in the role of the federal government as a granting source for states. The Social Security Act included programs for the needy elderly, dependent children, and the blind. It also provided fiscal incentives to establish state unemployment funds, financial assistance for maternal and child health and child welfare services, and additional grants to the states for state and local public health services. In 1950, the permanently and totally disabled were added to the list of eligible recipients.

As with any major piece of legislation, the Social Security Act has been amended extensively over time. Many of the amendments greatly increased the role of the federal government in paying for the delivery of health care services. The first amendment increasing the federal role in health services was the Kerr-Mills Act in 1960 which established a new program of medical assistance for the aged. Federal aid was given to the states to pay for medical care for medically indigent persons 65 years old and over. State participation was optional. The program, which became the forerunner of Medicaid, was implemented by 25 states.

The Social Security Amendments of 1965 established a program of national health insurance for the elderly, known as Medicare, and a program of health care for the indigent, known as Medicaid. Special project grants for comprehensive services for children and youth including maternal and infant care projects were also a part of the 1965 amendments. A new act, Title XVIII was added to the original Social Security statute. Part A of this title provided basic protection against the cost of hospital and certain post-hospital services. Inpatient hospital services of up to 90 days during any episode of illness and psychiatric and inpatient services for up to 190 days in a lifetime were included. Extended care services, such as nursing home care, were covered for up to 100 days during any episode of illness. Some home health services and hospital out-patient diagnostic services were covered.

Part B, providing supplemental medical insurance benefits, was a voluntary insurance program, financed by premium payments from enrollees, along with matching payments from general social security revenues. Physician and related services, such as x-rays, laboratory tests, supplies and equipment were covered, as are additional home health services. Both Part A hospital services and Part B physician and related services involved cost-sharing by the social security recipient in the form of deductibles and copayments.

Claims and payments were not handled directly by the Social Security Administration, but were paid through fiscal intermediaries such as Blue Cross/Blue Shield. The social security recipient and the institutional providers, such as hospitals and nursing homes, were not directly reimbursed for health care services by the federal government, but received payments from the fiscal intermediary in their geographic area. Institutional providers had to meet conditions of participation, such as utilization reviews, that were aimed at ensuring a minimum quality level of care.

The 1965 Social Security Act Amendments also created Medicaid, a program of medical assistance for public welfare recipients, through Title XIX. As with all federal-state matching programs, participation by any particular state was voluntary. The variability across states in coverage and amounts of services funded was great. Not all states included a medically needy category under Medicaid. States had the option of extending eligibility to medically indigent persons not on welfare, who had a borderline poverty level of income but earned too much to be eligible for federally subsidized welfare. Some states also provide welfare (and thus Medicaid) to two-parent families under Aid to Families of Dependent Children with Unemployed Fathers (AFDC-UF).

Under Medicaid, all states were required to provide at least some of five basic services: inpatient hospital services, outpatient hospital services, other laboratory and x-ray services, skilled nursing home services, and physician services. A large number of optional services, such as optometric services, were available to states under Medicaid. States could also opt to provide more extensive mental health coverage, ambulance transportation, and dental care, but were not required by the federal government to do so.

Amendments to both Medicare and Medicaid between 1966 and 1971 had the impact of extending either the type or the amount of services provided under each of these programs. Changes were also made in institutional eligibility requirements and reimbursement schedules. More extensive amendments to both Medicare and Medicaid were passed in 1972. Many of the changes were technical and related to reimbursement methodologies. Some new services were added such as chiropractic services and speech pathology. Family planning services were added to the list of basic Medicaid services.

Two significant changes were incorporated into the 1972 amendments. One was the creation of Professional Standards Review Organizations (PSROs) to address problems of cost, quality control, and medical necessity of services. Associations of physicians reviewed the professional activities of physicians and other practitioners within institutions. The use of PSROs by Medicaid was made optional in 1981, and subsequently federal funding for PSROs was eliminated. The second change extended Medicare services to people who required hemodialysis or renal transplants for chronic renal disease by declaring them disabled and eligible for Medicare coverage under Title XVIII. While this expansion represented a numerically small category of people covered under Medicare, the average medical expenses for members of the category proved to be quite high.

A major set of amendments dealing with antifraud and abuse in both Medicare and Medicaid were passed in 1977 which strengthened criminal and other penalties for fraud, included federal monies for state Medicaid fraud units, and required uniform reporting systems for participating health care institutions. A large number of changes concerning cost containment and cost efficiency were included in 57 separate sections of the 1980 Medicare and Medicaid amendments. Small rural hospitals were authorized to use beds on a "swing" basis for either acute or long-term care beds as needed. "Swing-bed" demonstration projects were allowed. The home health services provisions of the Medicare legislation were changed in several ways, including the removal of the 100-visit-per-year limit. Some new services and providers were added such as alcohol detoxification under Part A of Medicare, and nurse midwifery under Medicaid.

As in other facets of national health policy, the Reagan administration supported major legislative changes. The majority of both proposed and enacted changes in Medicare were attempts to deal with problems of health care costs. The 1982 amendments made large changes in the method of payment for hospitals by shifting to diagnostic-related groupings (DRGs), and small changes that directly affected recipients. After the 1982 amendments, Medicare beneficiaries paid $12.20 per month as premiums for physician care under Part B. The recipient-paid premiums under those amendments were to increase to equal 25 percent of the Part B costs. The Reagan administration proposed further increases in the share of cost borne by the recipient of up to 35 percent by 1988.

Cutbacks in federal Medicaid funds for states, and greater flexibility for states in determining the structure of their program were passed as part of the Omnibus Budget Reconciliation Act of 1981 and the Tax Equity and Fiscal Responsibility Act (TEFRA) of 1982. These changes represented a retrenchment in Medicaid and increased state variability. In 1981, matching federal Medicaid payments to the states were reduced by 3 percent in fiscal year 1982, 4 percent in fiscal year 1983, and 4.5 percent in fiscal year 1984, although the cutback could be lowered by 1 percent in each fiscal year if a state operated a qualified hospital cost review program, had an unemployment rate over 15 percent of the national average, and had an effective fraud and abuse recovery program.

Prior to 1981, Medicaid required states to offer recipients freedom of choice in the selection of providers. After 1981, states could apply for waivers of the freedom of choice requirements and could require Medicaid recipients to receive care from a specially designated pool of providers. Copayments for basic services, previously prohibited by federal statute, were made optional for states under the 1982 amendments. The Reagan administration proposed even further cost-shifting to recipients by advocating mandatory copayments.

THE ECONOMIC OPPORTUNITY ACT OF 1964

Known as the Antipoverty Program, the Economic Opportunity Act of 1964 created the Office of Economic Opportunity (OEO) to combat poverty in a number of spheres, including a small health-related component. Through Community Action Programs (CAPs), OEO neighborhood health centers in poor, inner cities and later in rural areas provided a comprehensive range of outpatient services to residents. In the mid-1970s, the neighborhood centers were transferred to the PHS.

THE NATIONAL ENVIRONMENTAL POLICY ACT OF 1969 AND RELATED ENVIRONMENTAL LEGISLATION

The National Environmental Policy Act of 1969 consolidated programs dealing with air pollution, water pollution, urban and industrial health, and radiological health. Forerunners of this act were the Water Pollution Control Act of 1956, and the Clean Air Act of 1963 (Peters 1982). The former was amended by the Federal Water Pollution Control Act of 1965 which switched enforcement responsibilities from the Department of Interior to the Department of Health, Education, and Welfare. It required states to set standards for water quality. The impact of this act in controlling water pollution was minimized by competition among states to attract new industries. States set water pollution standards low to accommodate industrial needs to remain competitive in appeal to industry. The Clean Air Act of 1963 was similar in its functioning and structure to the earlier water control efforts. It relied on conferences and voluntary compliance.

The National Environmental Policy Act established guidelines for environmental controls for projects that involved the federal government. The act included a major new mechanism of environmental impact statements. Before a project could be approved, an environmental impact statement detailing the effect of the project, its potential negative consequences, and possible alternatives had to be filed with the newly created advisory body — the Council on Environmental Quality. The act also allowed for citizen participation by permitting citizens to challenge a project on environmental grounds.

In 1968, the Consumer Protection and Environmental Health Service (CPEHS) was formed within HEW to deal with environmental issues impacting on health. The Food and Drug Administration was a part of the CPEHS at that time. In January of 1970, the functions of the Consumer Protection and Environmental Health Service were split. Two separate agencies were established within the PHS. The Food and Drug Administration handled the consumer protection functions of CPEHS, focusing on food and drug product safety. The Environmental Health Service was created to handle environmental functions.

Late in 1970, the Environmental Health Service within the PHS was abolished when President Nixon created the independent Environmental Protection Agency (EPA). Nearly all PHS environmental programs were transferred to the newly created EPA. EPA was also charged with implementation of environmental legislation passed in 1969 and the related air and water quality legislation. In 1970, the Clean Air Act was amended to allow EPA to establish ambient (surrounding) air quality standards. Emission standards for plants with high-polluting potential were also established, as were strengthened automobile emission standards. In 1972, amendments were passed to the Water Pollution Control Act which set national rather than state standards for both water quality and sewage treatment. A nationwide discharge permit system was established, allowing the EPA to specify the levels of effluents which could be released, and to monitor compliance. Air pollution and water pollution laws were further strengthened by amendments in 1977.

Other environmental legislation dealt with toxic substances, waste disposal, pesticides, and safe drinking water. The 1972 Environmental Pesticide Control Act required registration of pesticides, and gave the EPA authority to ban the use of hazardous pesticides. The Safe Drinking Water Act of 1974 set standards for allowable levels of pollutants and chemicals in public drinking water systems. The Toxic Substances Control Act of 1976 regulated chemical substances affecting health and the environment, including banning the manufacture and use of PCBs. The Resource Conservation Recovery Act of 1976 and later amendments controlled discarded material and hazardous wastes. In 1980, the Comprehensive Environmental Response, Compensation, and Liability Act was passed. This act established a $1.6 billion federal superfund to clean up chemical dumps and toxic wastes. The act authorized the EPA to sue companies responsible for toxic spills to recover government clean-up expenses.

As in other areas of health policy, the Reagan administration advocated budget and staff cuts for the EPA. A 60 percent cut in purchasing power for the agency resulted from the combined effects of inflation and budget cuts during the first six months of the Reagan administration. The proportionate drop was even higher for EPA's research and development activities, areas which experts contend are critical to a strong national environmental policy. Due to technical complexity, the control of toxic substances requires more policy-relevant research, and a greater linkage between policy making and science, so that reductions for R&D funds for toxic substance impacts were particularly limiting.

EPA became the focus of great controversy during 1982 and 1983. Its chief administrators (Ann Gorsuch, EPA director, and Rita Lavelle, head of the Superfund charged with cleaning up toxic waste sites) were severely criticized in the popular press. Lavelle was accused of inappropriate links to the regulated industries, while Gorsuch was accused of incompetence and of hostility to EPA's environmental regulatory functions. Observers of the EPA felt that it had moved through the life cycle for regulatory agencies very quickly, shifting from zealous enforcement of environmental standards to advocacy for the regulated industry in a short ten-year span. After the departure of Gorsuch and Lavelle in 1983, William Ruckleshaus, the first EPA director, was reappointed to head the agency. He remained respected among proenvironmental groups, who expected him to enforce existing legislation more vigorously than his predecessors.

THE OCCUPATIONAL SAFETY
AND HEALTH ACT OF 1970

Until the passage of the Occupational Safety and Health Act of 1970 (OSHA), the federal government played no active role in protecting the health of workers. Working conditions were determined by state law and market forces. OSHA gave the Secretary of Labor strong standard-setting authority. It specified minimum levels of worker protection against many hazards. Initially, OSHA adopted preexisting industry standards concerning working conditions. Subsequently, public hearings gave impetus to higher standard levels.

OSHA has been severely criticized by opponents of government regulation who contend that many of the standards for worker protection are needless and expensive, often failing to strike a reasonable balance between risk and cost. Proponents argue that while emphasis on detail may have been excessive at times, market forces have been insufficient to adequately protect worker safety and lives. In addition to standard setting, regulatory enforcement was a second OSHA function. One continuing debate between industry and labor was whether unannounced spot inspections of work places are necessary to ensure adequate enforcement. Management contended spot enforcements were needless interference and harassment, while labor contended they were necessary for OSHA to achieve its preventive goal of maintaining worker health and avoiding illness.

SUMMARY

The structure of U.S. government places extreme emphasis upon decentralization. Decentralization of power occurs both from the split of functions between the national and the state governments, and from the separation of powers among the executive, legislative, and judicial branches. This extreme structural decentralization and fragmentation is reinforced by the underlying attitudes supporting liberal and capitalistic traditions. Extreme decentralization leads to multiple veto points in the policy process, where the power to block exceeds the power to initiate. Running the gamut of hurdles for policy initiatives is very difficult. Far more initiatives and changes fail than succeed. Only when an initiative is fueled by strong public dissatisfaction and appropriate timing are policy proposals in the U.S. system typically enacted. The development of health laws has proved typical rather than exceptional of policy development, legislative initiatives, and organizational changes.

Ad hoc crisis-oriented development of legislation has produced a system of patchwork categorical programs. The long and convoluted history of the Public Health Service Act with its numerous amendments illustrates the addition, across time, of new categories of clientele and incrementally accreted services. In mental health, groups and types of substance abuse were incrementally added on a piecemeal basis. With Medicare, services were expanded from the initial focus on the elderly to include a category for renal disease.

The shifts and changes in the Public Health Service Act also partially illustrate the instability of federal health agencies. Organizations and reorganizations have been the norm. While some structural changes and reorganizations are the direct result of new or amended legislation, others occur due to changes in the executive branch of the government. Both personnel changes at the presidential level and the top administrative levels of agencies often result in reorganization within the agency. This has been particularly true in the Department of Health and Human Services. While there has been an organizational entity entitled the Public Health Service for over 40 years, its functions have expanded and contracted at various points in time as administrative reorganizations have occurred.

The combined effect of crisis development, categorical legislation, incremental expansion, and numerous organizational changes has been a lack of overall coherence and coordination in national health policy. The Reagan administration deviated from the categorical approach to health legislation with its emphasis upon block grants. Despite their departure from the categorical program format, block grants have failed to increase national health policy coordination. Not only was the block-grant mechanism employed to reduce overall federal financial support for health services and functions, but it also further diluted the role of the federal government in health policy development by devolving further power to the states. Therefore, a less-clearly defined national policy resulted. States were able to emphasize their own special problems at the cost of acquiring a coordinated and coherent national health policy.

CHAPTER SIX
DEMAND FOR HEALTH CARE

THE INTERACTION OF DEMAND AND SUPPLY

While the health care delivery systems of many industrialized countries follow a model of central governmental planning and resource allocation, the health system in the United States operates under more complex conditions sometimes resembling a private market. Both providers of health care and the general public adhere to capitalism in theory if not always in practice. Under free markets, both product prices and total quantities produced result from the interplay of supply and demand.

The equilibrium price and the equilibrium quantity produced occur where supply and demand intersect (see Figures 6-1 through 6-3). If each producer and each consumer is left to pursue his or her own individual/institutional interests, total output will be maximized. Due to the unique status of health care in preserving human life, notions of private markets, free enterprise, supply, and demand have been transferred into health policy only with great difficulty and considerable theoretical slippage.

To the economist, "supply" reflects a relationship, often depicted graphically on a Cartesian coordinate system where the X axis represents total quantity produced and the Y axis represents the price. The relationship reflected by such a supply curve is that of market price and the amounts of goods that producers are willing to supply at that price. Implicit in the supply curve is a fixed technological and regulatory environment. Supply curves typically slope

FIGURE 6-1
DEMAND AND SUPPLY CURVES

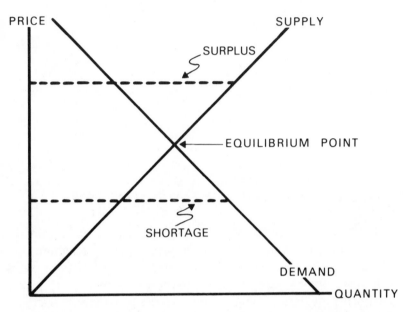

upward from the lower left to the upper right, implying that as the price of a service or product increases, producers are willing to supply greater quantities.

Movements up and down a fixed supply curve are distinguishable from shifts in the curve itself. Under competitive conditions, movements up and down a fixed supply curve indicate the entry and exit of producers in the particular market so that more or fewer producers are available to supply the product or service. Classically, economists view the prevailing market price to be determined by the total quantity, which results from the autonomous decisions of numerous independent producers.

By contrast, shifts in a supply curve reflect a change in the relationship between price and the quantity producers are willing to supply at that price, resulting from changes in either the technology used in production, or from legal changes in the regulatory environment. Changes which alter the basic supply relationship impact on the costs of production. Under competitive conditions, technological innovations which lower the unit cost of production imply that more service or product units can be generated for the same input costs, and result in shifting the supply curve to the right.

If two otherwise identical supply curves are adjacent, one to the left of the other, at the same price level, greater quantities of the service in question will be produced by suppliers for whom the supply curve on the right is relevant. Lesser quantities would be supplied by producers for whom the curve on the left is relevant. Shifting the supply curve in an industry or service sector has the same effect.

One crucial characteristic of both supply and demand curves is their respective slopes. Slopes mathematically express the change in one variable (usually the dependent variable) relative to the change in a second variable (usually the independent variable). With supply

FIGURE 6-2
AN EXPANSIONARY SHIFT IN THE DEMAND CURVE INCREASING THE EQUILIBRIUM POINT

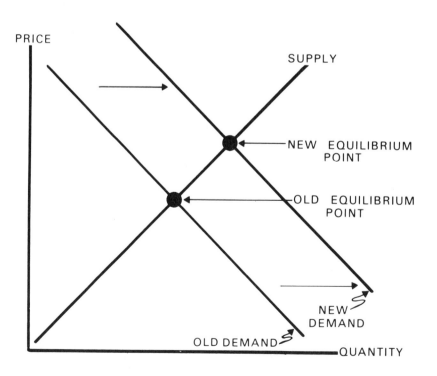

FIGURE 6-3
*A CONTRACTIONAL SHIFT IN THE DEMAND CURVE
DECREASING THE EQUILIBRIUM POINT*

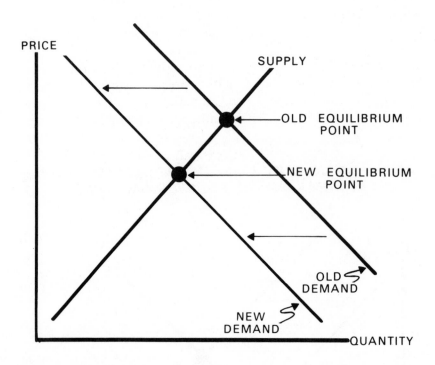

and demand curves, the slopes reflect the change in price relative to the change in quantity of services produced. The closer the slope of either supply or demand is to zero, the flatter the curve.

A related concept to slope is elasticity. While the slope depends on absolute changes in price and quantity, the elasticity depends on relative changes in those two things. High elasticity reflects a small change in price relative to a large change in quantity. By contrast, small elasticity reflects a great change in price relative to a small change in quantity of services. When the curve is vertical, supply or demand are said to be inelastic, where price is not responsive to changes in quantity of services (see Figure 6-4).

Elasticity coefficients can be calculated for a demand curve. Coefficients may vary in numerical value across the range of a demand curve, so that one curve has several coefficients, depending on the portion of the curve examined. They are calculated numerically as a ratio between the percentage change in quantity demanded and the percentage change in price. An elasticity coefficient of one is called unitary elasticity and represents an equal percentage change in quantity demanded relative to a percentage change in price.

Elasticity coefficients greater than one represent elastic demand, where the percentage change in quantity demanded exceeds the percentage change in price. The larger the value of the coefficient is relative to one, the greater the demand elasticity. With very high

FIGURE 6-4
DEMAND ELASTICITIES

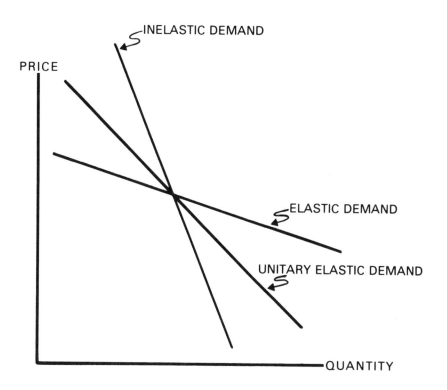

elasticities much greater than one, a large change in quantity demanded occurs with even small percentage changes in price. By contrast, elasticity coefficients less than one are inelastic. Inelastic coefficient values imply that only very small percentage changes in quantity demanded occur with percentage changes in price. The closer the elasticity coefficient value is to zero, the greater the inelasticity.

Elasticity coefficients also have signs, indicating the direction of the percentage changes in quantity demanded and price. Demand elasticities are typically negative, indicating that a percentage increase in quantity demanded results from a relative decrease in price. Conversely, a percentage decrease in quantity demanded results from a relative increase in price. By contrast, supply elasticities are typically positive, indicating that a relative increase in price results in a percentage increase in quantity supplied, or that a relative decrease in price results in a percentage decrease in quantity supplied. Quantity and price are inversely related in the demand curve and positively related in the supply curve, a fact which is reflected in the sign of the two respective elasticity coefficients.

Demand curves also depict a relationship between price and quantity of services produced – in particular, the total quantity of services or products consumers are willing to purchase at a particular price. As with supply curves, movements along the demand curve reflect consumer responses to a change in service prices within the context of a stable relationship between price and quantity. Leftward and rightward shifts of the curve reflect a change in the relationship itself. A leftward shift implies less consumer willingness to purchase services at any price, possibly from a change in technology regulation making more attractive substitutes available (see Figure 6-3). A rightward shift implies more consumer willingness to purchase services at any price, possibly resulting from substitutes becoming less available or unavailable (see Figure 6-2). Additionally, changes in personal income of consumers can shift demand curves.

HEALTH CARE DEMAND AND UTILIZATION

Demand is not synonymous with need in health care, although the two concepts may, at times, be erroneously used interchangeably. Need is the amount of care which health care professionals believe is necessary for maintenance of quality of life, while demand is the actual use of health services (P. Feldstein 1973). While need is defined by professionals often independent of resource constraints, demand is defined by consumers within their resource constraints. Economic analyses are traditionally based upon demand rather than need. Government policies and political debates more often employ need than demand.

The idea of professionally defined need usually includes the concept of homeostasis. Homeostasis means maintenance of a steady state (Arrow 1963). Related to the homeostatic need is the question of whether the individual can be trusted to maintain a steady operating state, or whether professionals are necessary to perceive homeostatic needs and to ensure that those needs are met.

The concept of homeostasis can also be applied beyond the individual to the whole society. In this realm, some of the thornier ethical issues of determining appropriate need occur. How much health care services should a society provide to an aging or dying person in a world of scarce resources and opportunity costs? How long should a terminally ill patient be kept alive by artificial means in the absence of the ability to communicate and relate to relatives and friends? Should maintenance services be provided to an elderly or dying person at the expense of providing preventive health care services to the young and healthy? No easily derived professional or lay consensus exists on appropriate need from this perspective.

Nor is demand synonymous with consumer tastes. Tastes to a health economist are nonprice-related factors affecting intensity of demand for medical and health care. The general theory of demand assumes that the quantity of any service is a function of the price of that service, the price of other goods and services, consumer income, and consumer tastes. Sometimes tastes are called wants, and are influenced by consumer background factors such as health status, educational background, age, sex, race, and values (Jacobs 1980). In traditional economics, tastes are assumed to be relatively constant and stable. In health, however, controversy exists over the stability of tastes for individual medical care. Partially, tastes depend on the health of the individual which is variable across individuals and for the same individual across time. Physicians can influence the tastes of consumers for health care by changing the consumer's image of what is desirable in medical care.

Health care demand differs from normal demand in classical economic theory in one regard: traditional demand theory assumes that the consumer makes the purchasing decision based on service or product price. In health care, purchasing decisions and their derivative – total quantity of services produced – are often made by producers rather than consumers. The complexity and technical expertise of health care are cited as justifications for physicians and other providers making dual purchasing decisions for the consumers and production decisions for themselves.

While the consumer makes the initial decision to visit a physician, many of the subsequent decisions about utilization of health care services are actually made by the physician. Physician-written prescriptions are prerequisites for consumer purchases of many drugs. The impact of physician-producer decisions in inducing consumer patient demand is reflected in the statistic that, on average, one prescription is written for every outpatient visit to a doctor's office (Fuchs 1974). Similarly, only physicians can order diagnostic tests or x-rays, both of which are a major generator of health care costs.

There is also another important way in which the physician functions as a gatekeeper to the production of medical care services and thus induces patient demand for medical care services. Physicians must admit patients to hospitals, making use of the hospital services and the associated generated costs: the basic room charge; the charge for diagnostic tests, drugs, and consumable supplies; possible charges for operating rooms, anesthesiologists, and other surgical services, are all examples of physician-generated demand. Of every $100 spent for health care, the largest portion (over $40) goes to hospital care and another $10 goes to drugs, versus only a little over $20 which is spent directly on physicians' services. Physicians generate demand for services and costs for the health care system which average two and one-half times their own charges.

USE OF HEALTH CARE SERVICES

Demand and the Two-stage Decision Process

Health care demand differs from normal demand in a second way as well: health care demand is often described as inelastic.

Decision making for health services is essentially a two-stage process. First, the consumer decides whether or not to enter the system. Once having decided to enter the system, consumers make subsequent decisions about further use of health care services based on the physician's recommendations.

Many factors affect the first stage of the decision to seek health care. How a person feels, how the individual reacts to feelings of illness, opinions held by relatives and loved ones on the appropriate role of health care, personal and family income, education, job status, occupation, type of health care insurance, and the availability of health care all affect the first-stage decision concerning entry into the system. Analysts from various disciplines have categorized this complex of factors into three groups: (1) background factors such as education which affect individual predisposition to use health services; (2) enabling factors such as personal or family income and type of health insurance which enable an individual to use health services, and the available supply of health services; and (3) the condition or state of illness (Andersen 1968; Andersen and Newman 1972; Kronenfeld 1978; Wolinsky 1978).

Of these categories, the predisposing, personal enabling, and health factors primarily affect demand for health services; service availability constitutes supply. Economists combine predisposing factors and individual state of illness into a single category of consumer tastes where tastes are all nonincome and nonprice factors affecting demand. Additionally, economists argue that geographic accessibility factors (or supply) affects demand (Long 1981).

It is the second stage of the decision process to use health care which particularly contributes to demand inelasticity. If demand were elastic, consumers would be responsive to price changes in health services. As prices of health services rose, consumers would respond by purchasing less health and medical care. Since consumers, however, rely primarily upon physician advice in stage two as to what health services are needed in what intensities, consumer responsiveness to price is muted. After an initial visit to a physician, most patients will allow the physician to determine the need for prescription drugs, future office visits, specialists' services, laboratory tests, and hospitalization. Physician control over patient use of health services is enhanced by relative consumer ignorance on the affect of medical care on health (Jacobs 1980).

The Impact of Different Types of Illnesses on Demand

Elasticity of demand varies by type of health care service. Physician services cover a broad range of categories with reasons for consumer visits varying from minor health irritations to major illnesses. Elasticity of demand is greater for minor illnesses, and for initial visits to a physician's office, than for major illnesses or for follow-up office visits. Preventive services, like minor illnesses, involve a greater degree of consumer discretion over treatment decisions. Elasticity of demand is higher for preventive services than for treatment of illness.

Demand curves for such preventive services as Pap smears for cervical cancer detection, stress tests in the absence of indicators of cardiovascular problems, and routine physical examinations illustrate this elasticity. Dental care demand is influenced by the greater elasticity for both preventive services and for minor illnesses. Routine cleanings, x-rays, and fluoride treatments are examples of common preventive services of dentists, for which there is great elasticity of demand. Most people also perceive dental care to be less critical to life preservation than other types of medical care, a factor which enhances dental care demand elasticity.

Health care is a special type of commodity. Often the linkage between health care services and state of health is unproven or tenuous, a factor that would normally increase elasticity of demand. This does not hold for health services relating to the preservation of life. On life and death questions, uncertainty of treatment impacts has the reverse effect. When the consequence of death is faced, even uncertain treatments appear to be worth any costs. In a life-threatening situation, such as a heart attack or traffic accident, the demand curve becomes vertical so that the patient would pay any price for treatments holding promises of preservation of life. Even with serious illness falling short of threats to the preservation of life, but which seriously impact on the quality of life, consumer price sensitivity becomes quite low, and demand becomes very inelastic. For example, demand for hospital care is relatively inelastic, both due to the seriousness of illness implied by hospitalization, and the influence of physician recommendations. The price elasticity for minor or elective diagnoses is greater than for other types of hospital care, but is still generally inelastic (less than -1.0).

Demand and Third-party Payments

Further inelasticity of demand is generated by third-party payments. Patients who rely on third-party payers, such as insurance companies and government, to pay a substantial proportion of their health care costs, are less price sensitive than are patients who do not. Recognizing this fact, many cost-containment schemes strive to lower the proportion of individual health care costs paid by third-party payers and to increase the portion paid by the individual patient, presuming that price sensitivity is enhanced as health care costs become a larger proportion of total consumer expenditures.

Analysts do not agree, however, on the appropriate strategy for lowering overall health care demand. Those interested in immediate cost reductions emphasize a high deductible so that the individual is discouraged from entering the system unless health care needs are great. Those interested in long-term cost reductions through a greater emphasis upon preventive care rather than treatment of illness stress low deductibles to encourage people to enter the system before minor health problems become major illnesses.

Related to the impact of third-party payments on demand is the concept of user price. User price for health services refers to the total absolute costs paid by the consumer for particular services versus the costs borne by the third-party payee. In the case of no third-party payments where the entire cost of health services is borne by the patient, the user price equals the nominal or stated price. In the case of third-party payments, however, the user price is generally lesser than and some proportion of the total service costs.

The effective user price is a function of the initial deductible, the proportion of subsequent amounts over the deductible paid by the third party, maximum limits on third-party payments, and the total price of the service. As the deductible decreases, the third-party-paid proportion above the deductible increases, the maximum third-party-dollar payment increases, and the user price declines. Conversely, as the deductible increases, the third-party-paid proportion above the deductible decreases, the maximum third-party-dollar payment decreases, and the user price increases.

User price may not be highly correlated with nominal service price. A service with a high nominal price such as hospital care may have a relatively low user price. Over 90 percent of U.S. citizens have some type of hospital insurance or coverage through a government program so that much of the high nominal price of hospitalization is borne by the third-party payer. The result is a comparatively low user price for hospital care.

Similarly, a service with a low nominal price such as dental care may have a relatively high user price. Dental insurance is rarer than coverage for other types of service. Only 30 percent of those under age 65 had dental insurance in 1979. For the remaining 70 percent, total dental costs must be borne by the consumer, making the user price equivalent to the nominal price. While the actual cost of a physician visit for preventive purposes may be similar to a physician visit for the treatment of illness, the latter is more typically covered by third-party payments while the former is not. The consequence is markedly different user prices for physician office visits consuming roughly equivalent amounts of physician time and with roughly similar nominal prices.

Even within the category of physician visits for illness treatment, the user price may vary. A common type of health insurance coverage requires a $100 to $200 deductible for services, including physician visits related to an illness and drugs, before the health insurance plan will reimburse the consumer for 80 percent of the cost of the visit. This payment reimbursement scheme results in significantly higher user prices for physician visits occurring before the deductible amount has been expended by the consumer than for physician visits occurring after the deductible amount has been expended in the designated time frame.

While theory suggests that cost sharing methods, such as deductibles and coinsurance, would lead to lower use of health services, empirical studies on this point are not conclusive. A number of data-based studies have found evidence that the extent of cost-sharing affected use, but the estimates in these studies differ by a factor of three or greater in the degree of increase in health service utilization when an average uninsured person becomes fully insured (Fein 1971; Beck 1974; Enterline et al. 1973; Feldstein 1977; Newhouse 1978; Newhouse and Phelps 1976; Newhouse, Phelps, and Schwartz 1974; Phelps and Newhouse 1972; Phelps and Newhouse 1974; Scitovsky and McCall 1977; Scitovsky and Snyder 1972). Some experts argue that fully insuring ambulatory services should reduce total health expenditures by increasing preventive care and encouraging more appropriate use of hospitals (Roemer et al. 1975). Other studies do not support this contention (Hill and Veney 1970; Lewis and Keairnes 1970).

Differential Individual and Group
Responses to Cost-sharing Schemes

Do different types of individuals respond to cost-sharing schemes similarly? There is also debate on this question. Canadian data suggest that the poor and those with larger families are more responsive to cost sharing, modifying consumption patterns as a function of total medical costs paid by third parties (Beck 1974). One U.S. study detected few differences in the responses of different income groups to cost sharing (Newhouse and Phelps 1976). Other studies report low-income groups respond more percentage-wise to coinsurance, although the absolute changes for different income groups are similar (Phelps and Newhouse 1972; Scitovsky and Snyder 1972). Similar confusion exists about the sensitivity of children to cost sharing. While some research supports the hypothesis that children are less sensitive than adults to cost sharing (Marmer 1977), other research supports the reverse hypothesis (NCHS 1972). Compounding the confusion were contradictory findings in 1972 NCHS data and 1979 NCHS data. The 1972 data found the rate at which children visit physicians more sensitive to cost sharing than that of adults, while this trend was ameliorated in the 1979 data.

The controversy over the effect of cost sharing on health care utilization induced the federal government to sponsor a social experiment to test this impact (Newhouse 1974). The controlled trial began with the selection of the first sites in 1974 and ended in 1982. Interim results from the study showed that per capita total expenditure (inpatient plus ambulatory expenditures excluding dental and outpatient mental health services) rose steadily as coinsurance fell. Expenditure per person in the most generous plan with all costs being borne by the third party was about 60 percent greater than in the 95 percent coinsurance plan where the consumer bore the predominant portion of costs until very high expenditures were reached. Expenditure per person in plans with less than 95 percent consumer coinsurance fell between the two extreme plans (Newhouse et al. 1982).

The response to the experimental plans by families at different income levels was similar, indicating that the poor are not necessarily more responsive to cost sharing. In this experiment, the actual cost shared was less for low-income families than for high-income families, so that while costs shared as a proportion of family income were constant across income groups, absolute costs shared varied. Expenditures for children were less sensitive to cost sharing than for adults. Since decisions concerning the purchase of health services for children are made by adults, adults were apparently more willing to spend their own dollars for health care for their offspring than for themselves. Once a patient was hospitalized, variations in cost sharing did not affect the amount of care consumed.

Constraints on the generalizability (external validity) of the interim results of the federally sponsored study on the impact of cost sharing include data limitations and the nature of experiments. The interim results do not include sites in which there were large numbers of blacks. Whether the interim findings will hold for minority groups is not clear. Crucially, none of the data on health status were included in the interim result, leaving ambiguous whether cost sharing induced reductions in health care use affected health status. The experiment measured how the demand of a small number of consumers varied with changes in cost sharing. Can these experimental results be generalized to a widespread plan of a similar nature? Universal delivery systems may experience different responses to cost sharing as waiting queues and other delivery problems develop than do systems covering a small fraction of the population.

The Impact of Organizational Structure on Demand

Other research has examined the question of whether organizational structure of health delivery systems affects utilization. Much of this research has been case studies of hospitalization in particular practices such as HMOs or in particular geographic areas (Pauley 1974). Supporters of HMOs claim that they contain the total cost of medical care due to the different economic incentives in HMOs when compared to conventional fee-for-service practices (Luft 1978a; Monsa 1970). Generally, prepaid group practices had lower rates of hospital utilization and lower in-plan costs than did more traditional insurance plans providing mainly fee-for-service coverage for inhospital services (Donabedian 1969). One deficiency of most of these studies, however, was the difficulty if not impossibility of telling whether the observed differences in utilization were the result of the way physicians were paid, the price incentives of consumers under the plan, the mode of organization of the plan, or the characteristics of plan members.

Luft (1978) has conducted a comprehensive review of all studies examining the role of HMOs in utilization and potential cost savings published since 1950. Most studies do support the claims and expectations that yearly medical care expenditures are lower for HMO enrollees when compared to people with conventional health insurance coverage. Almost all of these studies, however, examined cost differentials between the group practice form of HMO and conventional insurance. Most included a Kaiser plan, the largest group of HMOs geographically concentrated on the West coast, as one of the HMO groups. The Kaiser plans generally have the lowest expenditures of all HMO plans, a fact which may have biased findings in favor of HMOs. Luft could find no documented evidence that costs for enrollees in individual practice associations (IPA HMOs) were lower than costs for people with conventional health insurance.

Why are costs lower in HMOs? One explanation is the more efficient production of a given amount of services, while a second is changes in the number and mix of services provided. Most studies conclude that HMOs are not more efficient than fee-for-service provided in terms of costs for a specific day of hospital service or a specific physician visit (Luft 1978a; Saward and Greenlick 1972). The expenditure differentials reflect differences in practice patterns — the number and mix of services. Most savings come from reductions in hospitalization, since HMO enrollees receive at least as many, and according to some studies, more ambulatory services as enrollees in conventional plans (Luft 1978a; Broida et al. 1975; Perkoff et al. 1976; Shapiro et al. 1967). In Luft's summary of 17 studies of prepaid group practices, group HMO enrollees averaged 4.41 ambulatory visits per year, compared to 4.19 visits for those with conventional coverage. For the five studies examining IPA HMOs, the differential was substantially larger — 5.11 visits for IPA enrollees versus 4.32 visits for those with conventional coverage.

There are several ways to examine hospitalization. Researchers may examine an overall measure of hospital use, such as the number of inpatient days per hospital year. This overall measure is influenced by the number of admissions, and the average length of stay per admission. In Luft's review of 51 HMO-nonHMO comparisons,

HMO enrollees had fewer hospital days in 41 cases, and lower admission rates in 42 cases. Most of the cases where the hospital admission rate and number of days were higher for HMOs involved IPAs. The data on length of stay per admission are more mixed: lower for HMO enrollees in 29 cases, the same in 8 cases, and higher in 14 cases than for conventional enrollees.

One popular interpretation of lower hospital admission rates in HMOs is that HMO patients have less surgery. A general comparison of 23 HMOs paired with conventional practices did not support this contention. HMOs reduced hospital admissions equally in the surgical and nonsurgical categories (Luft 1978a). Eight surgical procedures which frequently have been criticized as overused are tonsillectomy, hysterectomy, hernia, cholecystectomy, cataract, hemorrhoidectomy, prostatectomy, and varicose veins. With the exception of tonsillectomies, HMOs did not differentially reduce these discretionary procedures.

THE ELASTICITY OF HEALTH CARE DEMAND

User prices affect elasticity insofar as user prices rather than nominal prices are the critical factor in determining quantity demanded. Price elasticity is the responsiveness of quantity of care demanded to changes in price, holding all other factors constant. A -0.23 price elasticity with respect to hospital services implies a 2.3 percent decline in hospital days with a 10 percent increase in price (Eastaugh 1981). Several later studies have attempted to actually measure elasticity of demand for various health services, using large data bases. Studies of price elasticity of demand for hospital services have yielded mixed results. A study by Paul Feldstein and Ruth Severson (1964) showed no price elasticity of demand for hospital services, while a study by Rosenthal (1964) found significant price elasticity for general hospital services, primarily in length of stay.

In their attempt to estimate demand elasticity for hospitalization, Davis and Russell (1972) studied state-aggregated data for 48 states in 1969. While prices differed among the states (measured as a ratio of revenue-to-patient and average room charge), these authors were able to calculate elasticities. They found price elasticities of -0.5 for hospital admissions, and -0.32 to -0.46 for hospital days. These figures clearly indicate significant price inelasticity in demand for hospital services.

Martin Feldstein (1971; 1973) used 1958 through 1967 state-aggregated data to estimate hospital demand. His price measurement was hospital cost per patient day. He considered an insurance payment to be equivalent to a reduction in price. Estimating both short-run (1963-67) and long-run (1959-67) demand for hospital days, the elasticity coefficient was −0.55 for the long run and −0.26 for the short run, indicating slightly greater short-run than long-run inelasticity.

Rosett and Huang (1973) used data on coverage and total medical expenditures for individual spending units rather than aggregated state data. Elasticities for hospitalization ranged from −0.35 at a 20 percent copayment to −1.5 at an 80 percent copayment. These findings imply that under a national health insurance plan, going from a zero copayment to a one-third copayment could double outlays for hospitals.

In a newer study, Martin Feldstein (1977) examines the price elasticity of demand for hospital days. Study elasticity coefficients were −0.29 for the short run (1966-73) and −0.13 for the long run (1959-65). Newhouse and Phelps (1976) found a similar coefficient of −0.23 for hospital days. For length of hospital stay (hospital days/number of admissions), Newhouse and Marquis (1978) found almost total price inelasticity (a coefficient of −0.05).

Estimates of elasticity of demand for physician services are available from a number of case studies (Scitovsky and Snyder 1972; Phelps and Newhouse 1972). In one study a 25 percent copayment for physician services was introduced in a prepaid comprehensive group practice for employees of Stanford University. The addition of this copayment reduced usage about 25 percent, resulting in an arc elasticity (using average price as a base) of 0.14.

This finding is similar to the results of a study of the imposition of a 41 percent copayment in Saskatchewan which found an arc elasticity of 0.13 (Phelps and Newhouse 1972). These elasticities were quite low, showing little response of quantity of physician services used by consumers to price. One possible explanation is that other controls within the two settings limited demand for services, making demand unresponsive to price. A second explanation is that the demand curve may have been linear rather than curvilinear. With a linear demand curve, elasticities vary across different portions of the curve. In the range of the curve where quantities demanded are low, elasticities are relatively inelastic.

With physician services, factors other than dollar costs affect demand. One example of a nondollar cost to the consumer of medical care is the time involved in obtaining services, including both the travel time to and from the physician's office and the waiting time in the office. Together, these constitute the time costs of obtaining care. Acton (1975) emphasized the importance of time costs in ambulatory demand function. The longer the consumer waiting time or travel costs, the lower the quantity of services demand.

CONSUMER UTILITY AND HEALTH CARE DEMAND

Insurance for the health care consumer provides a solution to the unpredictability and uncertainty of the occurrence of illness. Depending upon their tastes, incomes, the probability of illness, and the cost of medical care, consumers must decide how to react to potential sickness. When illness occurs, it results in medical care expenses, and a subsequent loss of income to the individual. The economic concept of utility relates to the consumer's decision about whether or not to purchase health care and insurance to partially pay for that health care.

To analyze such consumer decisions, economists employ the concept of consumer utility – the satisfaction derived from all sources, both pecuniary and nonpecuniary. By definition, a consumer with high utility is more satisfied than is a consumer with low utility. Marginal utility is the additional satisfaction derived by the consumer from purchasing the last unit of service or product. If a consumer purchases ten units of care, the relevant marginal utility is the satisfaction derived from the purchase of the tenth unit. For a consumer who purchases 50 units of care, however, the relevant marginal utility is the satisfaction derived from the purchase of the fiftieth unit.

Economic theory holds that consumer satisfaction will be maximized if the consumer continues to purchase service units until that point where the marginal utility derived from the last unit purchased equals the marginal cost to the consumer of that last unit. Marginal cost of the last unit is the amount the consumer must pay to secure its consumption. If consumers follow this purchasing rule, and producers follow the production rule of continuing to produce service units until that point where the marginal cost to the provider of production equals the marginal revenue derived from the sale of that service unit, both overall consumer welfare and overall production will theoretically be maximized.

Economists have noted that the marginal utility of purchasing service units for a single consumer does not remain constant across the entire range of units available for purchase, but rather typically declines as the number of units purchased increases and the consumer approaches satiation. The service in question becomes less attractive as marginal utility derived from purchasing additional units declines, and other services or products with higher marginal utilities where the consumer is not approaching satiation become relatively more attractive.

In health care, the nature of the service may affect the rate of relative decline in marginal utility with the purchase of additional service units. The more serious and life-threatening the illness a health service is designed to combat, the less likely the marginal utility will drop rapidly with the purchase of additional service units, since the more serious and life-threatening the illness, the less likely additional service units will move the consumer to satiation.

Despite an elaborate theoretical and mathematically sophisticated underpinning, marginal utility analysis of consumer purchasing decisions has provided little practical guidance for pricing either health care services or insurance coverage for those services. The problem lies in the difficulty of developing widely applicable interpersonally comparable objective measures of consumer utility. Suitable, easily obtainable, valid, and reliable measures of consumer utility have not yet been developed.

Because of measurement failure, actual pricing of health services and health insurance has taken place relatively independent of theoretical discussions of utility and marginal utility. Sometimes economists employ the concept of income loss to a consumer as a surrogate measure of utility loss. However, income loss is not equivalent to utility loss and provides only a rough approximation of the latter at best, especially in health care where utility is a function of many nonpecuniary factors which affect quality of life.

Related to the concept of consumer marginal utility is the idea of moral hazard, which refers to an increase in the quantity of services demanded if those services are covered by insurance (Jacobs 1980). Within the insurance industry, the term of "moral hazard" implies reckless use of services by consumers, relative to what they would purchase under the "marginal cost equals marginal utility" rule without insurance. The reckless use results from lowering the marginal cost of additional service units which raises the marginal utility to marginal cost ratio and causes consumers to expand service utilization. While the insurance industry attaches a pejorative connotation to expanded consumer service utilization under insurance coverage, from the point of view of economics, consumers are simply behaving rationally in accordance with the price quantity relationship implied in downward sloping demand curves.

FEDERAL LEGISLATION EMPHASIZING DEMAND

Early federal statutes affecting demand were largely small in scope and covered limited categorical groups (see Appendix 4). The act providing free services for merchant marine seamen in 1798 was the first statute with a demand component and covered a minuscule portion of the population. Over the next 100 years, federal legislation emphasizing demand was sparse (see Appendix 4). Even into the first half of the twentieth century, little federal legislation focused on demand, with those exceptions emphasizing selected groups. The Veterans Act of 1924 extended medical care to veterans not only for treatment of disabilities associated with their military service, but also for other conditions. Another group receiving attention with two separate pieces of legislation in the 1920s and 1930s were mothers and children. Federal legislation at this time gave limited grants to states to establish maternal and child health services. Much of the other federal legislation affected demand only in an indirect fashion. One goal of environmental health legislation was to reduce long-term demand for health care by preventing environmentally induced diseases.

In the 1960s, the federal role vis-à-vis health care demand changed radically. The Kerr-Mills Act of 1960 began programs on a limited scale providing direct medical assistance and payment for services to the elderly poor. Medicare and Medicaid legislation of 1965 greatly expanded direct federal involvement in affecting demand for health care. More specialized efforts affecting demand involved federal facilitation of special centers to serve underprivileged groups. Two such groups were migratory workers, and persons living in underserved low-income communities with access to Office of Economic Opportunity health centers.

In contrast to its previously expansionary thrust, the federal role in promoting health care demand under the Reagan administration was sharply curtailed. The Omnibus Budget Reconciliation Act of 1981 reduced demand by eliminating services in Medicare, by eliminating eligibles for Medicaid, and by reducing funding for a large array of health programs. The Tax Equity and Fiscal Responsibility Act of 1982 (TEFRA) also significantly reduced health care demand.

CHAPTER SEVEN
HEALTH CARE SUPPLY

Just as economic models may be employed to describe demand for health services, they may also be used to describe health care supply. Supply, like demand, is a relationship. A specific supply curve represents the various quantities of health services providers are willing to supply at different prices. Supply curves typically slope upward to the right, indicating a positive relationship between the price of a service and the amount of that service providers will produce. Under an upwardly sloping supply curve to the right, as the price of a service increases, the quantity of service providers are willing to produce increases. Conversely, as the price decreases, the quantity of service available from providers declines. The point of intersection between the upwardly sloping to the right supply curve and the downwardly sloping to the right demand curve represents equilibrium.

As with demand, providers may move up and down a given supply curve as price of health care changes, while the trade-off between the quantity of service providers are willing to produce at given prices remains stable. Alternatively, the supply curve itself may move to the right or the left, indicating a change in the relationship between price and quantity providers are willing to produce. A shift of the supply curve to the right implies that producers are willing to provide a larger quantity of services at the same price than they were willing to provide before the shift occurred (see Figure 7-1). One possible reason for such a shift may be cost efficient technological breakthroughs which have significantly dropped

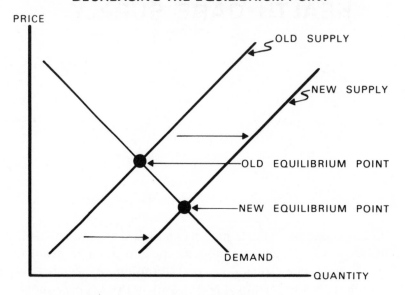

FIGURE 7-1
*AN EXPANSIONARY SHIFT IN THE SUPPLY CURVE
DECREASING THE EQUILIBRIUM POINT*

PRICE

OLD SUPPLY

NEW SUPPLY

OLD EQUILIBRIUM POINT

NEW EQUILIBRIUM POINT

DEMAND

QUANTITY

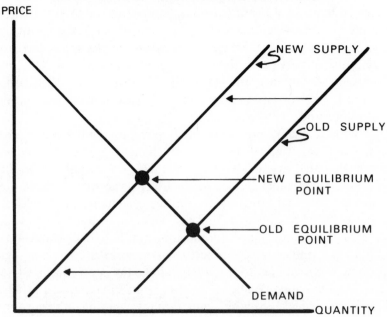

FIGURE 7-2
*A CONTRACTIONAL SHIFT IN THE SUPPLY CURVE
INCREASING THE EQUILIBRIUM POINT*

PRICE

NEW SUPPLY

OLD SUPPLY

NEW EQUILIBRIUM
POINT

OLD EQUILIBRIUM
POINT

DEMAND

QUANTITY

FIGURE 7-3
SUPPLY ELASTICITIES

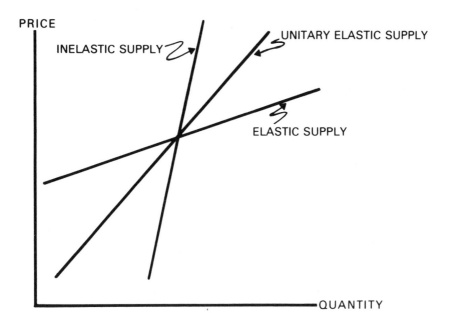

average unit costs. A shift of the supply curve to the left implies that producers are willing to provide smaller quantities of services at specific prices than they were willing to provide before the shift (see Figure 7-2). Underlying such a shift may be environmental or technological changes which have inflated unit service costs. Supply curves, like demand curves, may be elastic, inelastic, or have unitary elasticity (see Figure 7-3).

ECONOMIC MODELS OF PHYSICIAN BEHAVIOR

Many different types of suppliers of health care include physicians, hospitals, laboratories, drug companies, nursing homes, medical equipment companies, and blood banks. The major suppliers which have been modeled in economics are physicians and hospitals. Two different approaches have been used to model decisions about the nature and mix of health services physicians are willing to supply. The classical economic approach to modeling physician and hospital behavior is to use a profit maximization model which assumes that both physicians and hospitals strive above all else to maximize their total respective profits (Sloan 1976a; Sloan 1976b). This profit maximization model is a standard assumption and modeling procedure used by market economists to depict supply in any area.

Economists adhering to a profit maximization model for providers of health care prefer not to identify the unique aspects of the doctor-hospital-patient interaction which distinguish health care from other services and products, but prefer to apply a standard two-element utility function of profit and slack/leisure as the best approach to physician and hospital behavior (Pauley and Redisch 1973). They also argue that if both a multifaceted complex model and a simple model work almost equally well, the simple model should be used.

A second major economic approach is the utility maximization model (Feldstein 1970). Both the utility and profit maximization models assume some profit maximization in the physician's utility function. A physician-utility function includes profit, leisure time, professional status, complexity of case mix, study time to remain current, and possibly other factors. While the profit maximization approach emphasizes the predominant role of profit in explaining physician behavior, the utility maximization model pays greater attention to nonprofit factors. Under the utility maximization approach, a substantial component of physician utility may be derived from the treatment of an interesting complex of cases – a job enlargement concept acknowledged by industrial psychologists to be a major contributing factor to satisfaction derived from work. Sometimes the utility function is discussed in negative terms. Physicians may experience a disutility by working longer hours.

Most health economists agree that physicians have an unusually high ability to affect both the quantity and the price of the services they offer. Unlike the findings in other sectors that have employed traditional competitive economic analyses, higher physician density per capita correlates with unchanged or higher physician fees (Holahan et al. 1978; Institute of Medicine 1976b; Newhouse and Phelps 1974). The positive relationship between the number of suppliers in a geographic area and the price of services runs contrary to the normal notion of demand sloping downward to the right.

Physician Income Maintenance

Three main hypotheses about why physicians are able to maintain their income levels, despite increased physician density, have been suggested. Feldstein (1971) argues that when physician density increases, physicians merely reduce the proportion of patient need which goes untreated. This hypothesis assumes a market of permanent excess demand. The second hypothesis argues that new demand is created and that the new demand is physician-generated, rather than previously and permanently extant (Fuchs and Kramer 1973; Evans 1974). This second hypothesis essentially states that supply induces its own demand. The third hypothesis argues that if physicians are unable to maintain a target level of demand, they can nevertheless maintain a target income through increasing fees (Newhouse 1970). Physicians are partially able to raise fees in the face of increased supply, a phenomenon contrary to the normal laws of supply and demand, because they do not face a truly competitive market.

These hypotheses about whether or not there is supplier-induced demand relate to the public debate about appropriate health manpower ratios per capita and whether there is a need for greater production of physicians. Several examples from the field of surgery illustrate the policy issues. Bunker (1970) compared both the number of surgeons and the amount of surgery in the United States with the equivalent figures for Great Britain, finding that the United States had roughly twice as many surgeons and rate of surgical operations per capita, supporting the concept of physician-generated demand for surgery.

Other findings also support the hypothesis that physicians have the ability to generate a target income. Surgeons in a suburban community in the New York metropolitan area had a work load only one-third of what experts deemed a reasonably full schedule. They did not, however, spend the rest of their time in other kinds of medical work. Rather, they took more days and afternoons off and enjoyed longer weekends. Fee levels were high enough to ensure that even surgeons with small practices made a very comfortable living (Fuchs 1974).

Fuchs (1978) has also studied the surgeon manpower supply equilibrium. Surgeons do partially shift demand upward to compensate for an expansion in the supply of surgeons. They also increase prices to minimize the potential income reduction resulting from increased supply. Given these findings, the large number of people currently training in surgical residency programs may continue to contribute to rising health care costs and to produce a problem in cost containment. Any attempt to deal with cost containment by affecting the supply of surgeons takes a period of years, due to the long time involved in surgical training. It takes eight to ten years from the time students enter medical school to their initial independent practices, depending on the amount of advanced training involved and how specialized the surgeon becomes.

One recent major advisory study has generally accepted that there are negative consequences of an oversupply of physicians for consumers and for cost containment. The Graduate Medical Education National Advisory Committee Report to the secretary of Health and Human Services (GMENAC 1980) has projected an oversupply of 60,000 to 70,000 physicians by 1990. This report recommends a 17 percent reduction in medical school class size.

One major supply issue with policy implications is whether physicians work a greater or lesser amount as a result of changes in physician fees. Two major types of effects — the substitution effect and the income effect — potentially impact on physician response to fee changes. With a physician fee increase, under the substitution effect, physicians would decide to work harder because each hour of work becomes more financially lucrative. Physicians would substitute more patient care for leisure time, increasing the total amount of available patient care. The alternative income effect postulates that physicians would decide that their absolute income is sufficiently high with a fee increase that they can afford to purchase more leisure hours and work less.

In the case of fee increases or decreases and their impact on the quantity of physician labor hours available, the substitution effect and the income effect have opposite consequences. While the substitution effect increases the quantity of physician labor, the income effect reduces the quantity of physician hours available, given a fee increase. If the income effect outweighs the substitution effect, the net effect of a fee increase on physician hours available will be a decrease in the quantity of physician labor. When this occurs, the labor curve at higher fee rates may actually bend backward. While a normal supply curve slopes upward to the right throughout the entire rate of relevant fee rates, a backward bending labor supply curve only slopes upward to the right throughout the range of relatively lower fee rates. At higher fee rates, the supply curve begins to bend backward, sloping slightly upward to the left, indicating the decline in labor quantity from the dominant income effect.

Research results are mixed as to whether the income or substitution effect is actually the stronger. Feldstein (1970) finds strong support for the backward bending supply curve and the dominance of the income effect, while Sloan (1976a) finds no empirical support for a backward bending physician supply curve. Vahovich (1977) finds results falling between Feldstein and Sloan, reporting evidence of a slightly backward bend in physician supply. Reinhardt (1975) used data from individual physician practices and supports the backward bending labor supply hypothesis.

Brown and Lapan (1979) employ aggregate time series data, and also corroborate the backward bending supply hypothesis. They also find that nonphysician inputs, such as the availability of physicians' assistants and nurse practitioners, can substitute for declines in physician labor resulting from the income effect, making the overall supply curve for physician labor positively sloped throughout its entire range. One implication of the Brown and Lapan study is that the inflationary impact of increases in physician prices might be reduced if nonphysician inputs were readily available as substitutes (Eastaugh 1981).

Physician Supply

One supply issue in health care deals with the adequacy of the quantity of the supply of physician labor. Debates over this policy issue are longstanding. At the turn of the century, the Flexner Report (1910), which is best known for criticizing the quality of the physician supply, also criticized the oversupply of practicing physicians. Due to the report, both low quality and oversupply were justifications for closing a large number of U.S. medical schools.

By the 1930s, the Flexner Report had been so successfully implemented that studies were then concerned with estimating the shortage of physicians. In a classic study, Lee and Jones (1933) tried to estimate the shortage by using medical standards to translate levels of mortality and morbidity into number of required physician hours. This approach had great technical difficulties arising from problems in reasonably estimating mortality and morbidity, as well as translating those estimates into manpower projections.

Most studies in the 1940s and 1950s estimated physician-to-population ratios as an indicator of number of physicians needed to bring the country to a desirable standard, a technically simpler task (President's Commission on the Health Needs of the Nation 1953; Bane 1959). Despite the comparative ease of estimation, difficulty in ascertaining an appropriate standard for desirable physician-to-population ratios remained. Studies often employed widely varied standards, resulting in markedly different conclusions about the adequacy of physician supply. A further difficulty with this approach is whether physician-to-population ratios need to be computed for smaller geographic units rather than for the entire country. As physicians become more specialized, a similar difficulty is whether physician-to-population ratios need to be computed for specific medical and surgical specialties, rather than for all physicians combined.

Beyond technical difficulties in the previous studies, an economist's critique of their approach is that demand and supply are estimated simultaneously. Future demands or needs are projected on the basis of a particular supply level. Economists typically advocate separate estimation of supply and demand. The first well-known study separating demand and supply estimation procedures was done by Fein (1967). He estimated demand functions, taking account of various characteristics of the population, such as size, age/sex/race distributions, income, education, urbanization, migration, and Medicare. He then projected the future value of each of the population demographics, and determined the increase in demand using projected population demographic values. Supply was independently estimated using data on the number of graduating physicians from U.S. and foreign medical schools across time. Fein concluded for 1967 that the estimated 19 percent increase in physician supply would be inadequate, given projected increases in demand, assuming constant physician productivity.

Fein's study paid greater attention to estimating demand than to estimating physician productivity and supply. Reinhardt conducted a careful study of physician productivity, examining the impact of increases in the number of auxiliary personnel, of greater expenditures on capital equipment, and of the reorganization of the practice setting. Reinhardt concluded that a large increase in the supply of physicians would occur into the next century, but left unresolved whether this increase would be adequate or too large. Potential changes in physician productivity, as well as changes in consumer demand, made final determinations of physician supply adequacy difficult.

The GMENAC Report

In April 1976, the secretary of the Department of Health, Education, and Welfare (now Health and Human Services) established a Graduate Medical Education National Advisory Committee (GMENAC) to advise the secretary on national health planning objectives related to physician manpower. The committee was charged to determine how many physicians were needed to meet the national health care needs, the appropriate specialty distribution of these physicians, a desirable geographic distribution of physicians, and appropriate methods of financing graduate medical education. The committee developed a needs-based model to predict physician manpower. Needs were established by the Delphi technique, where a panel of physician experts gave independent opinions on each round of needs assessment, using the estimates from the last round as the beginning basis for each subsequent round. Under the Delphi technique, rounds of expert assessments are continued until a group consensus emerges.

The GMENAC report to the secretary predicted a physician surplus of 70,000 physicians by 1990, and of 140,000 physicians by the year 2000. Over 100 different recommendations to deal with this oversupply, including cutbacks in medical school enrollments and restrictions on the entry of foreign-trained doctors were made. The committee recommended that medical schools reduce first-year class size by 1984 by at least 17 percent of the 1980-81 class size. Severe restrictions on the number of graduates from foreign medical schools allowed to enter and practice medicine in the United States were advocated, since it was estimated that the entry into medical practice in the United States of 40,000 to 50,000 graduates of foreign medical schools accounted for over half of the predicted 1990 surplus. No specialty or subspecialty would be allowed to increase or decrease the number of first-year trainees in residency or fellowship programs in 1986 by more than 20 percent of the 1979 figure.

Other GMENAC recommendations argued for greater support for family practice residency programs, since these programs are more likely to train providers who practice in geographically underserved areas. A discontinuation of capitation payments to medical schools for the purpose of increasing class size or influencing specialty choice was recommended, in view of the projected surplus of physicians. Similarly, the need to train nonphysician health care providers at current levels was targeted as an area needing further study and possible cutbacks, since the intended role of these providers was to substitute nonphysicians for the scarce labor of physicians.

The number of projected surplus physicians varied by subspecialty. Continued shortages were actually predicted for general psychiatry, emergency medicine, and preventive medicine. Balance was forecast for eight subspecialties, including some of the primary care fields of family practice, general pediatrics, and general internal medicine. The widely recognized oversupply of general surgeons was projected to continue with newly created oversupplies in other surgical fields as well. Oversupplies were anticipated for allergists and immunologists, cardiologists, obstetrics-gynecology, general surgery, neurosurgery, and orthopedic surgery, among others.

A number of critiques of the GMENAC approach have been made (Reinhardt 1981). One set of criticisms dealt with the methods of determining how much health care will be utilized in the future. The needs-based approach was criticized for using a panel of physician-experts to develop normative standards for health care utilization 10 to 20 years in the future. Some felt the physicians were not sufficiently well-trained in demography, epidemiology, and statistical projection techniques to be able to fulfill this task. Others believed that the shape of the future financing and delivery of health care is uncertain, and that there is not a sufficiently stable political and economic climate to be confident that an individual's perception of a need for medical intervention will actually be translated into effective demand. These critics argue that a demand-based projection model should have been employed.

There are also criticisms of the approach taken to predicting the supply of active physicians in patient care. While apparently easier than demand and utilization estimation, estimating supply has several methodological difficulties. One difficulty is the projection of physician immigration, a trend related to worldwide political and economic conditions. Other difficult aspects include estimating physician decisions on retirement, physician choice of professional activity, and the impact of the increasing percentage of female physicians in the overall supply.

Physician retirement decisions, physician choice of professional activity, and the gender composition of the supply of doctors each potentially affects the average hours physicians will work, an important factor in addition to the total number of physicians in predicting physician labor supply. In the past, physicians have maintained active practices beyond the usual retirement age, but it is unclear whether this trend will continue into the future. The long pipeline from the entry into medical school to actual practice, the ability of doctors to shift specialties while in training or practice, and the freedom to shift types of practice from a private one in which a physician might work 70 or 80 hours a week to salaried practice with a 40 or 45-hour work week, all make accurate predictions of the number of future available physician hours difficult. Past surveys of physicians have indicated that women physicians work fewer hours per week and per year, and tend to see fewer patients per hour than do their male counterparts. However, the GMENAC summary report failed to consider impending changes in the gender composition of the physician supply (Reinhardt 1981).

Overall criticisms of GMENAC focus on the clarity of the report recommendations. While normally more clarity is preferred to less clarity, critics argued that the report ignored the complexity of the medical field and the technical difficulties in modeling physician supply, making empirically unfounded recommendations straightforwardly. One technical criticism was that the summary report employed point estimates of future supplies rather than range estimates which would typically be more appropriate for conditions of uncertainty. Nor were substitution effects addressed in sufficient depth to mollify critics. The Delphi panels employed to assess health care needs and manpower supplies were developed within each specialty. Members of specialty panels may have tended to overestimate the relative importance of their own specialties, underestimating possible substitution effects among specialties as well as substitutions between physician and nonphysician labor. The GMENAC report was also faced with the conundrum: while physician labor supplies must necessarily be modeled for separate specialties to be useful in planning, the smaller the physician specialty being modeled, the less reliable is any single projection.

HOSPITALS AS SUPPLIERS OF HEALTH CARE SERVICES

Today, hospitals play a central role in the delivery of health care services. The typical person in the United States today is born in a hospital, dies in a hospital, and is admitted for treatment to a hospital at several points in between. Doctors would find medical practice almost impossible without hospitals and the availability of the modern technology and diagnostic tests that they provide. Hospitals employ about three-fourths of all health care personnel. Expenditures for hospital services account for nearly one-half of the total health care services dollars in the United States. Hospitals have been at the center of most government efforts to control costs in health care and to regulate health care quality.

Types of Hospitals

Hospitals may operate as either profit-making corporations (proprietary) or as nonprofit agencies. At the time of the Flexner Report in 1910, 56 percent of all hospitals were proprietary (Raffel 1980). Most of these hospitals were established by one physician in a community or a small group of physicians who wanted to ensure the availability of minimal community hospital facilities for their patients. As hospitals became recognized as important community resources by mid-century, these small early facilities gradually were either closed or sold to community organizations. The Hill-Burton Act, which provided government loans to communities after World War II — first for the building of new hospitals and later for the expansion and modernization of older facilities — accelerated the shift from small physician-owned hospitals to nonprofit community hospitals. The percentage of proprietary hospitals declined to 25 percent in 1941 and 11 percent in 1968.

Starting in the early 1970s, the number of proprietary hospitals began to increase. By 1977, 13 percent of all hospital beds were located in proprietary hospitals. The type of proprietary hospitals changed from small physician-owned hospitals to larger investor-owned hospitals that are part of multiunit for-profit hospital systems owned by large corporate chains such as the Hospital Corporation of America, Humana Corporation, or AMI. Due to the decline in the number of small physician-owned hospitals, the proportion of proprietary hospitals has changed little through 1980. Many large proprietary hospital chains own several hundred hospitals scattered across the United States, and in some cases, in foreign countries. These corporations may frequently negotiate management contracts with hospitals they do not own outright to provide management services, sometimes blurring the distinction between profit and nonprofit hospital status. The number of hospitals entering management contracts with hospital chains approximates the number of hospitals owned by chains.

In addition to for-profit hospital corporate chains, many nonprofit hospitals now join together in contractual arrangements to share services. These multi-hospital arrangements among nonprofit hospitals are used to enhance efficiency, but simultaneously make the hospital care delivery system considerably more complex. In 1978, an American Hospital Association Survey reported that 80 percent of U.S. hospitals shared at least one service, such as group purchasing of supplies, consortia for planning or education, or a formal affiliation with a medical school. Multi-hospital systems, with a single organization owning and managing more than one hospital, involved over 25 percent of all hospitals. This would include for-profit chains, as well as large HMO groups such as Kaiser-Permanente, and Catholic or other religious-owned hospital groups (Wilson and Neuhauser 1982).

By 1980, 90 percent of hospitals had some type of arrangement for sharing services and/or departments with neighboring hospitals; 26 percent were members of multi-hospital systems (Johnson 1980). Nonprofit multi-hospital systems are particularly popular in midwestern states, including Indiana, Illinois, Michigan, Wisconsin, Kansas, and Missouri. Investor-owned proprietary multi-hospital systems are more common in California, Texas, and other southern and southwestern states.

Hospital Utilization

Debate exists over whether hospitals serve preexisting demands for hospital services, or fill empty hospital beds independent of prior demand. While the hospital in an institutional sense cannot create demand, hospitals may indirectly control some incentives for physicians who have hospital privileges. If there is supplier-induced demand for hospitalization, physicians on the staffs of hospitals make the decisions to recommend hospital care. While physicians on a hospital staff benefit from financial stability for that hospital, it is questionable whether any one physician derives enough benefit from that stability to alter practice patterns. Hospitals with large numbers of empty beds might try to recruit additional staff members, who would subsequently hospitalize patients and increase the hospital occupancy rate. Unless a physician were recruited from outside the community, the total demand for hospitalization within the geographic area would not be increased, but part of the demand would merely be shifted from one supplying hospital to another.

A related issue in hospital supply is the degree to which excess capacity in hospital beds generates demand for hospitalization. One measure of hospital utilization is discharge rate per 1,000 population. Utilization rates of hospital bed capacity vary substantially among regions of the United States and among different organizational modes for practice (that is, HMOs versus fee-for-service). Luft (1978a and 1978b) has conducted a very comprehensive review of over 50 studies comparing hospital utilization rates in prepaid group practices, prepaid individual practice associations (IPAs), and traditional fee-for-service practices. When compared to traditional fee-for-service practices, rates of hospital days per 1,000 persons ranged from 25 to 45 percent lower in prepaid group practices, and 0 to 25 percent lower in IPAs.

Between regions, the Medicare discharge rate per 1,000 enrollees ranges from 264 discharges in the Northeast, to 328 discharges in the South – a 25 percent difference. Hospital days per 1,000 enrollees also shows great interregional variation, going from 2,867 in the West to 3,911 in the North Central region – a 36 percent difference (Gornick 1976). Within states there is also wide variation in hospital use. A study of Maine found that discharge rates per 1,000 population varied from 127 in the lowest area to 235 in the highest. Hospital days per 1,000 persons varied from 831 to 1,625 (Wennberg et al. 1975). Similar variability is found in other states. A report from Iowa indicates county variations in admission and hospital day rates ranging from more than 30 percent below to greater than 50 percent above the statewide mean, even with adjustment for the age/sex composition of each county (McClure 1982).

Most studies that have tried to explain these regional and state variations conclude that age, sex, mortality rates, and other general consumer demographic factors explain only about 15 percent of the observed variation (McClure 1982; Kelly and Schieber 1972). Researchers are increasingly turning to supply-side factors, such as manpower, facilities, and organization of practice to try to explain the variation.

General agreement exists that too few physicians or hospital facilities would result in inappropriately low-service use by a population. There are also some indications of the converse: that higher physician/population and hospital/population ratios lead to higher hospital use. Bunker (1970) reported that rates of surgery correlated with surgical manpower rates, a finding confirmed by several other researchers (Lewis 1969; Vayda 1973). Roemer's classic study reported that holding all other factors constant, the supply of hospital beds has an upward effect on hospital use. Other studies have corroborated Roemer's findings (May 1975; Chiswick 1976).

Why does the supply of hospital beds increase hospital utilization? One explanation suggests a pecuniary motivation on the part of physicians and hospitals. Hospitals with a large excess capacity of unused hospital beds have lower revenues than do equivalently sized hospitals with higher occupancy rates. While physicians can generate revenues for their practices in a number of ways, one important source of revenue generation is through the hospitalization of patients. Each time a physician visits a patient in the hospital, some revenue is created. If a physician has a large number of patients in the same hospital, substantial revenues result, since physician visits to hospitalized patients are relatively cost efficient.

Unused available beds represent substantial costs to hospitals. With lower-bed-occupancy rates, fixed costs for plant, equipment, heating and cooling, and janitorial staffs are amortized over a smaller number of service units, driving up the cost of each service unit provided. While theoretically these costs can be transferred forward to the consumer of hospital services in the long run, in the short run, payment reimbursal schemes by third-party payers may limit hospital flexibility to shift costs. Also theoretically variable costs, such as personnel costs, which could be cut if occupancy rates fell, in reality may be less variable than in theory. Hospital administrators wanting to retain a competent hospital nursing staff may have limited ability to reduce personnel costs with temporary declines in occupancy rates. In a study of Maryland hospitals, the long-run cost of an unoccupied bed, relative to occupied beds, was estimated to average 75 percent (Gianfrancesco 1980).

Some. unused bed capacity is desirable from the viewpoint of providing quality care, although not from an economic viewpoint. A hospital wishing to maximize revenues would strive for a 100 percent occupancy rate with substantial waiting lists for admissions so that all available beds would be constantly used. This strategy for revenue maximization, however, conflicts with the norm of providing high-quality care, since patients needing hospitalization on short notice for life-threatening conditions would have to wait for hospital admittance. Higher occupancy rates enhance revenue maximization for the hospital, but simultaneously lower the quality of care by creating admissions queues and increased waiting times for admittance.

Hospital occupancy rates are affected by specialization (the case mix). Case mix refers to the degree to which a hospital concentrates on specific diagnostic categories and the frequency of admissions in various categories. A very specialized hospital would have a limited case mix, whereas a general hospital would have a broad case mix. The broadest case mix often occurs in university teaching hospitals where the institution not only accepts a variety of different types of cases, but actually encourages a broad mix in order to train doctors to deal with a great variety of illnesses. University hospitals also have wide variety in the severity of the different illnesses that they treat.

For any particular hospital, the greater the specialization in a variety of different diagnostic categories, the less beds are interchangeable. The less beds are interchangeable, the lower the occupancy rate, because an unused bed designed for one specialty cannot be substituted and used for another specialty. A reduction in the number of diagnostic categories treated will lessen the variation in admissions over time, thereby reducing the required bed capacity which, in turn, will be reflected in higher occupancy rates (Gianfrancesco 1980).

Some experts question the interpretation that doctors and hospitals are primarily financially motivated to fill unused hospital beds with patients (McClure 1982; Bunker and Brown 1974). A study by Bunker and Brown (1974) reports that physician families are, themselves, higher than average users of hospital care. Physicians do not hospitalize patients more than they hospitalize their own families.

Critics of the hypothesis that unused hospital beds generate hospital utilization point out that other factors besides bed capacity and hospital facilities affect utilization rates. The amount and type of insurance is but one example of other factors which impact on consumption of hospital services. The organizational and financial structure of medical practice also affects hospital occupancy.

Occupancy rates for hospitals are related to but differ from the concept of oversupply. An oversupply of hospital beds results in lower occupancy rates, and overall higher health care costs, given the high costs of an unoccupied bed. While occupancy rates are calculated for individual hospitals, the concept of oversupply is typically used to apply to a metropolitan area. With oversupplies in the number of physicians some potential for mobility exists so that oversupplied physicians in one area could, given appropriate incentives, move to areas with physician shortages. With oversupplies in the number of hospital beds, no potential for mobility equalizing areas of over- and undersupplies exists.

Given the permanency of hospital bed oversupplies and the associated high costs, federal policy has been concerned with controlling the growth of new beds and orderly closure of unnecessary beds in oversupplied areas. While rapidly growing areas have experienced temporary shortages in hospital beds, the nation as a whole has experienced an oversupply. An excess of 100,000 to 130,000 acute care hospital beds was estimated in 1976 (Institute of Medicine 1976; Ensminger 1976). Oversupplies of hospital beds have particularly plagued areas with declining populations, including the older cities of the Northeast and the Midwest.

Hospital Reimbursement Schemes

In addition to occupancy rates, third-party reimbursement schemes affect hospital revenues. For most patients during the 1960s and 1970s, hospitals were reimbursed by third parties who paid on the basis of the hospital's actual cost. Two other large groups of patients had bills paid by Medicare and Medicaid. Although these governmental programs did include requirements at various points for quality control mechanisms or other special requirements, until recently, the reimbursement methodology they have employed has been cost based. Reimbursement of hospitals was traditionally retrospective, so that the third party or government paid for expenses already incurred.

Four variants of the traditional retrospective reimbursement schemes for hospitals are cost based, charge based, cost-plus based, and minimum payment. Under cost-based schemes, the hospital is fully reimbursed for costs already incurred. Charges are the publicly stated rates established by the hospital for various services. Under charge-based schemes, charges rather than actual costs are the basis for reimbursement. With cost-plus reimbursement, the hospital receives payments for its allowable costs, plus some specified amount (usually never more than 2 or 3 percent) of total cost. With minimum payment reimbursal, the hospital receives the lower of either the cost or charge-based method of calculation. Cost calculation in a hospital is technical and complex for wide variations exist. Factors included in cost calculations vary by payment plan. For example, Medicaid traditionally did not allow depreciation and interest on debt for unapproved capital expenditures to be included as costs in Medicaid reimbursement, while most third-party plans allowed depreciation as cost factors.

Economists criticize the retrospective reimbursement schemes, arguing that they encourage organizational expansion and insulation of both the producer and the consumer from market discipline (Ro and Auster 1969; Hornbrook and Rafferty 1982; Jacobs 1980). Efficiency incentives are undercut with retrospective reimbursement, since most insurance companies simply pay the majority of hospital requests. When reimbursement is assured and costs can constantly be shifted forward via the third-party payer ultimately to the general consumer, hospitals have few incentives to minimize long-run costs. Nor are consumers disciplined since the specific consumer of hospital services at any point in time is a small subset of the general consumer of health insurance bearing the ultimate costs.

Although still less commonly used, prospective reimbursement schemes provide an alternative to retrospective reimbursals. All variants of prospective reimbursement involve setting the basis for payment before expenses are incurred. Different types of prospective reimbursement include payments based on a fixed total budget, a per service rate, a per diem rate, a per admission rate, or a case type rate. Conceptually, a fixed total hospital budget is the simplest plan. This method has been used in Rhode Island, Michigan, and Washington states (Allison 1976; Baker 1976; Hellinger 1976 and 1978). The states negotiate a total budget with the hospital to which the hospital must adhere. The costs implied by the hospital budget for various services become the standard for reimbursal by third-party payers.

The most common variant of the total budget reimbursement plan has focused on the rate of increase in the total budget, limiting projected cost increases to a negotiated percentage. Economists agree that the total budget basis for reimbursal provides incentives to reduce both admissions and average length of hospital stay (Dowling 1976; Hornbrook and Rafferty 1982). Some argue this budgeting scheme would also provide incentives to reduce complexity of case mix and to increase efficiency (Dowling 1976). Preliminary evaluation studies indicate that in Rhode Island, hospital costs increased more slowly than for the nation overall by approximately 3 or 4 percent (Hellinger 1978).

Per service, per diem, and per admission methods of prospective reimbursement are all variants of prospective schemes. Each method includes costs per service, services per patient per day, days of stay per admission, and number of admissions as components of total costs. Under per service reimbursement, the hospital receives a given rate set in advance for each service, such as an x-ray, kidney dialysis, or an operation. With per service reimbursement, an output maximizing hospital would expand services as long as the preset rate covered the cost of providing each service. Output could be expanded by either increasing the number of services per patient per day, the number of days a patient stays so that more services could be performed, or possibly the number of admissions (Jacobs 1980).

With per diem prospective reimbursement, a given rate is set for each day of patient care. This method provides no incentive to expand the number of services given to each patient per day, because the hospital is not directly reimbursed for such an expansion. As long as the per diem rate covers costs, the hospital derives economic advantage from expanding the number of patient days, either by increasing length of stay or possibly by increasing admissions. Since the most expensive services usually occur early in a hospital stay, the hospital would particularly benefit economically by expanding length of stay. The per diem system therefore requires some regulation of and quality control over length of stay.

A number of experiments using per diem reimbursement have attempted to evaluate the advantages and weaknesses of this payment scheme. The studies indicate some degree of success, tempered by mixed results. Studies in western Pennsylvania and New Jersey showed small but statistically insignificant positive effects on cost containment from per diem reimbursals (Gaus and Hellinger 1976; Hellinger 1976; Worthington 1976). By contrast, a New York State program demonstrated greater positive effects on cost containment. Under prospectively set per diem payments, New York State's average per diem costs and average costs per patient have risen at significantly lower rates than has the United States as a whole. Evaluators estimate that the plan has reduced average costs per patient day by almost 5 percent, and average costs per hospital stay by 8.5 percent (Hellinger 1978). New York's experience with cost containment using prospective per diem reimbursement is the most successful of these prospective payment schemes in containing costs.

A per admission prospective reimbursement mechanism would financially reward the hospital only for adding more patients. A hospital would have direct economic incentives to reduce length of stay, to attract more patients, and to encourage readmission of patients. The hospital would also have an economic incentive to shift case mix toward simpler more profitable cases using few services with short stays. Few experiments with this method have been conducted (Hornbrook and Rafferty 1982).

A newer, more sophisticated, and more complicated method of prospective reimbursement by third-party payers and governments is case mix cost accounting for diagnostic-related groups (DRG). DRG reimbursement was developed to counter the weaknesses of the previous prospective schemes. Across time, the problems with the simplicity of prospective schemes discussed so far became apparent since each focused primarily on a single cost factor in an environment where costs were determined by many factors. The DRG scheme tries to establish a product definition for hospitals, recognizing that what hospitals supply is patient care of various kinds and intensities over various durations. The methodology tries to develop a relationship between the case mix of hospitals, the resources a hospital consumes, and the costs a hospital incurs (Thompson et al. 1979; Mills et al. 1976; Theriault 1978). DRG-based payment is a major alternative to current hospital reimbursement methodologies. A national shift to prospective DRG-based reimbursement for hospitals is a major issue in current national health policy which will be discussed in greater detail in Chapter 10.

THE SUPPLY OF NURSES AND ALLIED HEALTH PROFESSIONALS

While the average patient in a hospital may not be able to differentiate between skill level differences of nurses, the three levels of skill in nursing care are Registered Nurse (RN), Licensed Practical Nurse (LPN), and nurse's aide. Nurse's aides perform the menial tasks of patient care, many of which involve personal hygiene. They are generally trained on the job, with scope, duration, and formality of training varying across institutions. Educational requirements to become a nurse's aide also vary, although most institutions require some high school education. Almost all nurse's aides are female. Men performing the same functions are called orderlies or attendants and are trained separately but similarly.

LPNs (called LVNs in California and Texas for Licensed Vocational Nurse) do a variety of tasks in hospitals and nursing homes under the general and often nominal supervision of RNs. The first LPN educational programs were established by the Vocational Educational Act of 1917 (Smith-Hughes Act). Today, the training programs range from 9 to 15 months and are usually found in community colleges, vocational schools, and sometimes in hospitals. All states have some licensing procedure for LPNs. In about half the states, licensing is mandatory, while in the other half, it is voluntary. Although a few states have a separate board to license LPNs, in most states the overall state nursing board fulfills that function.

Three types of training for RNs are two-year associate degree, three-year diploma, and four-year baccalaureate programs. The most recently created route to becoming an RN (1952) is a two-year program, often based in a community or junior college, leading to a two-year associate degree. Under associate programs, clinical experience is obtained in an affiliated hospital. These programs have increased rapidly in the last 20 years. By the end of the 1970s almost half of all new RNs graduated from two-year programs.

The three-year diploma programs are based in hospital schools of nursing and were the first type of training programs for RNs. The earliest of these schools began in the 1870s and were based on the nursing educational principles of Florence Nightingale in England. Traditionally, these schools were developed as integral parts of a hospital. In early years, much of the education employed an apprentice model. Student nurses were the mainstay of the hospital labor supply. Through the 1950s, the great majority of nursing graduates came from these programs. Currently, the percentage of diploma graduates and the total number of such programs is declining.

Several factors explain the decline. Both baccalaureate and associate degree programs have increased, causing a relative decline in enrollment in diploma programs. Hospital standards and public opinion made staffing predominantly by student nurses increasingly unacceptable. A greater need for an improved curriculum has made hospital diploma programs more expensive. Consequently, many hospitals have closed their three-year nursing diploma programs.

Four-year nursing programs leading to a bachelor of science degree are located in universities. While the first school of this type was established in 1910 at the University of Minnesota, in general, these schools were few in number until the 1930s. In recent years, baccalaureate programs have experienced a rapid rise, and over 30 percent of recent nurse graduates hold B.S.N. degrees. Periodically, movements arise to reduce the status of associate degree and three-year diploma degree RNs to a lesser title, leaving four-year programs as the only legitimate route to receiving an RN. These movements have to date been unsuccessful in achieving their goal of devaluing the two and three-year RN degrees. In 1965, the American Nurses Association argued that minimum preparation for beginning professional nursing practice should be a baccalaureate degree. Recently, nursing educators have again called for the two-year RNs to be technical nurses, and for all new RN nurses to have a B.S. degree.

Sex composition in the field of nursing has changed little during the last decade; 98 percent of nurses are still female. Many experts argue that the overwhelmingly female composition of the nursing force creates special issues relevant to maintaining an adequate labor supply. The array of career possibilities for women has broadened in the last 10 to 15 years, sometimes reducing the attractiveness of traditional careers, including nursing. Nursing as a career has many liabilities, such as relatively low pay, traditionally undesirable work schedules, and difficult working conditions.

One common perception about the nursing labor force is that large numbers of women trained as nurses do not practice nursing for an extended number of years. The typical pattern is high rates of employment immediately after graduation, with reductions in labor force participation rates beginning after age 25 as nurses begin to marry and raise children. A survey of Registered Nurses in 1972 found that 69 percent of respondents were actively employed at that time. There were some reductions in labor force participation with age. However, the lowest percent of any age cohort until the age of 60 was 65 percent of RNs employed in the age category 30 to 35 (*Facts About Nursing* 1973; *The Nation's Nurses* 1974). This percentage was much higher than popularly perceived.

Currently, if all nurses employed or looking for work are counted, the labor force participation rate for nurses is nearly 80 percent, higher than the labor force participation rate for women with comparable levels of education in other occupations (Aiken et al. 1981a). The total number of licensed Registered Nurses in the United States is now about 1.4 million, an all time high. The nurse-to-population ratio is also higher than ever (Weisman 1982). Nurses are the single largest group of employees involved in patient care, comprising 58 percent of the total supply of all active health professionals.

Nursing is poorly paid in comparison to other occupations demanding similar levels of education and involving similar responsibility. The income gap between nurses and physicians, for example, has increased dramatically since the end of World War II. In 1945, nurses' incomes averaged one-third of physicians' incomes. By 1980, doctors earned over five times as much as nurses (Aiken et al. 1981b; Mechanic and Aiken 1982). Nurses' current incomes also do not compare well with those in other female-dominated occupations. Nurses' salaries in 1980 were on a par with the national average for secretaries, even though the educational preparation was considerably greater for nurses (Aiken et al. 1981b). The typical salary structure also does not reward experienced career nurses.

A nurse beginning her first job will earn only slightly less than a nurse with years of clinical experience (Donovan 1980).

The salary of RNs is also not that much greater than the salary of an LPN or a nurse's aide, and the differential has been decreasing over the last 20 years. In 1960, LPNs earned 70 percent and nurse's aides 65 percent of what the average RN earned. By 1980, LPNs earned 76 percent and aides 71 percent of what the average RN earned (Aiken et al. 1981a; Demkovich 1981). During the nursing shortage of the 1960s, hospitals hired LPNs and nurse's aides to substitute for RNs. Today, the rationale for the substitution of LPNs and nurse's aides for RNs has diminished, because the average hospital patient is more severely ill than the average patient of 20 years ago, and medical technology has become more complex. Both of these factors have contributed to a reverse substitution of RNs for LPNs and aides, since RNs are the most versatile of the three types of nurses and, with the reduced salary gap, are not significantly more costly. In 1968, RNs constituted 33 percent of all hospital nursing personnel, whereas by 1979, they were 47 percent.

Over two-thirds of all nurses in the labor force work in hospitals. Traditional work schedules for these nurses are often undesirable. Nurses frequently were required to work rotating shifts in which they would spend several weeks on day shifts followed by several weeks on evening or late-night shifts. Schedules were also typically based on a seven-day work week, which meant that the average nurse had Saturday or Sunday off only about once a month. Being off-duty both weekend days occurred only once every seven weeks. In addition, nurses routinely worked many of the major holidays. Recently some hospitals have begun to experiment with innovative and more desirable schedules. One new schedule is to pay nurses working 2 weekend shifts of 12 hours each a full salary. This frees the weekends for nurses on other schedules.

Beyond scheduling, there are other negative aspects of a nurse's working conditions. A study of nurses in Baltimore found that perceived control over work, including the ability to make decisions on work conduct, was the strongest predictor of job satisfaction (Weisman et al. 1981; Weisman 1982). Nurses have little professional control, but great professional responsibility. While nurses are held accountable for any mistakes in patient care, most services provided to patients or medications given must be under a physician's order.

A nurse cannot unilaterally change a physician's order which she perceives as incorrect without a physician's approval.

The nurse's physical environment also falls short of desirable working conditions. The nurses' station is actually a multidisciplinary station housing the ward secretary, patient charts, telephone, and often medications. Physicians, social workers, and other members of the health care team confer in the nurses' station. In some hospitals, night nurses may not even have a place to obtain a hot meal or eat it in peace.

One argument that many economists make about the low wages of nurses in general, but especially for hospital nurses, is that the market for nurses is monopsonistic, or oligopsonistic. A monopsony occurs when there is only one buyer for a supply of labor or a product in a particular geographic area. With an oligopsony, there are a few buyers in a geographic area. In each case, free competition does not occur. If the suppliers (sellers) are many in number and unorganized in their negotiations with the buyer(s), then the buyer can drive down the price of the labor being sold, since the many and unorganized sellers who wish to work have no alternative source of employment (Yett 1970a; Yett 1970b). Evidence to support this argument is that over 70 percent of the hospitals in the United States are located in a one-hospital community, while many other communities are serviced by only a few hospitals (Yett 1970a). Since hospital nurses are the largest group of nurses, their wages set wages for nurses in other types of jobs. Using this analysis, the shortage of nurses is not an absolute shortage, but results from a shortage of nurses willing to work at the low wages monopsonistic and oligopsonistic competition allows.

A recent Institute of Medicine study argues that the nation's nursing shortage of the past two decades has largely disappeared ("Nursing and Nursing Education: Public Policies and Private Actions" 1983). According to the study, a nationwide shortage no longer exists, although there is a shortage in administrative posts, inner-city and rural areas, and nursing homes. Reasons for the reduction in shortage of skilled nursing care include recent wage increases and revised schedules which have helped to retain nurses, and the generally poor economic conditions of the last few years which have made switching to alternative careers less attractive.

Others contend that the shortage is still a problem, and that its elimination was more of a record-keeping change than a real change. Some evidence exists that hospitals have ceased to budget nursing positions for which funds were not immediately available, increasing the proportion of filled positions by eliminating positions rather than by increasing the number of nurses hired. While there is disagreement over whether the overall nursing shortage has abated, agreement is universal that nursing shortages are still a problem in rural and inner-city areas. Shortages in these geographic areas have been attributed to the generally less-desirable working conditions and lower wages which prevail there.

Less attention has been directed to the supply of allied health professionals, such as laboratory technicians, medical records professionals, occupational and physical therapists, and medical technologists of various types. Depending on the educational level required, these people are trained in varied settings, including proprietary schools, hospitals, junior and technical colleges, and allied health schools that are a part of university medical centers. One problem for many of these specialized jobs is lack of upward advancement, a phenomenon described as "phantom mobility." The highly specialized and technical nature of many of these jobs, coupled with licensing and regulatory restrictions reduce mobility from one allied health field to another.

Within each allied health field, there are only a few administrative positions to which allied health professionals can advance without acquiring different training to change their job designation. In a laboratory, for example, a medical technologist with a bachelor's degree may acquire supervisory responsibilities over other medical technologists and over technicians who have less training. Yet the head of the laboratory will generally be a pathologist — usually an M.D. but occasionally a Ph.D. Allied health professionals are similar to nurses in this regard. LPNs can never advance to become RNs without additional training, nor can nurse's aides advance to become LPNs. This rigid specialization with each occupation requiring specific training in health fields is distinguished from other sectors of the economy, including business, where experience and job performance are often sufficient grounds for advancement.

Midlevel health professional fields — nurse practitioners (NPs) and physician's assistants (PAs) — were created under federal aegis with federal training funds to alleviate the projected physician shortage. One pool of labor for recruiting PAs was medics trained in and leaving military service. Both of these midlevel occupations were designed to fulfill similar tasks of first-level patient care. A major distinction is gender, in that NPs are predominantly female, while PAs are predominantly male. Given the decline in the physician shortage (and according to some experts, the oversupply of doctors by 1990), the future role of these occupational specialties is in doubt. Since nurse practitioners begin their training as RNs, they can revert to nursing and stay within the health care field. This flexibility is less apparent for physician's assistants, since there is no traditional occupation to which they can return.

FEDERAL LEGISLATION EMPHASIZING SUPPLY

Early federal efforts to affect supply of health care services were two pronged: one aspect regulated the supply of drugs and health care products; a second aspect was federal provision of hospitals and staffing for the merchant marine and for general public health (see Appendix 5). In the 1930s and 1940s the creation of the National Institute of Health affected supply by offering training of health research personnel and research grants. The 1935 Social Security Act and the 1944 Public Health Service Act provided federal monies to establish state and local health departments to increase health care supply. After World War II, two new federal thrusts were manifested: federal monies to train general health care personnel and funds to increase the supply of nonfederally owned health care facilities. The Hill-Burton Act of 1946 began the tradition of providing federal funds for building and renovating hospitals and other health care facilities. The Community Mental Health Centers Act of 1963 extended construction and renovation to mental health centers. The Health Maintenance Organization Act of 1973 provided federal grants and loan guarantees to a special type of health facility. The Emergency Medical Systems Act of 1973 pushed the development of area medical systems.

Federal manpower legislation to expand the supply of nonfederal health care personnel other than researchers began with the Health Amendments Act of 1956 which provided traineeships for public health personnel and for some nurses. A 1958 amendment began formula grants to schools of public health. The 1963 amendments provided construction grants to most health professional schools and provided student loan funds to physicians. Later amendments through the 1960s and early 1970s expanded trainee-ships, loan funds, and capitation and formula grants to a broader array of health professional schools. As in other areas of health, federal funds augmenting supply were cut back during the Reagan administration. Funds to support new HMOs were eliminated, as was funding for capitation for nursing and medical schools. Trainee-ship and loan funds were severely reduced.

CHAPTER EIGHT
EQUITY IN HEALTH CARE

Two types of equity have been discussed in national health policy: geographic equity and income equity. When inequity existed, federal policy sometimes, especially in the recent past, was developed to increase availability of health services for groups where access was previously lacking. Equity is a complex issue. Several kinds of equity exist. Does equity imply equal access to health care for all groups, or equal health care, not just access? If the poor are less healthy than the nonpoor, would not equity require greater health care access by the less healthy?

EQUITY AND ACCESS

Related to the definition of equity is whether or not U.S. society regards health care access as a basic human right. While most other industrial societies have answered this question with a "yes" by creating either national health insurance or national health delivery systems, Americans have not yet reached the same conclusion. Two coexistent but contradictory traditions have developed in the United States. One holds that individuals are responsible for their own welfare, including health care. A second tradition contends that communities have a responsibility for providing health care access to all citizens, and especially to those unable to secure access on their own. At various points, one tradition has dominated the other.

The Committee on the Cost of Medical Care in 1932 was supported by private foundations and conducted one of the earliest national studies on the economics of health services. The committee negated a popular conception at the time that good medical care was widely available to the poor as well as the rich. Persistent gaps for different geographic units, rural and urban regions, and income groups were reported for medical care need, access, and supply (Falk 1983).

In 1952, the President's Commission on the Health Needs of the Nation concluded that "access to the means for the attainment and preservation of health is a basic human right" (President's Commission on the Health Needs of the Nation 1953). This philosophy guided policy makers for the subsequent three decades, leading to a number of federal programs designed to increase health care access.

A new presidential commission was formed in the 1980s to study ethical and legal implications of equity in health care (President's Commission for the Study of Ethical Problems 1983). The commission concluded that society has an ethical obligation to ensure equitable access to health care for all. The reasons cited were the special importance of health care in quality of life, and recognition that health care needs are generally beyond individual control. Balancing the societal obligation are individual obligations to pay a "fair share" of their own health care costs and to take reasonable steps to provide for such care.

What is equity? The 1983 presidential commission in a controversial recommendation defined it as access to a standard level of health care without incurring excessive burdens. This translated into a policy recommendation of a minimum level of adequate care below which no individual should fall. It did not preclude differences in health care access, or set a ceiling on amount of care. The commission emphasized the desirability of achieving equity through private market forces when possible. The final responsibility for health care access, however, rested with the federal government, working through a combination of government and private forces.

The commission embraced the ability-to-pay criterion for paying for health care access, arguing that no one sector, geographic area, or set of institutions should pay all access costs, but those with a greater ability-to-pay should pay a larger share. Greater priority was attached to giving some access to all than to giving better access to some who had already obtained a minimum standard. Efforts to contain total health care costs should not, according to the commission, justify limiting access for those below a minimum standard.

Equity, access, coverage, and use of health services are interrelated. Equity implies a standard by which to judge the distribution of health services among groups. Access is the availability of health services to various groups. Coverage — usually insurance or third-party payment coverage — affects access by making services available to groups who otherwise could not afford them. Use is the actual health care services consumed. While use or utilization patterns of health services among income groups is observable and measurable, and coverage is also observable and measurable, equity and access are not. Often, however, in the absence of better empirical measures, utilization patterns are used as surrogate indicators of access, obscuring the theoretical differences between the two. In theory, access could be broader and more extensive than actual usage.

Availability of health care has several dimensions. The narrowest definition is the physical availability of services, emphasizing supply and focusing upon geographic distribution. A fuller definition examines whether consumers are able to secure care when it is needed. Accessibility of health care is often discussed negatively as the absence of barriers to receiving health care. Some barriers are obvious: the lack of insurance or income. Others are more subtle: an inability to negotiate the complexities of the health care system, lack of transportation, or excessive time constraints or other opportunity costs.

HEALTH STATUS DIFFERENTIALS

Examining equity in health involves health status — the level of individual health. Variations in health status among population groups are important in two ways: poorer health status may be an indicator of inadequate access to health services; additionally, access to health service must be assessed in terms of need for services for various groups. Equitable access will not guarantee equality in health status, due to differences between individuals even within the same group. Nonetheless, group differences in overall health present a point of departure for analyzing equity.

Several measurement difficulties confound assessment of the health status of the poor. Health is a multidimensional concept, requiring multiple indicators, but the use of an overall index may mask important differences between groups in specific aspects of health status. Often data are not available broken out by income groups. Race has been used as a less than satisfactory surrogate measure for income, especially in examining mortality.

Many studies have consistently documented that the poor have lower health status than the nonpoor. Despite Medicaid, Medicare, and OEO-induced improvements in the access to health care of low-income groups, newer studies continue to demonstrate group differentials in health status (Kleinman et al. 1981; Davis et al. 1981; Davis and Schoen 1978; Lerner and Stutz 1977; Kane et al. 1976; Kitagawa and Hauser 1973; U.S. DHEW 1977).

Mortality rates are frequently used to measure health status. Overall mortality rates have been declining. At least one study has linked this drop to increased use of health services (Hadley 1982). Despite the mortality rate drop, the age-adjusted death rates for blacks were almost 48 percent higher than for whites (NCHS 1982). Causes of death with the largest racial differentials were diabetes mellitus, cirrhosis of the liver, diseases of early infancy, homicide, nephritis, and nephrosis (NCHS 1979a).

Infant mortality is even more sensitive to health service availability than are overall mortality rates. Some studies suggest that as much as half of all infant mortality is preventable by better access to health care (Usher 1977; President's Commission for the Study of Ethical Problems 1983). Infant death rates were relatively unchanged in the decade prior to the enactment of Medicaid. Since 1965, the overall infant death rate has declined from 24.7 per 1,000 live births, to 12.5. The disparity between the white and nonwhite infant death rate narrowed somewhat, but did not disappear (NCHS 1982). Infant mortality rates also vary by geographic area. Mortality in less-urbanized areas not adjacent to metropolitan areas was 20 percent higher than rates in suburban counties adjacent to metropolitan areas. Differentials between blacks and whites vary geographically and are larger in rural than in urban areas (NCHS 1980).

Another measure of health status less drastic than mortality and more reflective of daily fluctuations in quality of health is the number of days spent in bed as a result of illness (known as the bed day index). Number of bed days is chiefly, although not exclusively an indicator of acute conditions. Low-income persons report more bed days (ten) per year than the nonpoor (six). This gap between the poor and nonpoor holds for blacks and for whites.

An even less drastic indicator of health status for groups is average disability days — the number of days a person is unable to carry out his or her normal activities, including going to work or school due to illness or injury. Again, the poor as measured by family income report twice the number of restricted activity days as people in the highest income category. Poor children miss school 40 percent more than nonpoor children due to acute conditions. Blacks experience more restricted activity days per year than whites (President's Commission for the Study of Ethical Problems 1983; NCHS 1982; Starfield 1982).

A related measure of health status is the proportion of the population whose activities are limited by chronic conditions. There are large differences by income, with the poor almost twice as likely as the nonpoor to be limited by chronic conditions (22 percent versus 12 percent). While the types of chronic conditions are similar for the poor and nonpoor, the severity and prevalence are higher for the former (President's Commission for the Study of Ethical Problems 1983).

Self-assessment of health is also a useful indicator of health status which has been found to correlate well with clinical indications for the need of health care (Manning et al. 1982). Kleinman (1980) analyzed data on self-reported health status from the Health Interview Survey. He found that people in families with incomes below the poverty level reported themselves as being in fair or poor health three times more frequently than those with incomes greater than twice the poverty level. The percentage reporting lowered health status increased as income declined regardless of race or age. Persons living in rural areas reported lower health status than persons living in metropolitan areas (17 percent versus 11 percent). The rural/metropolitan gap was especially large for blacks.

HEALTH SERVICES UTILIZATION PATTERNS

The amount of utilization of health care services is frequently used as an intermediate or "realized" indicator of access. Not all variation reflects inequity. Analysts do not regard variation in use stemming from different levels of health as inequity, but rather expect variations in services utilization to accompany variations in health status. Additional variation in use may result from different attitudes and beliefs about when and whether to seek health care. Once the variation in health care use from these two sources — different health statuses and personal choice related to cultural differences — are taken into account, the remaining variation is argued to reflect inequity in access.

One major area of health care utilization is hospitalization. Inpatient hospital use was equivalent for the poor and nonpoor in 1964. Between 1964 and 1973, use of inpatient services by the poor rose dramatically, with the poor being hospitalized at higher rates than the nonpoor. After 1973, rates of hospitalization remained fairly stable for both income groups. In 1964, the poor had 14 hospital discharges per 100 persons, compared with 13 for the nonpoor. By 1973, utilization among the poor had increased to 19, while the nonpoor remained at 13. By 1979, these figures had changed very little. The increase in utilization among the poor reflected higher rates of illness, especially chronic illnesses, which were treated with hospitalization after the introduction of Medicare and Medicaid (Aday et al. 1980). Minority groups such as blacks and Hispanics continued to have lower hospital utilization rates than the white population. In 1977, whites had 15 hospital admissions per 100 persons, while blacks had 14 and Hispanics 12 (Taylor 1983).

Utilization of physician services has increased greatly among the poor and minorities during the 15 years starting in 1964. In that year, the nonpoor used 23 percent more physician services than the poor. Whites used 42 percent more physician services than blacks and other minorities. Using aggregate data unadjusted for differences in need, the disparities between these groups have largely disappeared. By 1980, some studies reported higher physician utilization by the poor (Kleinman 1980; Aday et al. 1980; Madans and Kleinman 1980). One explanation for the equalization of utilization rates is the introduction of Medicare and Medicaid. The equalization of group rates for the poor and nonpoor and for blacks and whites masks age differences. Poor children have lower utilization than children in families with higher incomes. Poor, nonelderly adults use more physician services than the nonpoor.

Since the poor have been sicker than the nonpoor, a fair comparison of utilization rates needs to adjust for health status. After controlling for health status, the poor made fewer physician visits per year, and blacks made fewer visits than whites. One approach employed for dealing with different health status among groups was to construct use/disability ratios. A second approach used multivariate statistical techniques, which can control statistically for other health use factors such as age, in addition to controlling for health status.

Two different versions of use/disability ratios appear in the literature. Aday et al. (1980) developed a ratio which measured the number of physician visits per 100 disability days for patients with at least one disability day, while Kleinman (1980) computed a ratio of number of physician visits to 100 bed-disability days. Both found that the poor made fewer physician visits than appeared to be the case when raw data unadjusted for health status were used. While Aday found the health status adjusted rates similar across all income groups, Kleinman used different data and found health status adjusted rates for higher income groups were twice as great as for low-income groups.

A number of studies have used multivariate techniques. Kleinman (1980) employed ordinary least squares regression analysis to control for health status, age, and sex while examining the impact of income, insurance, race, and residence on use of physician services. Persons with over twice the poverty income received 5.2 physician visits annually, compared with 3.5 to 4.0 visits for persons below the poverty income. There were small effects for race and residence, with both blacks and nonmetropolitan residents using fewer physician services. Link et al. (1980) used Tobit analysis to estimate utilization of physician services by the elderly. The elderly without a chronic condition and with incomes of $25,000 or more made 32 percent more physician visits than the elderly without a chronic condition and with incomes below $5,000. For the elderly with chronic conditions, there was an 11 percent differential in use.

A more recent study (Yelin et al. 1983) controlled for need differentials among income groups when examining differences in utilization patterns. The results of the Yelin study contradicted the earlier findings of Kleinman et al. (1981). While Kleinman et al. found the poor have between 7 and 44 percent fewer visits to physicians than those with incomes twice above the poverty level, adjusting for age and health status, Yelin et al. found no consistent differences in the number of physician visits made per year by income, race, education, insurance coverage, or region, controlling for need. Using data from the National Health Interview Survey of 1976, Yelin employed a stricter control for medical need which included both symptoms and discrete diagnoses, while Kleinman employed several less stringent measures of need ranging from self-assessment to the use/bed disability ratio. One explanation for the different findings was the different definition of need. Even using Yelin's more stringent definition of need, hospital utilization differences for some symptoms persisted across income and racial groups.

The poor have differed from the nonpoor not only in the amount of health care, but also in the source of that care. The poor have been less likely than the nonpoor to have a regular source of care. Families who have lacked a regular source of care have used fewer services, making a customary source of care an important variable in determining accessibility (Andersen 1968). The percent of U.S. population without a regular source of care has remained relatively stable in the 20-year period since 1963 at about 14 percent (Kasper and Barrish 1982). High- and middle-income groups were less likely to be without a usual source of care (12.2 and 13.8 percent) than were low-income groups (17.1 percent). Similar findings hold by race with 13 percent of whites without a usual source compared to 20 percent of blacks and 19 percent of Hispanics. Having a specific physician as a regular source of care is generally equated with a higher quality of care and is somewhat more common among high-income groups (Aday and Andersen 1975; Dutton 1980). In 1977, high-income persons received 71 percent of their visits in a physician's office or group practice, compared with 60 percent of low-income persons (NCHS 1979b). Hospital outpatient departments are used most frequently by low-income persons (Andersen et al. 1975).

Low-income persons have been less likely to receive preventive as well as acute care than have been high-income persons. Women from high-income families were 40 percent more likely to receive a breast exam from a physician than women from low-income families (Aday et al. 1980). High-income women were 40 percent more likely to have had a Pap smear to detect cervical cancer. Similar patterns occur with prenatal care, with high-income women 50 percent more likely to receive prenatal services in the first trimester of pregnancy. Racial differences also have occurred in access to preventive care. White children have been 70 percent more likely to receive polio vaccinations than minority children, and 30 percent more likely to receive measles vaccinations.

Across time the poor have gained increased access to physician services and hospitalization through an expansion of government programs. Wide gaps in utilization rates between the poor and the nonpoor exist in dental care, an area not often covered by government programs or insurance. Using 1982 data, 14 percent of people in the three lowest income categories including families making less than $15,000, had never been to a dentist versus 10 percent in the $15,000-24,999 category, and 6 percent in the category above $25,000 (NCHS 1982). Larger differentials existed in the percent who have visited a dentist in the past year, with a consistent pattern going from 37 percent in the lowest income group to 65 percent in the highest. Not only were high-income persons more likely to have seen a dentist in any given time period, they had twice as many visits (Aday et al. 1980). Most of the gap in access, however, was the lack of access initially. For people who visited a dentist in the previous year, the average number of visits was very similar across income categories (Rossiter 1982). Some differences in utilization between racial groups persisted. Ten percent of whites and 15 percent of blacks had never visited a dentist. Fifty-two percent of whites versus 34 percent of blacks had visited a dentist in the previous year. Whites who had visited a dentist in the previous year had an average of 3.1 visits, while blacks had 2.5 visits, indicating continuing gaps in use as well as initial access.

Eye care services increased for all groups with increases in age. Only small differences between income groups persisted, partially because corrected vision is crucial to immediate ordinary daily functioning, whereas dental care is less crucial. In 1977, 11 percent of persons and families with incomes below $12,000 had purchased or repaired glasses or contact lenses, while for the highest income category ($20,000 or above), this figure increased to 13.9 percent. Among racial groups, 14.1 percent of whites, 11.4 percent of Hispanics, and 9.1 percent of blacks had purchased or repaired corrective devices (Walden 1982).

GEOGRAPHIC ACCESS OF HEALTH SERVICES

Two aspects of geographic access to health services are their availability across geographic areas and use patterns in different areas. By the 1970s most Americans, excluding the rural and inner-city poor, had access to a wide range of health care institutions and providers. A substantial increase in the overall supply of health care during preceding decades contributed to increased geographic access. Between 1970 and 1979, the number of active physicians increased 34 percent, a two-thirds growth over the 1960 supply. The number of professionally active physicians per 10,000 population was 14.2 both in 1950 and in 1960. By 1970, that statistic had increased to 15.5. Dramatic increases occurred across the 1970s, so that by 1979, the equivalent statistic was 19.3 (NCHS 1980).

Community hospitals (all nonfederal short-term general and other special hospitals excluding the hospital units of long-term institutions) have been the dominant form of hospital in the United States, composing 98 percent of all short-term hospitals in 1978. Community hospitals' beds have increased, contributing to increased geographic access to health care, but have grown less rapidly than the number of physicians. Most of the change occurred between 1960 and 1975. In 1940, the number of community hospital beds per 1,000 population was 3.2. By 1950, this statistic was up slightly to 3.3, and by 1960, to 3.6. Larger increases occurred over the next 15 years, so that by 1970, the statistic was 4.3 and by 1975 was 4.6, becoming stable through 1980 (NCHS 1980).

Overall growth figures for physician-to-population and community hospital bed-to-population ratios mask regional and other geographic differences in health care access. In 1970, large regional differences in access to physicians existed. The Northeast had the highest nonfederal physician per 100,000 civilian population ratio of 178.7, followed by the West with 154.8, the North Central with 118.2, and the South with 111.5. One factor in the large regional variation is the greater proportion of rural areas in both the South and North Central regions. By 1980, the ratios had increased in all regions, but the relative differences remained. The Northeast had a 224.9 physician-to-population ratio, the West 208.0, the North Central 162.5, and the South 159.4.

Differences are even greater when comparing states. New York's physicians per 100,000 population in 1980 was twice as high as

-South Dakota's: 260.0 compared to 107.0. Even within regions, interstate differences remained: in the South, 238 for Maryland to 109 for Mississippi; in the North Central region, 196.5 for Minnesota to 107 for South Dakota; in the West, 233.9 for California to 114.4 for Idaho; and in the Northeast, 260 for New York to 151.2 for Maine (U.S. Dept. of HHS 1981).

Differences in community hospital bed to 1,000 population ratios also occur by region, with patterns changing between 1940 and 1978. The New England, Middle Atlantic, East North Central, Mountain, and Pacific states had ratios above the national average in 1940. All of these regions experienced either slow rates of increase in the ratio or actual drops between 1940 and 1960, and moderate increases during the period of overall national growth from 1960 to 1975. By 1978, all five regions were barely at or below the national average. The other major census divisions – the West North Central, South Atlantic, East South Central, and West South Central regions – had ratios substantially below the national average in 1940. These regions experienced large growth spurts in hospital beds-to-population ratios between 1950 to 1975. By 1978 these regions were all at or above the national average. Interstate variations existed within all regions.

Population-to-provider ratios have been one way of assessing differences in the availability of services, but do not indicate whether supplies are adequate to meet the needs in a particular area. Two different measures to designate geographic areas as underserved are the Index of Medical Underservice and the Health Manpower Shortage Area Criteria. Both were federally developed and used by different agencies. The Index of Medical Underservice is a weighted index including data on primary care physician-to-population ratios, physician ratios, infant mortality rates, and the proportion of aged and poor in the area. About 20 million Americans, predominantly in rural and inner-city communities, lived in areas classified as high priority underserved (President's Commission for the Study of Ethical Problems 1983). If a deficit of primary providers is emphasized, as with the Health Manpower Shortage Index, 16 million Americans live in underserved areas.

Geographic access includes travel time to health care facilities. While most Americans spend less than 30 minutes traveling to regular sources of health care, the elderly, blacks, Hispanics, low-income, and rural citizens generally have longer travel times. One study found the poor likely to travel 20 percent farther and to wait 40 percent longer (Aday et al. 1980).

HEALTH INSURANCE AND EQUITY

By the early 1980s, public or private insurance covered most Americans, with 85 to 90 percent either having private health coverage through their place of employment or public coverage such as Medicare or Medicaid. While the comprehensiveness of health insurance obtained through work varied, most employed persons had some health coverage through work, ranging from hospitalization, the most common type of coverage, to major medical, dental, and eye coverage. The best benefits have been provided in large unionized firms, while employees in small firms with half or more of the work force at the minimum wage were the least likely to have health coverage. In 1977, only 55.4 percent of employees in firms with 25 or fewer workers had health insurance versus 92 to 99 percent in all other firms (Taylor and Lawson 1981).

Beyond workers in small firms, people between the ages of 18 and 24, nonwhites, and rural residents have been more likely to lack health insurance coverage. A slightly higher probability of no coverage has occurred in the South and Western regions. In 1977, a government report estimated that 12.6 percent of the civilian noninstitutionalized population, or 26.6 million persons had no health insurance coverage (Kasper et al. 1980). The number of people without any health insurance during a 12-month period is larger than the number uninsured at any particular time during the year. Estimates were made that 34 million (16 percent of the population) were without coverage sometime during 1977 (President's Commission for the Study of Ethical Problems 1983). Survey data have shown that persons with lapsed coverage during some part of the year reduce utilization of health services during that period, even though their incidence of illness is not lower.

Two age groups were noticeable in their percentage without insurance coverage. Persons 18 to 24 years old were almost twice as likely to be without health insurance coverage as other age groups (22 percent versus 12 percent in 1977). The elderly were very unlikely to be without some insurance coverage (4.3 percent), demonstrating the comprehensiveness of Medicare in providing at least some health care access to senior citizens. Despite comprehensive coverage for elderly individuals, Medicare has not paid for all services. All Medicare recipients have hospitalization, and Medicare paid 75 percent of all hospital expenses for the elderly. Coverage for physician services has been optional and more restrictive, with 54 percent of physician expenses for the elderly being paid by Medicare (Davis et al. 1981).

Has the Medicare program equalized health services utilization among the elderly? Racial differences in use of physician services among the elderly have disappeared over time (Davis and Schoen 1978; Link et al. 1980; Madans and Kleinman 1980). Differences in utilization by income have also decreased, with no significant differences for senior citizens with chronic conditions existing by the early 1980s. For the 22 percent of elderly with no chronic conditions, high-income people continued to utilize more physician services than low-income people. The Medicare program has had less success in diminishing utilization differences among elderly living in different geographic areas. Medicare reimbursement per enrollee was 63 percent higher in counties with a central city than in nonmetropolitan counties in 1975, and utilization of services by the elderly was positively linked to the supply of physicians per capita (Davis and Schoen 1978; Davis et al. 1981).

While the Medicare program has contributed greatly to equalizing health care access among the elderly, one threat to continuing improvement is the fiscal solvency of the Medicare fund. A partial solution has been to increase the dollar amount paid by the consumer. Another proposed solution is to change the way providers are reimbursed for treating Medicare patients. The impact of these recent changes on differential access among groups of elderly cannot yet be assessed.

While Medicare provided access to most of the elderly, Medicaid has been less comprehensive in providing access to the poor. In the late 1970s, the poor were three times as likely to lack insurance as people with high incomes, and twice as likely as those with middle incomes. Of uninsured people under 65, 55 percent were in families with incomes below $8,000 (President's Commission for the Study of Ethical Problems 1983). While Medicaid has provided reasonable coverage for eligibles, almost two-thirds of the poor do not qualify for Medicaid (Davis et al. 1981).

Federal categorical restrictions (blind, members of one-parent families, indigent elderly) must be met to be eligible for Medicaid. In addition, all recipients must meet state-established income restrictions which are frequently below the federally set poverty level. In Texas, for example, the income standards have been set at one-tenth of the poverty level, so that a family of four with a monthly income above $144 was ineligible for Medicaid (Davis et al. 1981; President's Commission for the Study of Ethical Problems 1983). In 29 states the income cutoff for Medicaid eligibility is less than 50 percent of the poverty level. Considerable variability in Medicaid eligibility criteria exists across states. Some states allow Medicaid payments for families with unemployed heads of household and the medically needy, while many states do not.

For the poor eligible for Medicaid, the program has increased access and utilization. One study found that Medicaid eligibles without chronic conditions have double the number of annual physician visits as the non-Medicaid poor. Medicaid eligibles with chronic conditions have 20 percent higher use rates (Davis et al. 1981).

Medicaid has grown substantially from its initial inception. In fiscal year 1968, 11.5 million recipients were covered by Medicaid. By 1977, 24 million recipients were covered (Thompson 1981). Approximately 45 percent of all Medicaid recipients − the largest single category − have been dependent children. Another 20 percent have been adults in families with dependent children. The elderly have represented only 15 percent and the disabled 10 percent of the total. Average monthly payments are much larger, however, for the disabled ($265) and the elderly ($242) than for individuals in families with dependent children ($82).

The higher expenditures for the elderly and disabled stem from their use of costly nursing home care. Nursing home expenditures have consumed increasingly larger proportions of total Medicaid funds. Between 1973 and 1978, the expenditures for nursing homes rose 150 percent, while the costs of other services rose 90 percent. Nursing home expenditures consequently rose from 35 percent to 42 percent of Medicaid outlays (Congressional Budget Office 1981). Critics feel that the proportionate increase of Medicaid funding for nursing homes undercuts the thrust of providing access for the traditional poor, and especially for children. Many elderly Medicaid patients, while medically indigent due to the high costs of nursing home care, have not been poor throughout the greatest part of their lives. Increasingly, Medicaid is assuming the costs of prolonged dying for some of the middle class. Public relations problems and communications difficulties arise from combining nursing home payments for previously middle-class elderly with payments for the currently nonelderly poor. Popular opinion is more favorable toward the former than the latter. When the two categories are combined, the public often overlooks the growing portion of Medicaid outlays for nursing home care for the previously nonpoor and criticizes Medicaid outlay growth.

Despite Medicaid's success in increasing health care access for the poor, problems exist. While Medicaid was originally designed to allow the poor to use all community providers, the reality has been different. The paperwork, delays in reimbursements, and limits on the dollar amount of reimbursement for providers has caused some health care professionals and institutions to refuse to treat Medicaid patients. In 1975, Medicaid fees for specialists were 75 percent of Medicare fees, which are often below the general fee (Burney et al. 1978). A 1976 survey found Medicaid payments for routine follow-up visits to be 40 percent below usual fees (Sloan et al. 1978). Finding providers willing to serve Medicaid patients has been a problem in geographically underserved regions, especially rural areas (Davis and Reynolds 1976).

Even with the expansion of insurance coverage for health services and government programs for the poor and elderly, individuals still pay substantial out-of-pocket costs as copayments or deductibles, or for noncovered services. When viewed as a proportion of income, out-of-pocket health care expenses are regressive, with the poor paying a larger proportion of their total income in out-of-pocket expenses than the proportion of total income paid by the nonpoor. In 1977, those with incomes less than $3,000 paid an average of 10.2 percent of their incomes in out-of-pocket expenses. This proportion steadily declined as income rose, dropping to 7.7 percent for those with incomes between $3,000 and $4,999; 6.0 percent for $5,000 to $6,999; 3.4 percent for $7,000 to $9,999; 2.0 percent for $10,000 to $14,999; and 1.7 percent for above $15,000 (President's Commission for the Study of Ethical Problems 1983). The poor continue to pay proportionately more for health services than the nonpoor.

FEDERAL LEGISLATION

Federal health legislation prior to Lyndon Johnson's administration and the 1960s War on Poverty was not focused in any major way on expanding access to previously uncovered groups, although the Hill-Burton Act stimulated improved access to hospital services, especially in rural areas. While some expansion had occurred through the extension of federally financed individual coverage to marine seamen and to veterans, substantial advances in equity were made in the 1960s with the introduction of Kerr-Mills, Medicare, and Medicaid (see Appendix 6). Earlier federal attempts to increase access such as the Hill-Burton Act employed a different strategy — that of increasing overall access by increasing the supply of available health services and providers rather than focusing on a clearly defined categorical group.

The thrust of traditional pre-1960 public health legislation had equity overtones, since the poor were more likely to be beneficiaries of such acts as the Sheppard-Towner Act and Title V of the Social Security Act. The primary thrust of traditional public health legislation, however, also included goals of disease prevention and maintenance of an adequate supply for the general population. Much traditional public health legislation was not directed specifically to increasing access for previously uncovered groups (see Appendix 7).

Beginning in the 1960s, federal health legislation incorporated an emphasis on extending coverage to the elderly and the poor in addition to earlier legislative emphases on supply expansion and the provision of services for the entire population. The two largest programs expanding coverage during this period were Medicare and Medicaid. In addition to these statutes, other laws began to incorporate equity concerns. Federal legislation during this period established clinics for migrant workers, neighborhood health centers in low-income areas, and special services for low-income mothers, children, and youth.

Much federal legislation which increased the availability of health personnel began to include provisions to encourage health professionals to practice in underserved areas. While not directly increasing the access of any specific population group, a number of programs which provided for the construction of new facilities or for special projects addressed broad equity concerns by providing states with lower per capita incomes a higher federal match rate. Medicaid currently uses this provision.

The federal thrust toward increased equity for individuals in previously uncovered groups begun in the 1960s had faltered by the 1970s as health care outlays continued to escalate. Federal lawmakers, when considering new programs or statutory changes, often asked the question in the 1960s — how will this program or change affect equity? By the late 1970s, the fundamental question being asked about federal health care statutes was how will this program or change affect costs? Improving access had taken a back seat to cost containment.

With the beginning of the Reagan administration, the federal policy emphasis on health care cost containment at the expense of increased equity was accelerated. The political philosophy of the Reagan administration was to reduce the role of the federal government in domestic concerns, and to reduce federal expenditures to control swelling deficits. Both of these goals pushed the administration toward recommending and achieving substantial cuts in health programs.

Much of the cutback in health funding occurred via the Omnibus Budget Reconciliation Act of 1981 and the Tax Equity and Fiscal Responsibility Act of 1982. The 1981 act repealed the entitlement of merchant seamen to free care and closed the merchant marine hospitals. A large number of traditional public health service delivery programs were placed in block grants to the states, and the level of funding was cut by 25 percent. The number of community health centers supported by the federal government fell from 800 in 1981 to 587 in 1983. Other traditional areas of public health programs such as maternal and child health, control of venereal disease, and immunizations had large cuts in 1981. In maternal and child health, grants to states fell from $456 million in 1981 to $373 million in 1983, causing over 200,000 mothers and children to lose services.

The 1981 act also restricted eligibility for AFDC. Since all AFDC recipients are simultaneously eligible for Medicaid, the number of people automatically eligible for Medicaid was also reduced. One and a half million children lost AFDC and Medicaid coverage. As the result of federal and state cuts in Medicaid funds, over 30 states in 1981 reduced or eliminated services, eligibility groups, or provider payments for Medicaid. One common reduction was to remove 18 to 21-year-olds from eligibility. Other states placed severe restrictions on the number of reimbursable physician visits and hospital days. Some common restrictions for physician visits were limits of 12 to 24 per year. A few states restricted hospital days per year to as little as 12. The growth rate in Medicaid payments was substantially decreased: payments for fiscal year 1982 grew by only 9 percent over 1981, as compared to 17 percent in the two previous fiscal years — the largest reduction in the rate of increase since the program began.

Both the 1981 and 1982 laws created changes in reimbursement strategies and delivery methods for Medicare and Medicaid. State Medicaid programs may experiment with restricting access to designated providers, alternative prospective payment systems, different cost-based reimbursement systems for hospitals, and copayments for recipients of services. While the full impact of these changes on access and utilization has yet to be assessed, each change was passed to promote cost savings. The 1982 law proposed a major change in the Medicare reimbursement methodology for hospitals, employing diagnostic-related groups (DRGs) as the basis for hospital payments rather than traditional reimbursement methodologies which set fixed payments for hospital days and procedures. DRGs categorize treatments for illness with the diagnostic categories forming the basis for payments, much like industries formulate product groups for costing. Whether this methodology can decrease the growth rate of rising health care costs has yet to be determined, but DRGs are viewed as one alternative for future policy.

CHAPTER NINE

PREVENTION OF ILLNESS, MAINTENANCE OF HEALTH, AND PRESERVATION OF LIFE

A health care continuum can be envisioned which ranges from the prevention of illness for healthy people, to the maintenance and restoration of health for those with acute illness, to the preservation of life at the highest possible level for those with long-term and terminal illness. Likewise, federal policies may be placed along the same continuum. This chapter will examine changing patterns of diseases and mortality trends which underlie our shift in health care from a predominantly acute care orientation to greater emphasis on both prevention of illness and preservation of life.

The definition of health and our society's image of what we want from our health care system and our national health policy has been undergoing major shifts in the last 50 to 100 years. In an earlier era of medical knowledge and scientific achievement, the definition of health was simple — it implied the absence of disease. The goal of national policy was also simpler — health was predominantly viewed as a personal, not governmental concern. Early policies focused on preventing the spread of disease to unaffected parts of the population through use of quarantines and through special hospitals to treat diseased merchant seamen.

With the advent of the successes from microbiology and the germ theory of disease beginning at the turn of the century, definitions of health began to grow more complex and the possibilities of the health care system increased. Physicians could restore health and actually cure people and health care became a more desirable service for all segments of the society. The provision of health care for acute illness became more desirable as research and technology increased the effectiveness of that care.

In the post-World War II period, several trends occurred. Most infectious diseases were effectively conquered. The disease profile of the United States had shifted to a predominant emphasis on major chronic illnesses, such as cancer and heart disease, bringing with it increasing recognition of the complexity of the definition of health, of the causes of disease, and of the role of health policy. While infectious diseases were consistent with the simple cause and effect model of illness — sometimes described as the "magic bullet" approach — medical science was unable to find a magic bullet for most chronic diseases. A leading microbiologist discussed the "mirage" of health. Gradually the medical community recaptured an understanding of disease causation which again incorporated an important role for the individual's environment and lifestyle (Dubos 1959).

During the same time period, a broader definition of health as espoused by the World Health Organization became common — the definition of health not merely as the absence of disease or disability but as a complete state of physical, mental, and social well-being. Health policy also expanded beyond narrow concerns to a broader conceptualization including social and economic policy. During the same time period, the appropriate role of the federal government both in developing domestic policy and delivering services in such fields as education and health was considerably augmented.

Much of the thrust of health policy in the 1950s and 1960s emphasized the provision of more health care services, under the assumption that medical care equals health. In reality, more available medical care does not necessarily equal better health, and many of the factors that lead to good or bad health are not part of the traditional medical care system. Wildavsky (1977) has discussed the fallacy of the great equation that medical care equals health. One explanation for the fallacy is the "paradox of time." Under this paradox, past successes lead to future failures. Life expectancy has increased, and diseases that formerly led to death now lead to disability. Medicine is faced with an increasingly older population with more disabilities. Cure becomes harder and costlier to achieve, since easier problems have been successfully combated. As Wildavsky summarizes, "Yesterday's victims of tuberculosis are today's geriatric cases. The Paradox of Time is that success lies in the past and (possibly) the future, but never the present."

The other explanation for the fallacy of the great equation is described by Wildavsky (1977) as the principle of goal replacement. Any objective that cannot be obtained is replaced by another. He argues that in U.S. society there has been displacement from health objectives to other social objectives such as first health care in general and then access to health care. Ultimately this has led to the great emphasis in the United States on more and better technology. The provision of the maximal level of service and technology has become the standard of acceptable care.

A CONTINUUM OF HEALTH CARE
POLICY INTERVENTION

Health policy may be regarded as intervention along a continuum of care ranging from a policy to keep healthy people healthy, to a policy to help the terminally ill die gracefully and as painlessly as possible. This continuum may be simplified into three categories: preventing illness for healthy people, maintaining and restoring health for ill people who can be returned to normal functioning, and preserving life as fully and meaningfully as possible for those who cannot be returned to normal functioning.

Many factors affect individual health. One of the most useful ways to categorize factors affecting health was first developed in Canada by LaLonde (1975). He identifies four spheres: (1) human biology including genetic components; (2) the external environment, including the objects within it; (3) lifestyle − the customs and habits of living; and (4) health promoting and restoring systems of society, − including environmental control and regulatory measures, and preventive and medical treatment services of the health care system.

In most cases, two or more of the four spheres interact to determine the overall condition of individual health. Applying the model to risk factors for particular diseases or conditions produces varying degrees of overlap among the four spheres. In the case of a genetic disease, such as Tay-Sachs, human biology dominates. For cirrhosis of the liver and lung cancer, lifestyle factors of drinking and smoking dominate. For the nation's major health problems − heart disease and stroke − at least two and possibly three spheres are important determinants. High-blood pressure and family history are part of human biology, while smoking, diet, and exercise levels are part of lifestyle factors. Some researchers argue that stressful working conditions also play a role in the development of heart disease, making environment a third determinant in the development of the disease. Health promoting and restoring systems would figure into whether and how completely an individual returns to normal functioning.

SOURCES OF DEATH AND THE ROLE OF PREVENTIVE POLICIES

Life expectancy is a time specific concept, and is the age to which the average individual can be expected to live, given that person has reached a specified age. While the most commonly employed statistic is life expectancy at birth which is used to depict changes in overall population health, life expectancies may be calculated for various age cohorts. The average U.S. infant born in 1978 could be expected to live 26 years longer than one born in 1900 — a dramatic increase largely resulting from the prevention and control of communicable diseases which formerly were the major causes of death among both children and young adults.

Another way of examining improvements in life span is changes in the infant mortality rate. States first began to register births in 1915. At that time, 100 of every 1000 babies born alive died during the next 12 months. By 1950, this rate had fallen to 29.2 per 1000 and by 1982, was down to 11.1.

Major shifts in the most important causes of death have occurred between 1900 and 1977 (see Figure 9-1). Using age-adjusted data, the three most common causes of death at the turn of the century were influenza and pneumonia, tuberculosis, and diarrhea and related diseases, whereas in 1977, the three most common causes of death were heart disease, malignant neoplasms (cancer), and stroke. The change in major causes of death from 1900 to 1977 reflects the success in combating infectious diseases between the two periods, attributed to improvements in medical care and technology, and to increases in sanitary engineering and the general standard of living. While infectious diseases were the predominant cause of death in 1900, chronic diseases were the major killers in 1977. In addition to the shift in specific causes of death there was

FIGURE 9-1
AGE-ADJUSTED DEATH RATES FOR THE 5 LEADING CAUSES OF DEATH IN 1900 FOR 10 STATES AND THE DISTRICT OF COLUMBIA AND IN 1977 FOR THE UNITED STATES

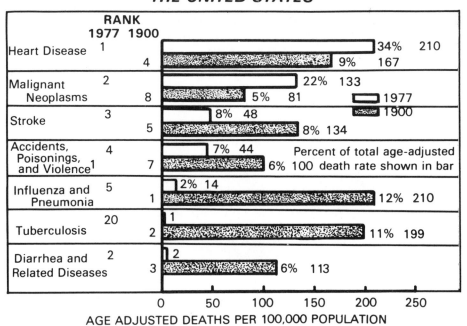

AGE ADJUSTED DEATHS PER 100,000 POPULATION

[1] Data for 1906 and 1977
[2] Not a ranked cause in recent years
Source: Health United States, 1980, National Center for Health Statistics

a greater variety of lethal illnesses in 1900. The four leading causes of death in 1977 were responsible for 71 percent of all deaths, while the four leading causes in 1900 accounted for only 40 percent of deaths (NCHS 1980).

In 1977, heart disease accounted for two in five deaths, cancer for one in five, stroke for one in ten, and accidents for one in ten (see Figure 9-2). The middle bar in the graph indicates the impact of leading causes of death on years of lost life. While heart disease and cancer are still the two most important causes of years of lost life, they account for a smaller proportion of lost years than of deaths, since those two diseases strike with higher frequency in older age groups. By contrast, accidents account for almost twice as high a proportion of years of lost life as deaths, since children,

FIGURE 9-2
NUMBER AND PERCENT DISTRIBUTION OF SELECTED CAUSES OF DEATH, POTENTIAL YEARS OF LIFE LOST, AND EARNINGS FORGONE: UNITED STATES 1977

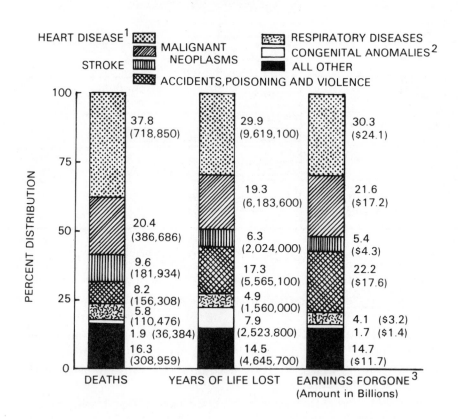

[1] Diseases of the circulatory system excluding stroke
[2] Includes certain causes of perinatal mortality
[3] Discounted at 10 percent
Source: Health United States 1980, National Center for Health Statistics

teenagers, and young adults are the most frequent victims of accidents and violence. The third bar shows the present value (discounted at a 10 percent interest rate) of lifetime earnings lost due to premature mortality. This distribution is very similar to that for lost earnings, since early deaths have a greater impact on lost earnings than deaths which occur later in life when fewer productive years are remaining.

Figure 9-3 shows ten of the major causes of death and risk factors associated with each. Some of the risk factors relate to personal lifestyle, some to inherited biological characteristics, and some to environmental hazards. Controlling these risks could require individual action, action by the medical and health care system, or public policy changes. For example, major risk factors for motor vehicle accidents include alcohol, seat belt usage, speed, roadway design, and vehicle engineering. While alcohol, seat belt usage, and speed can be controlled by individual action, roadway design and vehicle engineering changes to enhance safety may require public policy mandates. Public policy, though, can also control alcohol and seat belt usage as evidenced by lower accident injury rates in many European countries with more stringent safety laws. The leading killer of heart disease also is associated with individual, environmental, and inherited biological risk factors. Smoking and elevated cholesterol levels relate to personal lifestyle, although elevated cholesterol and family history are also part of inherited biological factors. Stress levels influenced by environmental factors as well as by lifestyle and biological factors also play some role in the development of heart disease.

Sources of death vary by age groups. The major risks to health for infants are associated with immaturity (low birth weight and birth-related conditions). Practice of better health habits throughout pregnancy (such as not smoking and reduced alcohol consumption) can reduce infant immaturity problems. Early identification and clinical management of medical risk factors can detect some but not all birth-associated risks.

The major cause of death of children ages 1 through 14 is no longer disease, but accidents, both motor vehicle related and other. Ways to control accidents include use of car safety restraints for younger children or safety belts for older children, and better supervision and control of environmental hazards such as toxic substances in the house or drownings. Young adults vary in cause of death by

FIGURE 9-3
MAJOR CAUSES OF DEATH AND ASSOCIATED RISK FACTORS

MAJOR CAUSES OF DEATHS, 1977		
CAUSE	*PERCENT OF ALL DEATHS*	*RISK FACTOR*
Heart Disease	37.8	Smoking[1], Hypertension[2], elevated serum cholesterol[1] (diet), lack of exercise, diabetes, stress, family history
Malignant Neoplasms	20.4	Smoking[1], worksite carcinogens,[1] environmental carcinogens, alcohol, diet
Stroke	9.6	Hypertension[1], smoking,[1] elevated serum cholesterol,[1] stress
Accidents other than Motor Vehicle	2.8	Alcohol[1], drug abuse, smoking (fires), product design, handgun availability
Influenza and Pneumonia	2.7	Smoking, vaccination status[1]
Motor Vehicle Accidents	2.6	Alcohol[1], no seat belts[1], speed[1], roadway design, vehicle engineering
Diabetes	1.7	Obesity[1]
Cirrhosis of the Liver	1.6	Alcohol abuse[1]
Arteriosclerosis	1.5	Elevated serum cholesterol[1]
Suicide	1.5	Stress[1], alcohol and drug abuse, and gun availability

[1] Major risk factors
Source: Health United States 1980, National Center for Health Statistics

race. Young whites die predominantly from accidents, while young blacks are murdered, followed by death from accidents. A major risk factor associated with both youth homicides and accidents is increased alcohol consumption. Changes in levels of alcohol consumption may be brought about by individual changes in lifestyle, as well as by public policy. Other risk factors of youth homicides and accidents which can be altered by both lifestyle and public policy are fast driving, seat belt usage, and easy access to firearms.

The major causes of death for adult groups, both those ages 25 to 64, and those 65 and over, are the same three major causes of death for the total population – heart disease, cancer, and stroke. While heart disease is the leading cause of death for men over 40, the mortality rate for heart disease among women is much lower but gradually catches up after menopause. While risk factors for heart disease have been identified, much of the incidence of heart disease, particularly in people 65 and over, remains unexplained. Cancer represents a group of diseases rather than a single disease, so that the environmental, lifestyle, and biological factors vary by the type of cancer. Lung cancer is the leading type of cancer for men, and is growing in importance among women. A lifestyle factor – cigarette smoking – is a major contributor to lung cancer. Smokers have ten times the frequency of lung cancer as do nonsmokers.

What are the costs associated with these major causes of death? What portion of national health expenditures is spent on conditions or the consequences of conditions which are partially preventable? Health economists separate direct from indirect costs. Direct costs are expenditures specifically for medical care. Indirect costs are dollars lost from earnings foregone because of illness, disability, or premature death (Cooper and Rice 1976). Four major causes of death (diseases of the circulatory system including heart disease and stroke; neoplasms; accidents, poisonings, and violence; and diseases of the respiratory system) together in 1975 cost $110.8 billion, or 46 percent of the total direct and indirect costs of illness in the United States in that year. Looking only at direct costs, 30 percent (approximately $35.6 billion) was for the same four disease groups, while for indirect costs, 62 percent ($74.6 billion) was for these four disease groups (NCHS 1980).

Health costs may be associated with specific risk factors, as well as with disease groups. Alcohol abuse has been linked with a variety of health problems: accidents, certain cancers, homicide and other violence, and cirrhosis of the liver. In 1975, one dollar out of every five dollars spent on hospital care for adults was for treatment of conditions associated with alcohol abuse. The total bill for these treatments was $8.4 billion. Other expenditures for treatment of health problems associated with alcohol abuse add another $4.3 billion. Nonhealth costs of alcohol abuse (extra costs for the social welfare system, for fire protection, and for the criminal justice system) totaled $2.7 billion in 1975.

Many experts describe cigarette smoking as the chief preventable cause of death in U.S. society. In addition to lung cancer, cigarette smoking has been identified as a culprit in heart disease, other cancers, and respiratory disease. One study estimated the direct health care costs from smoking to be $8.2 billion in 1976. The indirect costs were $19.1 billion, and property loss was $176 million (Luce and Schweitzer 1978). While it is difficult to estimate the cost of personal risk factors, general risk factors such as air pollution create even greater cost estimation problems. Lave and Seskin (1977) estimated the 1970 health costs from air pollution to be $4.3 billion.

SUCCESSES, FAILURES, AND GAPS
IN DISEASE PREVENTION POLICIES

Success attributable to health policies per se is difficult to measure. Success may be observed by positive changes in morbidity and mortality statistics, but causally linking positive changes to specific federal disease prevention policies is not possible. Nonetheless, whether changes in mortality rates are negative or positive is sometimes used as a rough measure of policy achievement.

Heart disease mortality has been decreasing since 1950, but the rate of decrease has increased dramatically since 1970. From 1970 to 1977, heart disease decreased by about 17 percent, the same amount of decrease during the 20-year period from 1950 to 1970. Death rates from stroke began to fall during the 1950s and 1960s, and were reduced 27 percent between 1970 and 1977. Death rates for accidents also began to fall slightly during the 1950s, with larger declines during the 1960s and 1970s. Small declines in influenza and pneumonia deaths occurred between 1950 and 1970, with a 36 percent decline between 1970 and 1977. Deaths from cirrhosis of the liver, which had increased during the 1950s and 1960s, began to decline in the 1970-77 period. Total cancer mortality started to decrease among people younger than 45 years old in the 1970s, but the rate for lung and other cancers of the respiratory system has continued to rise. Lung cancer is the most common cause of cancer death among men. While breast cancer is still the most common cause of cancer death among women, lung cancer is increasing rapidly.

No one change or program explains these trends. Important factors in the reduction of deaths from heart disease and stroke include the reduction of risk factors in the population due largely to education in schools, in work sites, and through the media. Better emergency medical services, better technology, and increased attention to rehabilitation have also contributed to the decline in heart disease mortality. One explanation for continuing high rates of death for cancers of the respiratory system is the high level of exposure to risks, including environmental exposures as well as self-induced risks from high rates of smoking.

A recent Harris (1978) survey found greater concern about preventive health and prevention among Americans than existed previously. Over 50 percent of all Americans, and an even higher percentage of leadership groups, are much more concerned about preventive health than they were a few years ago. Forty-two percent of the general public and 80 percent to 90 percent of business executives and union leaders surveyed by Harris agreed that the health system should give more emphasis to prevention and less to cure.

When given a list of 30 possible health threats, Americans today perceive environmental and lifestyle hazards as major threats. The top five threats were industrial wastes (59 percent perceiving as a threat), pollution (58 percent), marijuana (58 percent), cigarettes (55 percent), and crash diets (55 percent) (Yankelovich et al. 1979). On the same survey, when adults were asked what they could do to set a good health example for their families, the most common responses were changing personal habits, such as quitting smoking (29 percent), exercising regularly (19 percent), staying calm (18 percent), losing weight (15 percent), cutting back on sweets (13 percent), and eating more balanced diets (12 percent). An important change in personal habits not mentioned was use of seat belts while driving.

Americans have been reducing some potentially harmful habits. Smoking has been decreasing among adult males and females. Between 1965 and 1979, the percent of adult males who smoked cigarettes decreased by 28 percent, and adult females decreased by 13 percent. While the percent smoking cigarettes has also been decreasing among teenage boys (a 20 percent reduction between 1968 and 1979), teenage girls have greatly increased their smoking during that time period (a 51 percent increase). Smoking is a very difficult habit to break. Although there are over 30 million ex-smokers, often many attempts must be made to quit smoking before success is attained. In 1979, 53 percent of female smokers and 45 percent of males reported that they had made a serious attempt to quit smoking in the past two years (NCHS 1980).

Currently Americans are concerned both about the amount of food that they eat and the content of their diet. During the last 80 years, the mean (average) body weight of the total U.S. population has increased. Fourteen percent of men and 24 percent of women in the United States aged 20 to 75 are significantly overweight (over 120 percent of desirable weight for height and sex). Black women are one-third more likely to be overweight than are white women, although little differences in the likelihood of overweight exist between black and white men. Many Americans diet. In 1978, a Harris survey found that 16 percent of all adults were on a diet, and another 31 percent had dieted in the past (Harris 1978).

The types of foods that Americans are eating have been changing. In a 1978 survey, over 80 percent of adults believe that cholesterol and fat posed some or a great degree of threat to health, and 70 percent thought salt posed some threat (Yankelovich et al. 1979). Per capita consumption of butter decreased 28 percent between 1965 and 1979. Consumption of fluid milk and cream decreased 21 percent, and eggs 10 percent in the same time period. These dietary changes are responsible for the drop in the mean serum cholesterol in the United States between the early 1960s and the early 1970s of 12 percent for men and 22 percent for women (NCHS 1980).

Alcohol and drug abuse remain serious health problems. There was no decrease in the percent of adults who are heavier drinkers (2 or more drinks per day, or 14 or more drinks per week) between 1971 and 1976. Ten percent of the adult population have drinking problems, and 16 percent of all adults report that someone in their family drinks too much (National Institute on Alcohol Abuse and Alcoholism 1978). The average consumption of alcohol for people 14 years of age and older is 30 percent higher than 15 years ago. Use of alcohol has been increasing among young people. Eighty percent of 12 to 17-year-olds report having had a drink, and over half drink at least once a month. Since 1966, the percent of high school students intoxicated at least once a month has doubled from 10 percent to 20 percent. While adolescents may drink less regularly than older people, the occasions of intoxication are major health problems since alcohol-related accidents are the leading cause of death for people aged 15 to 24, and 60 percent of alcohol-related highway traffic deaths are among young people (Surgeon General's Report 1979a and 1979b).

While it is difficult to obtain accurate data on drug usage, heroin addiction, the most serious drug problem in the United States appears to be declining. Barbiturate-related mortality has also declined over the last ten years, partially due to physicians changing prescribing practices. Categories of drug usage which have increased over the last 20 years are marijuana and cocaine. Cocaine usage has been increasing rapidly in upper-middle class and high-income groups, and experience among teenagers and young adults with marijuana has increased greatly over the last 20 years. While in 1962, less than 2 percent of the population, including young people, had any experience with an illicit drug, 15 years later in 1977, 60 percent of 18 to 25-year-olds had tried marijuana, and among 12 to 17-year-olds, nearly 30 percent had tried the drug. Ten percent of high school students reported smoking marijuana every day (Surgeon General's Report 1979a).

The amount of physical activity depends both on exercise connected with employment and with leisure time. Most experts agree that the amount of physical activity required on the job or in typical activities of daily living, such as shopping and commuting to work, has decreased. Most people drive or ride to work and to shop. The percent of the population engaging in physical activity on the job has decreased. While 24 percent of men are estimated to engage in a great deal of physical activity at work, only 10 percent of women do. About 26 percent of men and 18 percent of women report some job-related physical activity.

The last ten years have evidenced tremendous growth of citizen interest in physical activity and fitness. Participation rates in activities such as tennis, bicycling, swimming, and especially running, have mushroomed. The likelihood of exercising is not spread uniformly throughout the population. In a 1978 Yankelovich family survey, 36 percent of adult family members received at least some planned physical exercise several times a week, while the remaining family members exercised only occasionally or not at all (Yankelovich et al. 1979). Regular exercisers are almost equally divided between men and women, and are most concentrated among people aged 18 to 34, followed by those 65 and over. Income is related to obtaining regular exercise. In households with less than $7,000 income, only 24 percent of adults exercise versus 56 percent in households earning $25,000 or more.

An important area of preventive health behavior which has been the focus of some policy changes is the area of safe driving, although changes in the behavior of the general population have been slow. All newer models of automobiles are required by federal law to be equipped with seat belts, but it is estimated that only 20 percent of the population currently uses seat belts. The proportion of the population using seat belts has increased very slowly. Usage of infant and child safety restraints has increased gradually, due to mandatory requirements in 21 states. These laws were passed after their effectiveness in reducing infant deaths was first demonstrated in Tennessee.

Another highway safety health hazard is drinking and driving. Very little improvement has occurred in this area. Public policy changes in the recent past include increasing the drinking age for teenagers to some age greater than 18, a reversal of an earlier trend among states to lower the age for legal consumption of alcohol. A subsequent increase in the number of highway accidents connected with alcohol among teenagers prompted some states to return to higher age limits for legal alcohol consumption. Stricter enforcement of DUI (Driving Under the Influence of Alcoholic Beverages) has also occurred recently.

Many other lifestyle characteristics have a relationship to personal health which must be considered in effective preventive health policies. While all people experience some stress, most experts now agree that there are positive and negative ways of responding to stress, and that poorly handled stress can result in physical, as well as mental, health problems. A more recent concern is the amount of work-related stress. One in four men and one in three women who work are estimated to be under a great deal of job stress (NCHS 1980). Despite the popular image of high-level executives as being under the most stress, low-level clerical, secretarial, and mid-level management jobs where job holders have little control over the work process but are expected to meet high-productivity demands have been found to have the greatest amount of stress.

Recent research indicates that social support may play a major role in modifying the deleterious effects of stress. Social support has been conceptualized as information that tells a person that he or she is loved and valued, and is part of a network of communication and mutual obligation (Cobb 1976). Studies suggest that social support can aid recovery from surgery, and from illnesses such as congestive heart failure, tuberculosis, and myocardial infarctions, and reduce psychological stress and physiological symptoms following job loss and bereavement (Egbert et al. 1964; Chambers and Reiser 1953; Chen and Cobb 1960; Mather 1974; Cobb 1974; Burch 1972). In fact, the absence of strong social support systems can present as strong a risk factor for premature death as factors of diet, exercise, and the absence of other more widely known attributes of a healthy lifestyle (Berkman and Syme 1979).

USE OF PREVENTIVE SERVICES

Despite the recent questioning by medical authorities of the value of yearly routine physical examinations, many Americans have accepted the idea that a regular physical exam is an important investment. In 1979, 59 percent of men and 70 percent of women reported a physical exam within the past two years (NCHS 1980). One important aspect of routine exams is checking for hypertension, a major risk factor for heart disease. Checks for hypertension are also available through special blood-pressure screening programs held in many communities. Most Americans do obtain blood-pressure checks. In 1979, 75 percent of men and 83 percent of women ages 20 through 64 had their blood pressure checked within the past year, and 88 percent of men and 94 percent of women had such checks within the past two years. Checks are important since the National Heart, Lung, and Blood Institute estimates that 60 million people have elevated blood pressure (over 140 mm Hg/90 mm Hg) and 35 million or 15 percent of the population have definite hypertension (160 mm Hg/95 mm Hg). Control efforts for hypertension include medication, weight loss, and dietary modifications to reduce salt consumption. Blacks have higher rates of hypertension than whites (28 percent versus 17 percent).

An important preventive measure that has been available for a number of years is immunizations against such diseases as poliomyelitis, diphtheria, rubella, pertussis (whooping cough), and measles. During the early 1970s, immunization levels among children began to fall. By 1976, over one-third of children under 15 years of age were not properly immunized, leading to a 63 percent rise in the number of rubella cases, and a 39 percent rise in measles cases. By the fall of 1979 following a major federal childhood immunization program, 91 percent of school children in kindergarten through eighth grade were protected against measles, polio, diphtheria, pertussis, and tetanus, and 84 percent were protected against rubella (NCHS 1980).

A number of important areas of preventive care are specifically for women. Breast cancer is still the leading cause of cancer deaths among women. Although there are no known primary prevention measures, early detection and treatment increase the chances for survival. In 1973, only 12 percent of women aged 24 to 65 had had a breast examination by a physician in the previous year. Substantial improvement had occurred by 1979, with 62.5 percent of women in the previous year and an additional 20 percent in the previous two years having undergone a breast exam by a physician.

Obtaining Pap smears is one important way to eliminate deaths from cervical cancer. In 1979, almost 60 percent of women aged 20 to 65 reported having a Pap smear within the previous year. Another 20 percent had one within the previous two years, and 6 percent had not had or did not know if they ever had the test. The 1979 figures represent an improvement over 1973, when 12 percent of similarly aged women had never been tested. Reflecting an increase in the use of screening tests between 1968 and 1977, deaths from cervical cancer fell by almost one-half for both black and white women. In 1978, black women continued to die at significantly greater rates from cervical cancer than white women (17.2 deaths per 10,000 population for blacks compared to 5.3 for whites).

Family planning helps to prevent unwanted births, and enables people to make their own decisions regarding reproduction. The percent of unplanned births has been decreasing, although rates of unplanned births are still much higher for blacks and for the poor. Between 1971 and 1976, 32 percent of white births were unplanned compared to 48 percent for blacks. The poor use birth control less frequently than the nonpoor, with 46 percent below the poverty line and 29 percent above it having unplanned births. Many unplanned births are to teenagers. Less than one-third of the births to teens were wanted, because use of contraceptives is lower among teenagers. While only 14 percent of married women at risk of an unplanned pregnancy in 1976 were not using some form of contraception, 25 percent of sexually active unmarried teenagers reported that they never used contraceptives and another 45 percent used them only occasionally. The large number of abortions in the United States in 1978 (1.37 million) indicates the lack of adequate contraceptive practice. About one out of every eight women of childbearing age in the United States had an abortion. One-third of these were obtained by teenagers, three-fourths of whom were unmarried (NCHS 1980).

Early prenatal care is important in the reduction of the number of low-birth-weight babies. In 1977, 26 percent of women giving birth had not made a prenatal visit in the first trimester of pregnancy. This figure is dramatically higher among mothers under 15 years of age, who are at higher risk of bearing low-birth-weight infants. During the first trimester 68 percent did not receive care. Among all mothers, 6 percent had no care during the first or second trimester, compared to 21 percent of mothers under 15.

Although use of preventive health care has increased in the past 20 years, the most common types of health insurance policies do not encourage utilization of preventive health services. A typical health insurance policy, such as those provided in many states by Blue Cross/Blue Shield plans or by priviate health insurance companies, does not cover office visits for preventive services, even under the major-medical portion. Immunizations for children, for example, are generally not reimbursed by health insurance plans, nor are visits for family planning or general health exams. While many plans do pay for all laboratory tests, others will not reimburse for lab costs for preventive tests such as Pap smears. Only as a result of recent federal court rulings do most plans now automatically cover prenatal and pregnancy care. Medicaid programs have not differentiated between preventive and acute care services.

Health Maintenance Organizations (HMOs) have been one alternative to traditional insurance plans. Advocates of HMOs have argued that they enhance preventive care by making preventive services available without an out-of-pocket payment at the time of the service, and by a preventive care ideology which encourages the use of preventive services to maintain health, lowering the long-term costs of health care. In a comprehensive review of use of preventive health services among HMO enrollees and enrollees in fee-for-service (FFS) plans, Luft concludes that HMO enrollees currently use more preventive services than FFS enrollees because of the lower out-of-pocket costs for office visits. In those FFS plans in which the third party covers preventive visits so that the actual coverage is held constant across different forms of delivery of health care, some preventive services are used more by HMO enrollees, and others are used more by FFS enrollees. The rhetoric of HMOs concerning preventive policies appears to have little impact on use of preventive services, while the reality of better financial coverage does (Luft 1978b).

FEDERAL LEGISLATION

Federal statutes affecting the continuum of care ranging from preventive care through acute care to restore health to long-term care oriented toward preservation of life are shown in Appendixes 8 to 10. Numerous federal laws have contained preventive legislative components. The preventive legislation was of four types: one type offered general or acute care services to particular groups, such as merchant seamen, victims of venereal disease, and mothers and infants in an attempt to prevent the spread of diseases or to increase the probability of those groups being healthy. A second legislative effort regulated environmental factors, such as water, air, food, and drugs for impurities and toxic conditions. Yet a third effort involved research into the nature of diseases in an effort to understand their causes and prevent their future occurrence. The fourth preventive effort involved vaccinations and immunization programs to prevent the spread of infectious diseases.

The U.S. federal government has also passed legislation with components concerned with acute health care to maintain and restore health once the onset of illness or disease has occurred. Although the federal government has occasionally directly provided services, as for merchant marines through Public Health Service hospitals or for veterans through Veterans Administration hospitals, much of the federal role in this area has been that of facilitator, encouraging state and local governments and private health providers to extend acute care. Federal involvement in acute care has been typical of health care in general — expanding services on a categorical ad hoc basis across time to groups previously excluded from federal largess.

Most of the federal legislation affecting long-term care with the goal of preserving life at reasonable quality level has been of two types. The first type offered monies for the physical construction and maintenance of facilities. The second type, especially Medicaid, offered financial access for long-term care to eligible population groups.

Although sparse, much early federal health legislation was preventive in nature. Over time, the federal government began to have greater interest in health policies which were oriented toward acute care to make sick people well. The proportion of federal legislation emphasizing acute care increased greatly in the period after World War II, and by the 1960s the major federal policy debates were not around preventive issues but were over the role of the federal government in financing or directly providing acute care, leading to the passage of Medicare and Medicaid.

With the major exception of the commitment for long-term care for veterans after World War I, long-term care was not a focus of federal health policy until the 1950s. One major factor was the general lack of emphasis placed on long-term care in the nation's health care system as a whole. As the proportion of elderly population began to rise, and as people survived initial bouts with chronic diseases to confront a life of disability, long-term care became more important in the general health care system and simultaneously a greater concern of federal policy. The Medicare and especially the Medicaid programs quickly became major sources of funding for long-term care, making the federal government a major actor in long-term care policy.

Prevention has become a major focus in the health care system in general since the mid 1970s. Much of this focus has been organized by federal government initiatives, such as the surgeon general's report on prevention entitled *Healthy People*, administrative directives to increase preventive emphases in major health agencies such as NIH and CDC, and by legislative mandates such as the 1978 requirement that DHHS submit a national disease prevention profile to Congress every three years.

CHAPTER TEN
NATIONAL HEALTH CARE POLICY IN THE FUTURE

National health care policy can take several directions in the future. This chapter will discuss the issue of overall funding levels for health, as well as jurisdiction for health programs between levels and units of government and between government and the marketplace. It will also discuss selected short-range and long-range options and changes. Examples of short-range debates include the role for federally supported planning and the use of diagnostic-related groups to reimburse hospitals for Medicare patients. The long-range issue examined is the debate over the structure of the U.S. health care system. Three different models for future structure are the competition model, national health insurance, and a national health system.

Both short and long-range issues in health care, as well as debates over which level of government should have jurisdiction over health policy are greatly influenced by escalating health care expenditures. Two environmental factors that will continue to make health care costs increase are an aging U.S. population and the dramatic recent escalation in the development and use of medical technology. Because of chronic diseases, the elderly are disproportionately heavy users of health services. Increasingly in the United States treatments for chronic diseases are financed in the public sector, so the graying of the population has a particularly great impact on federal health care costs.

The absolute number of elderly are increasing, as is the percentage of the population that is elderly. In 1900, only 3.1 million

Americans were over 65; currently there are 25 million elderly and future projections indicate growth in absolute numbers for the next 40 years (Vladeck and Firman 1983; Cowgill 1974). In 1900, 4 percent of Americans were elderly. By 1980, this figure had increased to 11.2 percent and is projected to be 12.2 percent by the year 2000. The peak in proportion of the population over 65 is estimated to be 18.3 percent in 2030 (Vladeck and Firman 1983). In addition, the elderly are getting older. In 1980, 40 percent of the elderly were 75 and over. By the year 2000, 49 percent of the elderly are projected to be 75 or older. The "old old," those 85 or older, are the heaviest utilizers of expensive services. Their rising numbers will increase even more dramatically.

While a proliferation of new medical technologies has precipitated an infusion of technology-based treatments into mainstream medical care, the contribution of this trend to rising costs has been the primary concern the last 15 years (Banta et al. 1983). Rising costs have generated attempts to control the diffusion of technology through health planning, certificate of need legislation, and mandated rate setting in selected states. Recent studies found that new technologies diffused more slowly in states with mandated rate setting, and that complex services diffused at about three-fourths the rate of a random national sample of hospitals in states with rate setting (Cromwell and Kanak 1982; Banta et al. 1983). Concern over malpractice suits has encouraged the widespread use of such technologies as skull x-rays and electronic fetal monitoring.

There are three factors which make it difficult to control the use of technology in the United States. First, the United States has a pluralistic and private sector orientation in which decision making is spread among large numbers of individual physicians, health policy makers, and hospital administrators. New technologies in the United States are frequently developed by for-profit drug and medical technology companies. These companies spend large amounts of money to promote the use of their products. With an industry pushing physicians to ever greater use of technology, the profit structure of the U.S. system encourages dissemination to a greater degree than in countries with different structures and incentive systems. Second, the adoption of any specific technological change will benefit some parties but harm others. Third, it is very difficult to evaluate the benefits, risks, and costs of any specific medical technology (Banta et al. 1983).

THE DEBATE OVER FEDERAL FUNDING
AND THE FEDERAL ROLE

Consensus reigns on the overall policy objective of holding down health care costs. But when alternatives for achieving this overall objective are discussed, consensus disintegrates, often along the classic liberal-conservative continuum. Liberals agree that health care cost containment is a desirable end, but place a higher priority on equity and access issues than do conservatives. Conservatives place less emphasis on equity and access issues, and are more concerned with holding down the rate of increase in publically funded health programs, and in making the best possible medical technology available through the marketplace.

At times liberals even question whether health care expenditures are, in fact, too high. What is the magic number that represents a totally unacceptable proportion of the GNP being allocated to health care? Liberals point out that while other countries may seem to have good health systems at lower proportionate expenditures, no one knows what a good health system in a country as large and heterogeneous as the United States should cost. In the absence of such knowledge, how much is too much remains unclear.

Nor do liberals and conservatives necessarily agree on what unit of government is most appropriate for funding and administering health care programs. Liberals have traditionally favored federal funding and administration, while conservatives have favored leaving health policy responsibility to the states. The different perspectives on appropriate governmental jurisdictions are congruent with the differing priorities that liberals and conservatives place upon access and equity. The higher the unit of government, the more economically heterogeneous the population and tax base, and therefore the greater the potential for redistribution. The lower the unit of government, the more economically homogeneous the populations and tax bases of the various subnational jurisdictions, and therefore the less the potential for redistribution.

Reinforcing the liberal-conservative bias stemming from different theoretical redistributive potentials between the state and national governments is the reality of social policy. The federal government has historically been the protector of the poor and of minorities. With the exception of a small number of states long recognized as innovators and leaders in social and health policy, states have generally not been the protectors of the poor but rather the unit where special interests and the landed aristocracy have maintained the status quo.

Nor have states been the big social program spenders that the federal government has been. Most states have constitutional requirements to balance their operating budgets, a factor which limits their spending for ongoing programs to current revenues and reinforces a prevailing state bias toward fiscal conservatism. The federal government has been less conservative fiscally, does not operate under a balanced budget requirement, and has experienced more rapid growth in tax revenues than have the states. State tax structures until recently have relied greatly on sales and consumption taxes which are regressive in their redistributional impact and consequently have experienced less elastic growth. By contrast, the personal income tax structure of the federal government has been progressive in distributional impact and has consequently been elastic in growth.

More rapid revenue growth at the federal level has allowed Congress to assume the role of a rich Uncle Sam vis-à-vis the states in funding health programs. The different distributional impacts of the tax structures at the federal and state levels also reinforce the liberal preference for funding health programs at the federal level and the conservative preference for funding programs at the state level. Health programs funded at the federal level are financed by a slightly more progressive tax structure than are those financed by state tax structures, a fact congruent with liberal redistributive goals.

Libertarians interested in minimizing the role of government have criticized the liberal position for failing to separate allocative issues and distributional issues. Government decisions may allocate scarce resources between functional areas (for example, health, welfare, defense) or may redistribute resources from one group of individuals or income class to another. Libertarians charge that liberals present health expenditures in allocative terms, when the funds are really redistributive in impact, both because the monies are raised through the progressive income tax, and because they are distributed by an equity criterion which holds that access to health care should be based on medical need and not income (Berki 1983b). The liberal defense is that all policies necessarily simultaneously have allocative and distributive impacts, including market laissez-faire strategies.

Since the end of World War II, the federal role in health care has been expansionary. The federal government enacted new programs in traditional areas of public health and stimulated the supply of health care institutions and providers. Later, programs in which the federal government actually became the payer for health care services provided in the private market to individuals were enacted. These new programs occurred within the context of a general expansionary economy at a time when continued economic growth was assumed. Starting with both the budget deficits of the late 1960s and early 1970s and the rapidly rising health care costs of that era, continuing economic expansion was questioned, costs became an issue, and accelerated growth in new health programs slowed.

When the Reagan administration assumed national power in 1980, its philosophy toward health care was a mixture of conservative and libertarian strands. Like conservatives, the administration placed a higher priority upon cost containment than on access and equity issues. The funding levels for traditional public health programs were cut. Eligibility standards for categorical welfare programs were tightened, reducing the number of Medicaid recipients. In addition, Medicaid funding was cut. Public health service hospitals were closed. A large proportion of federal manpower funding was either eliminated or reduced.

Like conservatives, the Reagan administration favored a reduction in federal power and a devolution of policy to the states. Not only were funding levels for health services and social welfare programs cut, but the role of the federal government in setting guidelines and standards was greatly diminished by changes in funding mechanisms from categorical grants in which the federal government determined priorities to state block grants, where states varied greatly in equity concerns. Under the administration's New Federalism proposals, in addition to the conversions of categorical programs to state block grants, part of health care was to be centralized at the federal level by making Medicaid totally a federal program. Yet appearances are deceiving since the federalization of Medicaid was half of a switch in which states would assume funding and administrative responsibility for a number of other jointly financed programs, including AFDC (Lee and Estes 1983). The federalization of Medicaid was viewed as the necessary price to secure greater overall decentralization of social policy to the states. New Federalism evoked negative reactions from governors who would have been confronted with mounting social program costs in an era of shrinking tax bases and rising citizen resistance to tax increases. The changes in the division of policy responsibility between the levels of government failed to win congressional support, although the block grant portion of New Federalism was implemented.

Like libertarians, the Reagan administration valued a reduction in the role of government and a return to market competition. Although supporting the concept of the HMO as a viable competitive mechanism for the delivery of services, the Reagan administration eliminated the federal government's role in the provision of planning and start-up funds to encourage the development of new HMOs, arguing instead that incentives within the private marketplace were adequate.

SHORT-RANGE CHANGES AND OPTIONS

Supplementing the debate over the appropriate level of federal funding for health programs and the role of the federal government in health policy has been debate over several short-range issues and options, including the desirable degree of federal involvement in state and local area planning and in manpower training. Nor has the issue of cost containment abated, since the perennial problem of rising Medicaid and Medicare expenditures remains. Concern over cost containment has led to the enactment of legislation which shifts the basis for hospital reimbursement from retrospective individualized assessments to prospectively determined diagnosis-related groups whose impact on reducing hospital costs is not yet known.

Federal involvement in health planning at the state and local level initially occurred through CHPs (Comprehensive Health Planning Agencies). Created by the 1966 Comprehensive Health Planning Act (Partnership for Health), CHPs engaged in the development of area health plans. The National Health Planning and Resources Development Act (PL-93-641), an amendment to the Public Health Service Act led to the replacement of CHPs by SHPDAs (State Health Planning and Development Agencies) and HSAs (Health Systems Planning Agencies). SHPDAs developed state health plans, while HSAs developed local area plans. Both SHPDAs and HSAs regulated capital expenditures for hospitals. HSAs issued certificates of need, approval hospitals were required to secure before making capital purchases. HSAs were typically nonprofit organizations consisting of a board of health consumers and providers.

Initially, CHPs were opposed by hospitals who viewed these planning and regulatory organizations as impediments to hospital growth. Across time, consensus among hospital administrators receded. Large forprofit hospital chains continued to oppose federal involvement in health planning as growth impediments, but older nonprofit hospitals in areas of declining population or economic base began to view HSAs as instruments for reducing competition from other and often newer hospitals.

During the late 1970s, the role and functions of HSAs continued to grow. However, the advent of the Reagan administration signaled a shift in philosophy from one of government intervention in hospital facilities planning to one of federal disengagement. Originally, the administration proposed the total elimination of HSAs, a proposal defeated in Congress. However, under the Omnibus Budget Reconciliation Act of 1981, governors were given the option of eliminating HSAs in their own states, leaving all hospital facilities planning at the state level. Some governors exercised this option. Under Reagan, the federal role in planning was reduced and the functions of HSAs were truncated. The authorizing legislation for HSAs expires in 1984. A number of proposals are currently under consideration by Congress. Most include a mandated role for state planning agencies but an optional role for local agencies. Despite the uncertainty about the exact form of the new legislation, decisions about the nature and type of capital facilities planning are devolving to the states in accordance with the administration's conservative philosophy of reducing the overall federal role in domestic policy and restoring power to the states.

As in the area of health planning, the federal role in health manpower training has been reduced under the Reagan administration from its earlier levels. The federal role in training has rarely been one of directly training health manpower, with the exception of medics and some military health personnel. Rather, the federal government has provided training monies to medical and allied health professional schools and to students through scholarships, student loan forgiveness programs, and the mechanism of capitation grants in which schools receive a fixed per capita allocation per student.

In addition to achieving the overall objective of increasing the supply of trained medical personnel, capitation grants have allowed the federal government to influence the mix of physician specialties. Under Reagan, most capitation grants, including those for medical schools, have been totally eliminated. Not only is this federal cutback congruent with administration philosophy, but many analysts believe that the United States has an actual and potential future oversupply of physicians, contributing to the low saliency of manpower issues on the federal health policy agenda. While there is much less consensus that health personnel oversupplies exist in related areas, such as nursing, the low saliency of the issue of physician training extends to these areas as well.

Medicaid, designed to deliver health services to the medically indigent, remains a troublesome area. Inherent tension exists between the overall administration objective of cost containment which would keep federal budget deficits at an acceptably low level, and the program objective of providing adequate health care for Americans currently excluded from the middle class. The Reagan administration has placed highest priority on the former. Cuts in Medicaid were enacted in the Omnibus Budget Reconciliation Act of 1981. Eligibility standards for categorical welfare programs were tightened, simultaneously making eligibility standards for Medicaid more stringent. Monies available to states on a per eligible recipient basis were reduced. While overall federal outlays to the states were not reduced, the reason lay in worsening economic conditions increasing the number of eligible recipients, rather than in constant or increased available funds per recipient. Less successful was an administration New Federalism proposal to assume total responsibility for Medicaid in exchange for states assuming total financial and administrative responsibility for many now joint federal-state categorical welfare programs, including AFDC and food stamps. Governors, facing shrinking tax bases and rising costs on a variety of fronts themselves, opposed this switch and it was not enacted.

Medicaid costs have continued to escalate, partially due to increased outlays for long-term care for the elderly. Still worried about rising costs in an era where retrenchment has been the norm, the Reagan administration made a controversial proposal to require middle-class, middle-income children of now-poor parents receiving nursing home services paid by Medicaid to assume greater financial responsibility for their aged mothers and fathers. The political opposition to legally imposing financial responsibility for parental medical and nursing home expenses on children has been considerable. The elderly, fearing financial dependence and becoming a burden to their children, have disapproved of the proposed restrictions on their eligibility for Medicaid. Nor have middle-aged children, potentially facing substantial financial costs for their parents at the same time they are confronting sizable college outlays for their own offspring, been supportive. A more politically feasible option for covering the health costs of the elderly is the development of long-term care insurance provided at least partially by private insurance companies, a type of coverage that is nonexistent in the United States today.

At the beginning of fiscal year 1984 in accordance with the requirement of the Tax Equity and Fiscal Reponsibility Act of 1982, the federal government changed the way hospitals are paid for Medicare patients. Hospitals are now paid prospectively (in advance) with payments based on types of treatments rather than services rendered. The state of New Jersey conducted an experiment in which payment levels for all public and private payers were based on over 300 diagnosis-related groups (DRGs) developed by Yale University researchers in 1975 (Horn et al. 1983a and 1983b; Berki 1983a). By the end of 1980, the program was implemented in 26 hospitals and is currently in place in all but 3 of the 116 acute care hospitals in New Jersey.

Only preliminary evaluation data for New Jersey are now available. These data can be interpreted in various ways. While the rate of increase in cost for all N.J. hospitals was approximately 5 percent below the rate of increase for all U.S. hospitals, a similar differential was true in years prior to the implementation of the DRG system. In the 26 hospitals that were paid for part or all of 1980 on a DRG basis, costs increased at a slower rate (13.1 percent) than for other hospitals in New Jersey (13.8 percent). The difference, however, was not statistically significant. Some evidence exists that the DRG system reduces the rate of increases in costs more for hospitals experiencing financial problems than for financially strong hospitals (Iglehart 1982).

Beginning in October 1, 1983, most acute care hospitals in the country will be reimbursed for Medicare patients using a fixed price schedule on a cost per case basis determined by 467 diagnosis-related groups. The federal government hopes that the DRG system will reduce the rising Medicare expenditures for hospitals by changing the incentives created by traditional hospital reimbursement schemes. Under traditional cost-based reimbursement, a hospital's management approach was to keep beds filled and to maximize the number of reimbursable patient procedures. With per case diagnosis-related payments, patients needing hospitalization are assigned a diagnosis by physicians which fits into one of the 467 diagnosis-related groups. Hospitals are reimbursed fixed amounts per patient, based on a reimbursement schedule for each DRG. Under DRG payments, hospitals are rewarded for keeping patients as short a period of time as possible, and for controlling the use of ancillary services. If a hospital's Medicare revenues are greater than costs, the hospital has discretionary use over the surplus. However, if the hospital's Medicare costs exceed its DRG revenues, the hospital must find ways to cover the deficit.

Skeptics of prospective reimbursement raise several issues. They note that the evaluation data from the New Jersey experiment are preliminary and inconclusive. Further, there is a lack of similarity between the New Jersey experiment, where all patients of a hospital were covered, and the federal changes which will affect only Medicare patients. In the average hospital, Medicare patients are considerably below 50 percent of the patient load and frequently constitute less than one-third.

A second criticism focuses on the fact that physicians determine the length of patient stay and the amount of tests and procedures any patient receives. DRGs do not alter the financial incentives for physicians, since it does not affect the payment method for physicians under Medicare. Physicians are still paid on a fee-for-service basis rather than a per case basis, and still have some financial incentives to extend the length of patient hospitalization and the procedures performed. While the TEFRA law recommends the study of per case reimbursement to physicians, many experts feel such a change is unlikely. The politically powerful American Medical Association and other physician groups would be likely to challenge such a proposal. Additionally, the technical and data problems of per case reimbursements to over 350,000 physicians are several magnitudes greater than the problems associated with per case reimbursement of over 5,000 hospitals. Architects of the DRG reimbursement scheme assumed that since hospitals now have direct financial incentives to hold down length and extent of patient care in the interest of cost containment, hospital administrators will somehow be able to persuade physicians, most of whom are not employees of hospitals, to adopt the same goals. Whether hospital administrators will be this persuasive is still an unproven issue (Iglehart 1983; Kukla and Bachofer 1983; Brown 1983).

The third criticism is that DRG reimbursement may distort behavior in unintended and undesirable ways. If the DRG payment system does work to change physician behavior, there is a risk that hospitals and physicians may undertreat patients to increase their profits. Alternatively, hospitals may prematurely release and then rehospitalize patients to secure multiple payments. While it is not clear that inappropriate service will occur, the specter of elderly patients being undertreated and shuffled in and out of hospitals is cause for concern (Brown 1983). Others worry about "DRG creep," a constant shifting and redefining of the diagnosis-related groups by physicians and hospitals in such a way as to maximize reimbursable revenues and therefore profits (Iglehart 1982). Nor are some critics convinced that the variability of costs due to different severities of illness within diagnosis groups is sufficiently small to make the approach viable (Berki 1983a).

The switch from retrospective to prospective reimbursement based on diagnosis-related groups is occurring during the Reagan administration but is inconsistent with administration philosophy. The Reagan administration has generally promoted less federal control and less regulation, yet the new DRG system exemplifies greater federal intrusion into hospitals' operations. DRGs definitely do not decrease and may increase the amount of federal hospital regulation. In the case of the administration's embrace of DRGs, practical concerns with cost containment have overridden philosophical preferences for reducing federal private sector involvement. Given the prevailing basic level of citizen support for government-sponsored health care for the elderly, a reduced level of federal involvement may be an impossibility in some instances, even when federal involvement contradicts conservative philosophy.

MODELS FOR THE FUTURE: COMPETITION, NATIONAL HEALTH INSURANCE, OR A NATIONAL HEALTH SYSTEM

Three basic models for future health policy in the United States are the competition model, national health insurance, and a national health system. All three lie along a continuum with degree of federal intervention in the current organization, structure and financing of the current health care system ranging from a moderately large degree of intervention for the competition model, to a greater degree for the national health insurance model, to the greatest degree for a national health system. All three represent comprehensive approaches to national medical policy and are, in some ways, means toward desired ends, rather than ends in themselves.

In political debates, the distinction between means and ends often becomes clouded, partially because consensus about national health policy goals does not always reign. Fundamental disagreements exist about equity; the degree health policy should emphasize technology; the resource trade-offs between prevention, acute care, and long-term care; and how much the system should assure individual choice of providers and types of care. The future portends even new policy conflicts: Can patients refuse medical care for themselves? Is abortion death? Can terminally ill patients choose when and where to die? Under what conditions are patients dead? Should vital organs be marketed and sold to the highest bidder? Focusing national health policy debate on conflict over strategies to achieve goals sometimes obscures conflict over the goals themselves.

The competition or consumer choice model is a modified market approach. The consumer choice model assumes competitive markets, where producers are small and unable to affect either the price or quantity of a service provided, and where consumers behave rationally under conditions of perfect information. Wide recognition exists among analysts, however that the medical care system does not currently operate like a free market (McClure 1981; Council on Wage and Price Stability 1976; Davis 1973).

Two major strategic alternatives to deal with this market failure are regulation versus structural changes to make the health care system more closely simulate a free market. While these two alternatives are commonly referred to as "regulation versus competition," the more accurate description would be direct economic regulation versus market reform. The first approach of regulation concedes defeat in achieving market conditions in health care, and argues for making theory approximate reality. The second approach holds that market conditions can be obtained even if they are not now present, and argues for making reality approximate theory.

Although general suggestions about market reform and an increased role for competition are not new, much of the current debate began in 1978 with Enthoven's formulation of the Consumer Choice Health Plan (Enthoven 1978a; 1978b; 1980). Enthoven argued that a large part of health cost escalation stemmed from the current structure insulating the consumer from the expense of health care and rewarded providers for inefficient use of health care resources. He targeted several aspects of the current system for change, proposing a specific pro-competition model. Current tax laws which exempt employer-paid health benefits from personal income taxes and retrospective cost reimbursement of providers were among those areas targeted for reform. The essence of the consumer choice health plan would provide more than one health insurance option for consumers with varying levels of benefits and with financial incentives for employees to choose less costly insurance. Most versions of the plan would set a maximum amount of employer contribution to health benefits excluded from income tax. The employer's contribution must be the same for all options. Employees who chose a plan costing less than the employer's uniform contribution should receive a cash rebate. Any employer-paid premium above the maximum excluded amount of health insurance benefits would be taxed as employee income.

In Enthoven's original formulation, health plans would be required to operate according to a set of rules intended to create fair and socially desirable competition. Enthoven proposed that the enrollment process be run by a government agency. His plan would charge the same premiums to all persons in the same actuarial category enrolled with the same benefits in the same area. Qualified plans would have to offer a low option limited to basic benefits to be defined in a national health insurance law. These plans must publish a clearly stated annual limit on individual or family out-of-pocket outlays for covered benefits. Beyond this limit, the plan would pay all costs. This requirement would lower the incentives for plans to compete by offering inadequate benefits that would leave the seriously ill uninsured. Plans could require that members obtain all their covered benefits from participating providers with whom they had prior arrangements concerning fees and utilization controls. Enthoven expected most plans to work this way.

To aid the informed consumer choice which Enthoven viewed as essential to the success of his proposal, all health insurance plans would be required to publish total per capita costs, including premiums and out-of-pocket costs. Every year during specified "open seasons," consumers would have the option of switching health insurance plans. An administrative agency would have the authority to review and approve these materials, and to supervise the financial disclosure process. In contrast to libertarian markets, Enthoven's markets allowed a substantial role for federal government intervention. The choices as to benefits and eligibility would be a matter of political judgment, since Enthoven argued that the principles of consumer choice could be applied to a broad range of packages and eligibilities; and to many possibilities of federal and state financing responsibilities. The exact form which Enthoven's proposal would take is unclear. His plan remains a model, absent legislative and regulatory detail. In 1981, three different statutory versions of Enthoven's ideas were introduced in Congress.

Enthoven's proposal is predicated on the assumption that consumers, when given a choice, will often pick the option of less health insurance. Yet data from the Federal Employees Health Benefit Program (FEHBP) reveal the opposite: that consumers prefer more insurance to less when confronted with competing options (Ginsberg 1980; *Competition and Consumer Choice* 1981). In addition, the periodic availability of a range of health benefit choices during open seasons might trigger what is known in the insurance business as "adverse selection." Under adverse selection, consumers who anticipate greater health care services or higher health care costs would select more comprehensive higher priced coverages, while consumers who regard themselves as unlikely to incur high services or costs, would choose less comprehensive coverages. Adverse selection raises the cost of insurance to those who need it most, and makes it difficult to market comprehensive coverage. Adverse selection has been demonstrated in the Federal Employee Health Benefits Program. New enrollees who choose the Blue Cross/ Blue Shield high service option during the open season have claims costs that are 145 percent of the average employee enrolled in the program for a longer time. Employees who leave during the open season have claim costs that are only 65 percent of the costs of the average group as a whole (*Competition and Consumer Choice* 1981).

The choice for consumers in Enthoven's plan would be among competing benefit packages, a break with current insurance offerings. Now little choice exists, especially in the work setting, for employees about the level and cost of benefits they will receive. To the degree Enthoven's concept of reforming the health care system by restructuring incentives worked, his plan might actually reduce consumer choice in that once a benefit package was selected, an employee would be locked into receiving continued service from that provider to a much greater degree than is currently the case. Enthoven assumes that in most cases consumer selection of a benefit system also presumes selection of a particular set of health care providers.

Unlike many advocates of market reforms, Enthoven expressed concern for equity in health care. He argued that the poor would need a higher subsidy to assure their access to the plan and proposed a voucher usable only as a premium contribution to the qualified plan of their choice. Vouchers would be administered through the cash welfare system, but would be available to all low-income welfare people, not just those presently eligible for welfare. The dollar value of their voucher would decline gradually with increasing income on a sliding scale to encourage work incentives.

Enthoven wanted to retain Medicare but only with fundamental reforms in the program. The major reform would be a freedom of choice provision, permitting beneficiaries to direct that an amount equal to their adjusted average per capita costs be paid to a qualified health plan of their choice. This change would allow beneficiaries to receive for themselves the benefits of joining an economical alternative health delivery system through reduced premiums, reduced deductibles and coinsurance, or more extensive services.

Enthoven's proposal was first drafted for Joseph Califano while secretary of DHEW in the Carter administration. Some prominent Republican congressmen, including former congressman David Stockman, subsequently the director of OMB in the Reagan administration, introduced three different variants of the consumer choice model. These incorporated the basic idea of increased consumer choice but did not exactly replicate all of Enthoven's specifics.

Two, for example, proposed no changes in Medicaid while one proposed no changes in Medicare. What all the plans had in common was the notion of competition, both giving consumers the means to identify more efficient health care providers and the financial incentives to choose those identified options. None of the three variants have secured congressional approval. Congress is an institution which responds to crises and short-term forces. The more competition plans emulate Enthoven's original proposal, the more they raise short-run costs in the interest of gaining long-run efficiency. These trade-offs are not made easily by politicians who must deal with frequently recurring elections and interest groups.

The prospects for the competition strategy are uncertain, both technically and politically. The market arguments are still largely theoretical. No nation has a competitive strategy. Despite evidence from selected cities where the competitive model is partially in place, the full model has not been proved anywhere. The normal skepticism over the translation of any theoretical possibility into reality applies to market strategies. Politically, the competition strategy is still poorly understood by providers, employers, insurers, and public programs. More crucially, the strategy would take five to ten years to accomplish. It is highly debatable whether U.S. health policy can follow a consistent direction for that duration of time. Most experts agree, however, that attempting to implement the policy too quickly would doom the strategy to failure (McClure 1983).

Comprehensive national health insurance does not now exist in the United States, isolating the United States from the developed nations of Western Europe and Canada which all have some type of coordinated governmental health policy assuring universal coverage. Proposals to adopt some form of national health insurance have been introduced into Congress at various points over the last 80 years. None have survived. Instead, the United States has pursued the categorical approach to extending governmentally financed health benefits, especially with the adoption of the Medicare and Medicaid programs in 1965. Carried to its ultimate conclusion, extensions of categorical coverage will result in universal coverage. Yet the categorical approach has not yet resulted in complete coverage of the poor, unemployed, or those employed in many low-wage industries. Nor is current coverage of the middle class by private insurance mandated in any way.

There are several different variants of national health insurance. In one sense, the competition models discussed earlier are a subset of national health insurance models. In the original Enthoven proposal, employers were mandated to provide a form of health insurance adhering to governmental guidelines. A second variant is catastrophic insurance which provides coverage of very large consumer health bills once a substantial deductible has been satisfied. A third variant is comprehensive national health insurance.

Several criticisms have been levied at the catastrophic model of national health insurance. Under a catastrophic plan which does not intervene in the current mechanisms for paying providers nor alter the current organization of health care institutional arrangements, medical costs may continue to increase rapidly, since medical coverage would increase demand for high cost services. Emphasis on catastrophic rather than first dollar coverage would exacerbate the current allocation of resources toward high technology medicine and life-extending technologies rather than on primary and preventive care.

Comprehensive national health insurance is difficult to discuss as a concept, because the details of any specific plan could radically alter the plan's impact on costs, access, and service delivery. One of the most comprehensive versions of a national health insurance plan introduced in the last few years was the Kennedy-Waxman proposal. This plan proposed a total reform of current insurance arrangements and provider payment mechanisms, rather than simply addressing gaps in coverage. All citizens and legal residents would automatically receive comprehensive insurance coverage without cost sharing, although Medicare beneficiaries would continue under separate but equally comprehensive coverage.

The Kennedy-Waxman plan would be financed through general revenues, the continued use of the payroll tax and beneficiary premiums for Medicare, and income-related premiums. An annual national health insurance budget would be set, with budget increases related to the average rate of increase in GNP over the preceding three years. The national budget would be allocated among states who would set prospective budgets for their hospitals and other institutions as well as maximum fee schedules for physicians. The plan would initially raise costs to many employers through the mandated coverage, potentially causing labor costs to employers to rise in the short run. While the bill had the potential for cost containment and controls on resource allocation decisions through a coordinated budget, there are questions as to whether the cost containment mechanisms would be effective. Desires to increase the program's acceptability to providers and the public might lead to initial delays in imposing expenditure controls, resulting in massive increases in health expenditures. Setting budgets for physician expenditures would be difficult, given initial data limitations. Politicians might respond to desires of providers, states, or federal policy makers who wish to allow health expenditures to rise faster than the GNP (Feder et al. 1981).

In some ways, Enthoven's Consumer Choice Health Plan was also an example of comprehensive national health insurance. It was distinguished by its theoretical assumption that competition would work to constrain costs. While the Kennedy-Waxman plan relied on public sector budgets and centralized resource allocation decisions, Enthoven's plan relied on the availability of consumer options and the assumption that when confronted with choice, consumers would be financially motivated and would pick low-cost options. Enthoven disagrees with arguments which state that demand for health care services including insurance, due to their special life-preserving nature, are relatively inelastic and that health care consumers are insensitive to price changes. He assumes that market models are applicable to health care.

A third model for future U.S. national health policy is a national health system. Under this model, government directly provides comprehensive health services universally available on a need basis. The crucial contrasts between a national health system as in Great Britain and proposals for national health insurance are that hospitals would be governmentally owned and managed institutions rather than private; health care providers would be employees of the state rather than self-employed or private sector employees; and there would no longer be a role for third-party payers such as Blue Cross/Blue Shield or private health insurance firms. While such proposals were introduced into Congress in the mid-1970s, this third model seems the least politically feasible alternative in the United States, given the historical biases toward private markets and providers.

Which of the future models for national health policy the United States embraces partially depends on which political party is in power. Neither party has strong advocates of a national health system at this time. The choice appears to be between a national health insurance model theoretically based on competition versus other variants of national health insurance versus the incremental strategy of muddling through with piecemeal, uncoordinated changes designed to respond to crises and interest group pressures. The non-model of muddling through may be the most likely in the short term under either Democrats or Republicans unless health becomes an issue of high political salience as it has been at various points over the last 20 years. If more comprehensive reform of health care becomes a major issue, Republicans are more likely to favor a theoretically based competition approach which assumes health care markets can be made to work efficiently, while Democrats are more likely to favor a public sector budget and allocation approach.

Whatever political party is in power, the issues of rising health care costs, the increasing role of technology in medical care and all the ethical questions surrounding the use of such technology, and the difficulty of effectively evaluating the impact of health care policy remain. For the next 20 to 40 years, these issues will be linked with the reality of an aging population and the pressures such a population will generate on the U.S. health care system. While other national policy areas may force health to take a back seat to defense, the economy, the environment, and education, in the next four decades the aging of the population, technology, and costs will force health to become an issue of high national priority.

APPENDIXES

APPENDIX 1

Selected Federal Legislation with Research Components

Commission Corps Act of 1899: became a device for hiring physicians for research.

Federal Food and Drug Act of 1906 (the Wiley Act): provided impetus to develop scientific testing procedures and standards to ascertain food and drug purity.

Veterans Act of 1924 and amendments: extended medical care to veterans, not only for treatment of disabilities associated with military service, but also for other conditions requiring hospitalization. Across time VA hospitals became linked with medical schools and research functions increased.

Ransdell Act of 1930: created the National Institute of Health from the Hygienic Laboratory.

National Cancer Act of 1937: created the National Cancer Institute and authorized research in NIH laboratories, grants to non-government scientists, and fellowships to train scientists and clinicians.

Federal Food, Drug, and Cosmetic Act of 1938 and amendments: included a stronger emphasis on testing drugs, therapeutic devices, and cosmetics before marketing.

Public Health Service Act of 1944: incorporated the National Institute of Health into the Public Health Service; authorized research and investigation into selected diseases and health problems.

Mental Health Act of 1946 (amendment to PHS Act): included mental health problems in the grant-in-aid programs in the PHS Act, and established the National Institute of Mental Health.

Mental Health Study Act of 1955 (amendment to the PHS Act): authorized grants to facilitate a research program into methods and resources for care of the mentally ill.

Amendments to Title V of the Social Security Act in 1963: provided grants for research projects related to maternal and child health and crippled children services.

Mental Retardation Facilities and Community Mental Health Centers Act of 1963 (amendment to PHS Act): assisted in construction of research facilities for mental retardation; amended in 1968 to provide research grants relating to alcoholism and narcotics addiction; in 1970 broadened to include research monies for drug abuse.

Federal Water Pollution Control Act Amendments of 1965 and amendments: switched enforcement responsibilities for water control from the Department of Interior to DHEW and required states to set standards for water quality; 1972 amendments set national rather than state standards for both water quality and sewage treatment; subsequent amendments strengthened the standards; included monies for research and demonstration for into waste treatment management and drainage and water pollution problems.

Heart Disease, Cancer, and Stroke Amendments of 1965 to the Public Health Service Act (Regional Medical Program): established regional cooperative programs among medical schools, hospitals, and other research institutions; developed programs of research, training, and continuing education in those three disease categories.

Amendments to the Clean Air Act of 1970 and 1977: allowed EPA to set ambient air quality standards, and set admission standards for plants with high pollution potential; included air pollution research monies.

Family Planning Services and Population Research Act of 1970 (amendment to the PHS Act): authorized research grants and contracts for family planning programs and services (except abortion).

National Sickle Cell Anemia Control Act and National Cooley's Anemia Control Act of 1972 (amendments to the PHS): authorized grants and contracts for research related to these diseases.

Toxic Substances Control Act of 1976: regulates chemical substances affecting health and the environment; provides grants to the states; included the development of a data system for research and regulation.

Omnibus Budget Reconciliation Act of 1981: created a new research program into adolescent family life and teenage pregnancy problems (the chastity amendment); included genetic defect research monies in maternal and child health block grant.

APPENDIX 2

Selected Federal Legislation with Planning and Regulation Components

Marine Hospitals Services Act of 1870: provided a national agency with central headquarters to oversee merchant marine hospitals and staffing.

Federal Quarantine Act of 1878 and amendments: gave the Marine Hospital Service the authority to develop quarantine laws for ports that lacked state or local regulation; was expanded to give the service full responsibility for foreign and interstate commerce.

Public Health and Marine Service Act of 1902: legitimized the overall coordinating role of the federal government in public health by establishing a communication system for state and territorial health officers.

Biologics Control Act of 1902: gave the Public Health Service the responsibility to license and regulate biologically derived health products.

Food and Drug Act of 1906 (Wiley Act): allowed the Bureau of Chemistry in the Department of Agriculture to prohibit shipment of impure foods and drugs across state lines.

Vocational Educational Act of 1917 (Smith-Hughes Act): provided funds to establish early licensed practical nursing (LPN) programs.

Maternity and Infancy Act of 1921 (Sheppard-Towner Act): provided grants to states to plan maternal and child health services.

Title V of the Social Security Act of 1935: provided grants to states for maternal and child health and child welfare services and for services to crippled children.

Federal Food, Drug, and Cosmetic Act of 1938 and amendments: regulated market entry of new drug, cosmetic, and therapeutic products for safety.

Venereal Disease Control Act of 1938: coordinated state efforts to combat syphilis and gonorrhea.

Public Health Service Act of 1944: specified a role for the Public Health Service in working with state and local health departments; incorporated the provision of the Biologics Control Act as a PHS responsibility; allowed use of quarantines and inspections for the control of communicable diseases.

Hospital Survey and Construction Act of 1946 (Hill-Burton Amendment to PHS): provided grants to states to inventory existing health care facilities and to plan for new ones; required the establishment of state planning agencies.

Water Pollution Control Act of 1956: created regulatory programs to combat water pollution; urged states to set standards for clean water.

Amendments of 1958 to Public Health Service Act (PL-85-544): established a program of formula grants to schools of public health.

Clean Air Act of 1963 and subsequent amendments in 1965, 1966, 1967, and 1969: urged states to set standards for clean air; established cooperative planning with states to set regulations to limit particulate pollution.

Health Professions Education Assistance Act of 1963 (amendment to the PHS Act): provided construction grants for facilities that train physicians, nurses, dentists, podiatrists, pharmacists, and public health personnel and student loan funds to schools of medicine and osteopathy; later amendments extended loan funds to a variety of health and allied health professions.

Mental Retardation Facilities and Community Mental Health Centers Construction Act of 1963 (amendment to the PHS Act): provided construction grants for community mental health centers and for centers for mentally retarded; facilitates programs to train teachers of mentally retarded, deaf, and other handicapped children; authorized special project grants for training and surveys in community mental health; revised extensively community mental health programs in 1980, including provisions for comprehensive state mental health systems.

Nurse Training Act of 1964 (amendment to PHS Act): authorized separate funding for construction grants for schools of nursing with associate degree and diploma programs; established student loan funds at schools of nursing.

Federal Water Pollution Control Act Amendments of 1965 and amendments: switched enforcement responsibilities for water control from the Department of Interior to DHEW and required states to set standards for water quality; 1972 amendments set national rather than state standards for both water quality and sewage treatment; subsequent amendments strengthened the standards.

Heart Disease, Cancer, and Stroke Amendments of 1965 to the Public
Health Service Act (Regional Medical Program): established
regional cooperative programs among medical schools, hospitals,
and other research institutions; developed programs of research,
training and continuing education in those three disease categories.

Health Professions Educational Assistance Amendments of 1965:
authorized basic improvement (institutional grants), special
improvement grants, and scholarship grants to schools of medicine, dentistry, osteopathy, optometry, and podiatry; authorized
scholarship grants to schools of pharmacy; expanded student
loan program.

Health Insurance for the Aged of 1965 — Title XVIII of the Social
Security Act (Medicare) and amendments: through the provision
of health insurance for the aged with federal funds, becomes the
mechanism for later federal regulations dealing with quality
assurance, institutional minimum standards, utilization review,
and cost controls.

Grants to the States for Medical Assistance Programs of 1965 —
Title XIX of the Social Security Act (Medicaid) and amendments: through the provision of health services for low income
federal public assistance recipients and the medically needy,
becomes a mechanism for federal regulation of quality assurance,
institutional minimum standards, utilization review, and cost
controls in health care.

Comprehensive Health Planning and Public Health Service Amendments of 1966 (Partnership for Health): provided for the state
and local planning through A and B agencies.

Allied Health Professions Personnel Training Act of 1966 (amendment to PHS Act): construction and improvement grants and
traineeships for allied health professions; revised student loan
program.

Health Manpower Act of 1968 (PHS Act amendment): extended
and modified previous health manpower legislation.

National Environmental Policy Act of 1969: consolidated programs
dealing with air pollution, water pollution, urban and industrial
health, and radiological health; established guidelines for environmental controls for projects involving the federal government;
included a new mechanism of environmental impact statements
before new projects are begun; allowed for citizen participation;
established the Council on Environmental Quality.

Amendments to the Clean Air Act of 1970 and 1977: allowed EPA to set ambient air quality standards, and set admission standards for plants with high pollution potential; set initial deadlines for auto emission standards.

Water Quality Improvement Act of 1970: established liability for oil spills; increased restrictions on thermal pollution from nuclear power plants.

Health Training and Improvement Act of 1970 (PHS Act amendment): provided institutional grants for new schools of health professions and special project grants for allied health.

Communicable Disease Control Amendments of 1970 (amendments to the PHS Act): reestablished categorical grant programs to control communicable diseases such as tuberculosis, venereal disease, measles, rubella.

Family Planning Services and Population Research Act of 1970 (amendment to the PHS Act): established an Office of Population Affairs under the assistant secretary for Health and Scientific Affairs for family planning.

Emergency Health Personnel Act of 1970 (amendment to the PHS Act): authorized the secretary of HEW to assign commissioned officers and other health personnel in the PHS to areas in critical need of manpower; provided the statutory basis for the National Health Service Corps which sent physicians and other health personnel into geographic shortage areas in exchange for education loan forgiveness.

Occupational Safety and Health Act of 1970 (OSHA) and amendments: created a strong standard setting authority vested in the Secretary of Labor to set a minimum level of protection for workers against specified hazards.

National Health Planning and Resources Development Act of 1974 (amendment to the Public Health Services Act PL-93-641): created a system of local and state planning agencies supported through federal funds; regulated funds for new capital expenditures and for renovations for health institutions.

Comprehensive Health Manpower Training Act of 1971 (PHS Act amendment): complex series of amendments that replaced institutional grants with a new system of capitation grants; set up project grants and financial distress grants; and revised loan and scholarship provisions.

Nurse Training Act of 1971 (PHS Act amendment): extended construction grant program, broadened special project grants, provided financial distress grants, provided capitation grants for nursing schools, and revised scholarship and loan programs; extended in 1975 to include advanced nurse training/nurse practitioner programs; extended in 1979 to nurse anesthetists.

Environmental Pesticide Control Act of 1972: required registration of pesticides; gave EPA authority to ban use of hazardous pesticides.

Health Maintenance Organization Act of 1973 (amendment to the PHS Act) and amendments in 1976, 1978, and 1981: specified the basic medical services which an HMO had to provide to be eligible for federal funding; specified requirements for fiscal responsibility for broad population enrollment and a policy making board; mandated that every employer of 25 or more persons offer an HMO option; amendments mitigated the stringency of the original requirements for HMO service provision to be eligible for federal funding.

Emergency Medical Services Systems Act of 1973 (amendment to the PHS Act): established grants and contracts for the development and improvement of area emergency medical systems and for related planning.

Safe Drinking Water Act of 1974: set standards for allowable levels of pollutants and chemicals in public drinking water systems.

Health Professions Education Assistance Act of 1976 (PHS Act amendment): extended capitation and special project grants to schools of public health and health administration programs; broadened startup grants, special project grants, and construction and traineeship grants; changed capitation grant prerequisites to emphasize primary care; placed some restrictions on entrance of foreign physicians into the U.S.

Toxic Substances Control Act of 1976: regulates chemical substances affecting health and the environment; provides grants to the states; included the development of a data system for research and regulation; banned manufacture and use of PCBs.

Resource Conservation Recovery Act of 1976 and amendments: developed management and review plans for safe disposal of discarded material; regulated management of hazardous wastes.

Clean Water Act of 1977: created best (conventional) technology standards for water quality by 1984; raised liability limits on oil spill cleanup costs.

Comprehensive Environmental Response, Compensation, and Liability Act of 1980: created federal superfund to clean up chemical dumps and toxic wastes; authorized EPA to sue responsible parties for toxic spills for recovery of government cleanup expenses.

Omnibus Budget Reconciliation Act of 1981: replaced categorical programs in areas of prevention, alcohol and drug abuse and mental health, primary care, and some areas of maternal and child health with block grants; eliminated requirements for local HSAs, cut their funding, and increased gubernatorial discretion concerning their future role; made the use of PSROs (Professional Standard Review Organizations) in hospitals optional for patients covered under government programs; made some changes in reimbursement and methodology for both Medicare and Medicaid; reduced Medicaid funding for states, but allowed a partial gainback for improved program administration, including fraud detection and error rate reduction; eliminated capitation payments for nursing and medical schools and reduced capitation payments for selected other health professional schools; greatly reduced funding for new entrants into the National Health Service Corps.

Tax Equity and Fiscal Responsibility Act of 1982: included changes in both Medicare and Medicaid. For Medicaid: tightened regulations on acceptable error rates and overpayments and made a number of changes in payment methodology. For Medicare: made extensive changes in reimbursement methodologies for hospital related services under Medicare; began a shift to case-mix (diagnostic related groups) for reimbursements for most acute care hospitals; eliminated nursing salary cost differentials and private room subsidies; eliminated the lesser of cost or charge provision; made reimbursement changes for HMOs.

APPENDIX 3

Selected Federal Legislation with Services Components

Merchant Marine Services Act of 1798: provides health services to U.S. seamen.

Marine Hospitals Services Act of 1870: revitalized and extended services to U.S. merchant seamen.

Commission Corps Act of 1899 and amendments: hired physicians and health personnel to provide public health services.

Maternity and Infancy Act of 1921 (Sheppard-Towner Act): provided grants to states to develop maternal and child health services.

Veterans Act of 1924 and amendments: extended medical care to veterans, not only for treatment of disabilities associated with military service, but also for other conditions requiring hospitalization.

Venereal Disease Control Act of 1938: provided services through states to combat venereal disease.

Title V of the Social Security Act of 1935: provided grants to states for maternal and child health and child welfare services and for services to crippled children.

Public Health Service Act of 1944: provided grants to states for the treatment of VD and TB and for establishment and maintenance of health departments; continued maintenance of marine hospitals; provision of services to penal and correctional institutions.

Hospital Survey and Construction Act of 1946 (Hill-Burton Amendment of PHS): provided grants for hospital construction; amendments to Hill-Burton provided additional monies for medically related nonhospital institutions and for modernization of hospitals.

Health Amendments Act of 1956 (amendment to the PHS Act): added special project grants dealing with problems of state mental hospitals.

Health Amendments Act of 1956 to the Public Health Service Act: authorized traineeships for public health personnel and for the advanced training of nurses.

Social Security Amendments of 1960 (Kerr-Mills Act): established a program of medical assistance for the aged which gave payments to states for medical care for medically indigent persons 65 and over; state participation was optional, with only 25 states participating.

Health Services Act of 1962 for Agricultural Migratory Workers (amendment to the PHS Act): established a program of grants for family clinics and other health services for migrant workers.

Amendments to Title V of the Social Security Act in 1963, 1965, and 1967: added special project grants for maternity and infant care for low-income mothers and infants; comprehensive services for low-income children and youth; added special project grants for child dental services.

Mental Retardation Facilities and Community Mental Health Centers Construction Act of 1963 (amendment to the PHS Act): adds mental retardation services into previous grant and facilities construction programs; 1965 amendments provide personnel grants to staff community mental health centers; 1968 amendments add grants to construct and staff alcoholism programs; the 1970 amendments extend alcoholic and narcotic addiction services and include drug abuse and drug dependence; added child mental health services; 1970 and 1975 amendments included developmental disabilities and other neurological handicapping conditions.

Economic Opportunity Act of 1964 (Antipoverty Program): OEO neighborhood health centers were established through community action provisions.

Health Insurance for the Aged of 1965 — Title XVIII of the Social Security Act (Medicare) and amendments: established a program of national health insurance for the elderly; Part A provided basic protection against the costs of hospital and selected post-hospital services; Part B was a voluntary program financed by premium payments from enrollees with matching federal revenues and provided supplemental medical insurance benefits; amendments added patients who received cash payments under the disability provisions of the Social Security Act and later patients who required hemodialysis or renal transplants were included as disabled for Medicare.

Grants to the States for Medical Assistance Programs of 1965 — Title XIX of the Social Security Act (Medicaid) and amendments: created a federal-state matching program with voluntary state participation to partially replace the Kerr-Mills program; participating states had to provide five basic services: inpatient and outpatient, other laboratory and x-ray, physician, and skilled nursing home services; states could include a number of other optional services; required and optional services changed with amendments; federal categorical welfare recipients were eligible; by option, states could include medically needy with incomes too high for cash federal welfare payments.

Comprehensive Health Planning and Public Health Service Amendments of 1966 (Partnership for Health): provided block grants to state health departments for discretionary purposes.

Family Planning Services and Population Research Act of 1970 (amendment to the PHS Act): authorized monies for family planning programs and services, except abortion.

National Sickle Cell Anemia Control Act and National Cooley's Anemia Control Act of 1972 (amendments to the PHS): authorized grants and contracts for screening, treatment, counseling, and information related to these diseases.

Health Maintenance Organization Act of 1973 (amendment to the PHS Act) and amendments in 1976, 1978, and 1981: provided grants and contracts to determine the feasibility of and plan HMOs; provided grant contracts and loan guarantees for initial development and loan guarantees for initial operating costs; amendments provided loans for acquisition of facilities, equipment, and training of administrators and directors.

National Health Planning and Resources Development Act of 1974; an amendment to the Public Health Services Act (PL-93-641): provided assistance for modernization or construction of inpatient and outpatient facilities.

Omnibus Budget Reconciliation Act of 1981: created block grants in some areas of prevention, primary care, and some areas of maternal and child health; reduced funds by 25 percent in the process of replacing categorical programs with block grants; replaced all mental health and alcohol and drug abuse programs including those under the 1963 Community Mental Health Centers Act with a single block grant and a 25 percent reduction in funding; eliminated new funding for planning and start-up of HMOs; closed or transferred to state or local authority Public Health Service hospitals and clinics; eliminated some Medicare services (for example, alcohol detoxification, occupational therapy to qualify for home health services) and increased Part B deductibles; gave states discretion as to whether to cover 18- to 20-year olds under Medicaid; reduced number of Medicaid eligibles indirectly by tightening requirements for AFDC; cut federal funds for Medicaid; added adolescent pregnancy services; allowed states to waive Medicaid consumer freedom of choice about physicians.

Tax Equity and Fiscal Responsibility Act of 1982: included changes in both Medicare and Medicaid. For Medicaid: allowed enrollment fees, cost-sharing, and similar charges for some categories of recipients and services. For Medicare: added payments for some portions of hospice care; made extensive changes in reimbursement methodologies for hospital related services under Medicare; began a shift to case-mix (diagnostic related groups) for reimbursements for most acute care hospitals; eliminated nursing salary cost differentials and private room subsidies; eliminated the lesser of cost or charge provision; made reimbursement changes for HMOs; recipient-paid premiums increased to 25 percent of Part B costs.

APPENDIX 4

Selected Federal Legislation with Demand Components

Merchant Marine Seaman Act of 1798: provided free services for U.S. merchant marine seamen.

Federal Quarantine Act of 1878 and amendments: controlled movement of individuals suspected to have diseases and affected their demand for health care; lowered demand from foreign nationals by preventing their entry into the U.S.

Maternity and Infancy Act of 1921 (Sheppard-Towner Act): provided grants to states to plan maternal and child health services.

Veterans Act of 1924 and amendments: extended medical care to veterans, not only for treatment of disabilities associated with military service, but also for other conditions requiring hospitalization.

Title V of the Social Security Act of 1935: provided grants to states for maternal and child health and child welfare services and for services to crippled children.

Venereal Disease Control Act of 1938: made venereal disease services more available.

Water Pollution Control Act of 1956: created regulatory programs to combat water pollution; urged states to set standards for clean water. One goal was to reduce long-term demand for health care.

Social Security Amendments of 1960 (Kerr-Mills Act): established a program of medical assistance for the aged which gave payments to states for medical care for medically indigent persons 65 and over; state participation was optional, with only 25 states participating.

Health Services Act of 1962 for Agricultural Migratory Workers (amendment to the PHS Act): established a program of grants for family clinics and other health services for migrant workers.

Clean Air Act of 1963 and amendments of 1965, 1966, 1967, and 1969: urged states to set standards for clean air; established cooperative planning with states to set regulations to limit particulate pollution.

Amendments to Title V of the Social Security Act in 1963, 1965, and 1967: added special project grants for maternity and infant care for low-income mothers and infants; comprehensive services for low-income children and youth; added special project grants for child dental services.

Economic Opportunity Act of 1964 (Antipoverty Program): OEO neighborhood health centers were established through community action provisions; emphasized stimulation of demands for health care services in underserved low-income communities.

Health Insurance for the Aged of 1965 – Title XVIII of the Social Security Act (Medicare) and amendments: established a program of national health insurance for the elderly; Part A provides basic protection against the costs of hospital and selected post-hospital services; Part B is a voluntary program financed by premium payments from enrollees with matching federal revenues and provides supplemental medical insurance benefits; amendments added patients who receive cash payments under the disability provisions of the Social Security Act and later patients who required hemodialysis or renal transplants were included as disabled for Medicare.

Grants to the States for Medical Assistance Programs Act of 1965 – Title XIX of the Social Security Act (Medicaid) and amendments: created a federal-state matching program with voluntary state participation to partially replace the Kerr-Mills program; participating states had to provide five basic services: inpatient and outpatient, other laboratory and x-ray, physician, and skilled nursing home services; states could include a number of other optional services; required and optional services changed with amendments; federal categorical welfare recipients were eligible; by option, states could include medically needy with incomes too high for cash federal welfare payments.

Federal Water Pollution Control Act Amendments of 1965 and amendments: switched enforcement responsibilities for water control from the Department of Interior to DHEW and required states to set standards for water quality; 1972 amendments set national rather than state standards for both water quality and sewage treatment; subsequent amendments strengthened the standards designed to reduce long-term health care demand.

National Environmental Policy Act of 1969: consolidated programs dealing with air pollution, water pollution, urban and industrial health, and radiological health; established guidelines for environmental controls for projects involving the federal government; included a new mechanism of environmental impact statements before new projects are begun; allowed for citizen participation.

Amendments to the Clean Air Act of 1970 and 1977: allowed EPA to set ambient air quality standards, and set admission standards for plants with high pollution potential; set initial deadlines for auto emission standards.

Water Quality Improvement Act of 1970: established liability for oil spills and increased restrictions on thermal pollution from nuclear power plants.

Occupational Safety and Health Act of 1970 (OSHA) and amendments: created a strong standard setting authority vested in the Secretary of Labor to set a minimum level of protection for workers against specified hazards; intended to reduce demand for health care services by lowering the incidence of occupational and work-related diseases.

Environmental Pesticide Control Act of 1972: required registration of pesticides; gave authority to EPA to ban use of hazardous pesticides.

Safe Drinking Water Act of 1974: set standards for allowable level of pollutants and chemicals in public drinking water systems.

Toxic Substances Control Act of 1976: regulates chemical substances affecting health and the environment; provides grants to the states; included the development of a data system for research and regulation; banned manufacture and use of PCBs.

Resource Conservation Recovery Act of 1976 and amendments: development management and review plans for safe disposal of discarded material; regulates management of hazardous wastes.

Clean Water Act of 1977: created the best (conventional) technology standards for water quality by 1984.

Comprehensive Environmental Response, Compensation and Liability Act of 1980: established the federal superfund to clean up chemical dumps and toxic wastes.

Omnibus Budget Reconciliation Act of 1981: created block grants which reduced funding for consumers of health care; increased Medicare Part B deductible to decrease demand and eliminated several previously covered services; allowed states to eliminate Medicaid coverage for 18- to 21-year olds and reduced number of eligibles by tightening AFDC requirements.

Tax Equity and Fiscal Responsibility Act of 1982: included changes in both Medicare and Medicaid. For Medicaid: allowed enrollment fees, cost-sharing, and similar charges for some categories of recipients and services to lessen demand for services. For Medicare: added payments for some portions of hospice care to increase demand for hospice care.

APPENDIX 5

Selected Federal Legislation with Supply Components

Merchant Marine Seaman Act of 1798: provided for construction and maintenance of hospitals in selected port cities.

Merchant Hospitals Act of 1870: focused on staffing of merchant marine hospitals; extended the number of hospitals.

Commission Corps Act of 1899: hired physicians and other health personnel for public health services and merchant marine.

Public Health and Marine Service Act of 1902: coordinated supply of state and local public health officials.

Biologics Control Act of 1902: regulated the supply of biologically derived health products.

Food and Drug Act of 1906 (Wiley Act): regulated the supply of processed food products and drugs across state lines.

Vocational Educational Act of 1917 (Smith-Hughes Act): provided funds to establish early licensed practical nursing (LPN) programs.

Veterans Act of 1924 and amendments: extended medical care to veterans, not only for treatment of disabilities associated with military service, but also for other conditions requiring hospitalization; led to growth of VA hospitals and long-term care institutions.

Ransdell Act of 1930: created the National Institute of Health from the Hygienic Laboratory.

Title VI of the Social Security Act of 1935: authorized annual federal grants to states for investigation of the problems of disease and sanitation, leading to the creation of new local health departments.

National Cancer Act of 1937: created the National Cancer Institute and authorized research in NIH laboratories, grants to non-government scientists, and fellowships to train scientists and clinicians.

Federal Food, Drug, and Cosmetic Act of 1938 and amendments: strengthened the regulation of the supply of new drug, cosmetic, and therapeutic products for safety.

Public Health Service Act of 1944: provided funds for establishment of state and local health departments, for maintenance of marine hospitals, and for medical services for penal and correctional institutions; expanded the Commission Corps to nonphysician health professionals.

Hospital Survey and Construction Act of 1946 (Hill-Burton Amendment to the PHS): greatly expanded the supply of hospitals initially and later of medically related nonhospital facilities; provided funds through amendments for hospital modernization.

Mental Health Act of 1946 (amendment to PHS Act): included mental health problems in the grant-in-aid programs in the PHS Act, and established the National Institute of Mental Health.

Mental Health Study Act of 1955 (amendment to the PHS Act): authorized grants to facilitate a research program into methods and resources for care of the mentally ill.

Health Amendments Act of 1956 to the Public Health Service Act: authorized traineeships for public health personnel and for the advanced training of nurses; added special project grants dealing with problems of state mental hospitals.

Amendments of 1958 to Public Health Service Act (PL-85-544): established a program of formula grants to schools of public health.

Health Professions Education Assistance Act of 1963 (amendment to the PHS Act): provided construction grants for facilities that train physicians, nurses, dentists, podiatrists, pharmacists, and public health personnel and student loan funds to schools of medicine and osteopathy; later amendments extended loan funds to a variety of health and allied health professions.

Mental Retardation Facilities and Community Mental Health Centers Construction Act of 1963 (amendment to the PHS Act): added mental retardation services into previous grant and facilities construction programs. The 1965 amendments provided personnel grants to staff community mental health centers. The 1968 amendments added grants to construct and staff alcoholism programs. The 1970 amendments extended alcoholic and narcotic addiction services and included drug abuse and drug dependence; added child mental health services. The 1970 and 1975 amendments included developmental disabilities and other neurological handicapping conditions.

Economic Opportunity Act of 1964 (Antipoverty Program): OEO neighborhood health centers were established through community action provisions.

Nurse Training Act of 1964 (amendment to PHS Act): authorized separate funding for construction grants for schools of nursing with associate degree and diploma programs; established student loan funds at schools of nursing.

Federal Water Pollution Control Act Amendments of 1965 and amendments: switched enforcement responsibilities for water control from the Department of Interior to DHEW and required states to set standards for water quality. The 1972 amendments set national, rather than state, standards for both water quality and sewage treatment. Subsequent amendments strengthened the standards; included training and scholarship monies for environmental health workers.

Health Professions Educational Assistance Amendments of 1965: authorized basic improvement (institutional grants), special improvement grants, and scholarship grants to schools of medicine, dentistry, osteopathy, optometry, and podiatry; authorized scholarship grants to schools of pharmacy; expanded student loan program.

Heart Disease, Cancer, and Stroke Amendments of 1965 to the Public Health Service Act (Regional Medical Program): established regional cooperative programs among medical schools, hospitals, and other research institutions; developed programs of research, training, and continuing education in those three disease categories.

Comprehensive Health Planning and Public Health Service Amendments of 1966 (Partnership for Health): provided block grants to state health departments for discretionary use; included training monies for public health personnel with 15 percent specifically allocated to mental health personnel.

Allied Health Professions Personnel Training Act of 1966 (amendment to PHS Act): provided construction and improvement grants and traineeships for allied health professions; revised student loan program.

Health Manpower Act of 1968 (PHS Act amendment): extended and modified previous health manpower legislation.

Health Training and Improvement Act of 1970 (PHS Act amendment): provided institutional grants for new schools of health professions and special project grants for allied health.

Communicable Disease Control Amendments of 1970 (amendments to the PHS Act): reestablished categorical grant programs to control communicable diseases such as tuberculosis, venereal disease, measles, rubella.

Family Planning Services and Population Research Act of 1970 (amendment to the PHS Act): authorized monies for family planning programs and services, except abortion.

Emergency Health Personnel Act of 1970 (amendment to the PHS Act): authorized the Secretary of HEW to assign commissioned officers and other health personnel in the PHS to areas in critical need of manpower; provided the statutory basis for the National Health Service Corps which sent physicians into geographic shortage areas in exchange for education loan forgiveness.

Comprehensive Health Manpower Training Act of 1971 (PHS Act amendment): complex series of amendments that replaced institutional grants with a new system of capitation grants; set up project grants and financial distress grants; revised loan and scholarship provisions.

Nurse Training Act of 1971 (PHS Act amendment): extended construction grant program, broadened special project grants, provided financial distress grants, provided capitation grants for nursing schools, and revised scholarship and loan programs. Extended in 1975 to include advanced nurse training/nurse practitioner programs; extended in 1979 to nurse anesthetists.

National Sickle Cell Anemia Control Act and National Cooley's Anemia Control Act of 1972 (amendments to the PHS): authorized grants and contracts for screening, treatment, counseling, and information related to these diseases.

Health Maintenance Organization Act of 1973 (amendment to the PHS Act) and amendments in 1976, 1978, and 1981: provided grants and contracts to determine the feasibility of and plan HMOs; provided grant contracts and loan guarantees for initial development and loans guarantees for initial operating costs; amendments provided loans for acquisition of facilities, equipment, and training of administrators and directors.

Emergency Medical Services Systems Act of 1973 (amendment to the PHS Act): established grants and contracts for the development and improvement of area emergency medical systems and for related planning.

National Health Planning and Resources Development Act of 1974; an amendment to the Public Health Services Act (PL-93-641): created a system of local and state planning agencies supported through federal funds; regulated funds for new capital expenditures and for renovations for health institutions; provided construction and modernization funds for inpatient and outpatient health institutions.

Health Professions Education Assistance Act of 1976 (PHS Act amendment): extended capitation and special project grants to schools of public health and health administration programs; broadened start-up grants, special project grants, and construction and traineeship grants; changed capitation grant prerequisites to emphasize primary care; placed some restrictions on entrance of foreign physicians into the United States.

Omnibus Budget Reconciliation Act of 1981: eliminated funding for new entrants into the National Health Service Corps; eliminated capitation funding for medical and nursing schools and reduced capitation funding for other health professional schools; closed or transferred authority for Public Health Service hospitals; discontinued planning and start-up funding for new HMOs; gave governors authority to eliminate local HSAs and cut federal HSA funding.

Tax Equity and Fiscal Responsibility Act of 1982: included changes in both Medicare and Medicaid. For Medicaid: tightened regulations on acceptable error rates and overpayments and made a number of changes in payment methodology. For Medicare: added payments for some portions of hospice care; made extensive changes in reimbursement methodologies for hospital related services under Medicare; began a shift to case-mix (diagnostic related groups) for reimbursements for most acute care hospitals; eliminated nursing salary cost differentials and private room subsidies; eliminated the lesser of cost or charge provision; made reimbursement changes for HMOs.

APPENDIX 6

Selected Federal Legislation which Promotes Equity

Merchant Marine Seaman Act of 1798: provides health service access to a previously uncovered merchant marine seamen.

Maternity and Infancy Act of 1921 (Sheppard-Towner Act): provided grants to states to plan maternal and child health services; had the effect of extending services to blacks.

Veterans Act of 1924 and amendments: extended medical care to veterans not only for treatment of disabilities associated with military service but also for other conditions requiring hospitalization; preference was given to veterans who could not afford private care.

Title V of the Social Security Act of 1935: provided grants to states for maternal and child health and child welfare services and for services to crippled children.

Public Health Service Act of 1944: extended services to inmates of penal and correctional institutions.

Hospital Survey and Construction Act of 1946 (Hill-Burton Amendments to PHS): promoted geographic equity by providing funds for hospitals in underserved areas; allocated disproportionate funds to low-income areas through a distribution formula partially based on per capita income; mandated recipient hospitals to provide some services to indigents.

Social Security Amendments of 1960 (Kerr-Mills Act): established a program of medical assistance for the aged which gave payments to states for medical care for medically indigent persons 65 and over; state participation was optional, with only 25 states participating; federal participation varied from 50 to 83 percent of costs, according to the per capita income in the state.

Health Services Act of 1962 for Agricultural Migratory Workers (amendment to the PHS Act): established a program of grants for family clinics and other health services for migrant workers.

Amendments to Title V of the Social Security Act in 1963, 1965, and 1967: added special project grants for maternity and infant care for low-income mothers and infants; comprehensive services for low-income children and youth; added special project grants for child dental services.

Mental Retardation Facilities and Community Mental Health Centers Construction Act of 1963 (amendment to the PHS Act): provided construction monies for community facilities for the mentally retarded and for community mental health centers; provided a higher federal match rate for states with lower per capita income; 1970 amendments included special provisions to encourage grants in poverty areas.

Economic Opportunity Act of 1964 (Antipoverty Program): OEO neighborhood health centers were established through community action provisions; emphasis on provision of health care services in underserved low-income areas.

Health Insurance for the Aged of 1965 – Title XVIII of the Social Security Act (Medicare) and amendments: established a program of national health insurance for the elderly. Part A provided basic protection against the costs of hospital and selected post-hospital services; Part B was a voluntary program financed by premium payments from enrollees with matching federal revenues and provides supplemental medical insurance benefits. Amendments added patients who received cash payments under the disability provisions of the Social Security Act and later patients who required hemodialysis or renal transplants were included as disabled for Medicare.

Grants to the States for Medical Assistance Programs of 1965 – Title XIX of the Social Security Act (Medicaid) and amendments: created a federal-state matching program with voluntary state participation to partially replace the Kerr-Mills program. Participating states had to provide five basic services: inpatient and outpatient, other laboratory and x-ray, physician, and skilled nursing home services. States could include a number of other optional services; required and optional services changed with amendments; federal categorical welfare recipients were eligible; by option, states could include medically needy with incomes too high for cash federal welfare payments.

Comprehensive Health Planning and Public Health Service Amendments of 1966 (Partnership for Health): allocated discretionary block grant funds to state health departments according to a formula partially based on per capita income.

Family Planning Services and Population Research Act of 1970 (amendment to the PHS Act): authorized monies for family planning programs and services, except abortion; became a primary provider of family services for low-income women and adolescents.

Emergency Health Personnel Act of 1970 (amendment to the PHS Act): authorized the Secretary of HEW to assign commissioned officers and other health personnel in the PHS to areas in critical need of manpower; provided the statutory basis for the National Health Service Corps which sent physicians into geographic shortage areas in exchange for education loan forgiveness.

Occupational Safety and Health Act of 1970 (OSHA) and amendments: established strong standard-setting authority in the Secretary of Labor to set a minimum level of protection for workers against specified hazards; attempted to increase the safety for hazardous jobs to that of nonhazardous jobs and impacted disproportionately on blue-collar occupations.

Comprehensive Health Manpower Training Act of 1971 (PHS Act amendment): loan provisions were broadened to provide up to 85 percent cancellation for three years practice in shortage areas; increased scholarships for needy students and increased scholarship funds to schools enrolling higher numbers of low-income students.

Nurse Training Act of 1971 (PHS Act amendment): loan provisions were broadened to provide up to 85 percent cancellation for three years practice in shortage areas.

Health Professions Education Assistance Act of 1976 (PHS Act amendment): continued loan forgiveness for practice in shortage areas.

APPENDIX 7

Selected Federal Legislation Which Does Not Enhance Equity

Merchant Marine Hospital Act of 1870: maintained services to previously covered merchant marine seamen.

Commission Corps Act of 1899: hired physicians for on-going public health services.

Federal Quarantine Act of 1878 and amendments: prevented spread of diseases among general population.

Public Health and Marine Service Act of 1902: coordinated general public health services at the state and local levels.

Biologics Control Act of 1902: regulated general availability of biologically derived health products sold across state lines.

Food and Drug Act of 1906 (Wiley Act): regulated general availability of food and drug products shipped in interstate commerce.

Vocational Educational Act of 1917 (Smith-Hughes Act): provided federal funds for early licensed practical nursing (LPN) programs.

Ransdell Act of 1930: created the National Institute of Health and established health fellowships for researchers.

Title VI of the Social Security Act of 1935: authorized annual federal grants to states for investigation of the problems of disease and sanitation, leading to the creation of new local health departments.

National Cancer Act of 1937: created the National Cancer Institute and authorized research in NIH laboratories, grants to non-government scientists, and fellowships to train scientists and clinicians.

Federal Food, Drug, and Cosmetic Act of 1938 and amendments: strengthened the Food and Drug Act of 1906.

Venereal Disease Control Act of 1938: made venereal disease services more available.

Mental Health Act of 1946 (amendment to PHS Act): included mental health problems in the grant-in-aid programs in the PHS Act, and established the National Institute of Mental Health.

Mental Health Study Act of 1955 (amendment to the PHS Act): authorized grants to facilitate a research program into methods and resources for care of the mentally ill.

Health Amendments Act of 1956 to the Public Health Service Act: authorized traineeships for public health personnel and for the advanced training of nurses; added special project grants dealing with problems of state mental hospitals.

Water Pollution Control Act of 1956: created regulatory programs to combat water pollution; urged states to set standards for clean water.

Amendments of 1958 to Public Health Service Act (PL-85-544): established a program of formula grants to schools of public health.

Clean Air Act of 1963 and amendments of 1965, 1966, 1967, and 1969: urged states to set standards for clean air; established cooperative planning with states to set regulations to limit particulate pollution.

Federal Water Pollution Control Act of 1965 and amendments: switched enforcement responsibilities for water control from the Department of Interior to DHEW and required states to set standards for water quality; amendments established national rather than state standards which were subsequently strengthened.

Health Professions Education Assistance Act of 1963 (amendment to the PHS Act): provided construction grants for facilities that train physicians, nurses, dentists, podiatrists, pharmacists, and public health personnel and student loan funds to schools of medicine and osteopathy; later amendments extended loan funds to a variety of health and allied health professions.

Nurse Training Act of 1964 (amendment to PHS Act): authorized separate funding for construction grants for schools of nursing with associate degree and diploma programs; established student loan funds at schools of nursing.

Heart Disease, Cancer, and Stroke Amendments of 1965 to the Public Health Service Act (Regional Medical Program): established regional cooperative programs among medical schools, hospitals, and other research institutions; developed programs of research, training and continuing education in those three disease categories.

Health Professions Educational Assistance Amendments of 1965: authorized basic improvement (institutional grants), special improvement grants, and scholarship grants to schools of medicine, dentistry, osteopathy, optometry, and podiatry; authorized scholarship grants to schools of pharmacy; expanded student loan program.

Allied Health Professions Personnel Training Act of 1966 (amendment to PHS Act): construction and improvement grants and traineeships for allied health professions; revised student loan program.

Health Manpower Act of 1968 (PHS Act amendment): extended and modified previous health manpower legislation.

National Environmental Policy Act of 1969: consolidated programs dealing with air pollution, water pollution, urban and industrial health, and radiological health; established guidelines for environmental controls for projects involving the federal government; included a new mechanism of environmental impact statements before new projects were begun; allowed for citizen participation.

Health Training and Improvement Act of 1970 (PHS Act amendment): provided institutional grants for new schools of health professions and special project grants for allied health.

Communicable Disease Control Amendments of 1970 (amendments to the PHS Act): reestablished categorical grant programs to control communicable diseases such as tuberculosis, venereal disease, measles, rubella.

Water Quality Improvement Act of 1970: established liability for oil spills and increased restrictions on thermal pollution from nuclear power plants.

Clean Air Act Amendments of 1970 and 1977: established ambient air quality standards, strengthened automobile pollution standards, and set emission standards for high pollution plants.

National Sickle Cell Anemia Control Act and National Cooley's Anemia Control Act of 1972 (amendments to the PHS): authorized grants and contracts for screening, treatment, counseling, and information related to these diseases.

Environmental Pesticide Control Act of 1972: required registration of pesticides; allowed EPA to ban use of hazardous pesticides.

Health Maintenance Organization Act of 1973 (amendment to the PHS Act) and amendments in 1976, 1978, and 1981: provided grants and contracts to determine the feasibility of and plan HMOs; provided grant contracts and loan guarantees for initial development and loan guarantees for initial operating costs; amendments provided loans for acquisition of facilities, equipment, and training of administrators and directors.

Emergency Medical Services Systems Act of 1973 (amendment to the PHS Act): established grants and contracts for the development and improvement of area emergency medical systems and for related planning.

National Health Planning and Resources Development Act of 1974; an amendment to the Public Health Services Act (PL-93-641): created a system of local and state planning agencies supported through federal funds; regulated funds for new capital expenditures and for renovations for health institutions; provided construction and modernization funds for inpatient and outpatient health institutions.

Safe Drinking Water Act of 1974: set standards for allowable levels of pollutants and chemicals in public drinking water systems.

Toxic Substances Control Act of 1976: regulated chemical substances impacting on health and the environment; provides grants to the states.

Resource Conservation Recovery Act of 1976: developed management plans for safe disposal of discarded materials; regulated the management of hazardous wastes.

Clean Water Act of 1977: created best (conventional) technology standards for water quality by 1984.

Comprehensive Environmental Response, Compensation and Liability Act of 1980: created federal superfund to clean up chemical dumps and toxic wastes.

Omnibus Budget Reconciliation Act of 1981: repealed the entitlement to free care at Public Health Service hospitals of merchant seamen; reduced numbers of Medicaid eligibles and federal dollars to states for Medicaid; eliminated funding for new entrants for the National Health Service Corps.

Tax Equity and Fiscal Responsibility Act of 1982: increased cost sharing by Medicaid recipients; little expansion of eligibility for services; increased proportion of Part B Medicare Costs borne by recipient to 25 percent.

APPENDIX 8

Selected Federal Legislation with Preventive Components

Merchant Marine Seaman Act of 1798: goals included maintaining health of merchant marine seamen and prevention of epidemics through ports.

Merchant Marine Hospitals Act of 1870: codified preventive and acute care services for merchant marine seamen.

Commission Corps Act of 1899: was intended to facilitate control of epidemics and infectious diseases through maintenance of on-going public health services.

Federal Quarantine Act of 1878 and amendments: used quarantine laws to control spread of diseases.

Public Health and Marine Service Act of 1902: stimulated state and local public health disease campaigns against trachoma, typhoid fever, and pellagra.

Biologics Control Act of 1902: regulated preventive vaccines.

Food and Drug Act of 1906 (Wiley Act): designed to prevent illness from impure food and drug products.

Maternity and Infancy Act of 1921 (Sheppard-Towner Act): provided grants to states to provide maternal and child health services to prevent future health problems of children.

Ransdell Act of 1930: created the National Institute of Health from the Hygienic Laboratory which conducted research into etiology of diseases.

Title V of the Social Security Act of 1935: provided grants to states for maternal and child health and child welfare services and for services to crippled children, including services to children suffering from conditions which might lead to crippling.

Title VI of the Social Security Act of 1935: authorized annual federal grants to states for investigation of the problems of disease and sanitation, leading to the creation of new local health departments.

National Cancer Act of 1937: created the National Cancer Institute and authorized research in NIH laboratories, grants to nongovernment scientists, and fellowships to train scientists and clinicians.

Federal Food, Drug, and Cosmetic Act of 1938 and amendments: strengthened the Food and Drug Act of 1906.

Venereal Disease Control Act of 1938: made venereal disease services more available to prevent the spread of syphilis and gonorrhea.

Public Health Service Act of 1944: specified working relationships with state and local health agencies to prevent spread of communicable diseases; incorporated the preventive aspects of the Biologics Control Act; continued authority for the use of quarantines and inspections to control the spread of communicable diseases.

Water Pollution Control Act of 1956: created regulatory programs to combat water pollution; urged states to set standards for clean water.

Clean Air Act of 1963 and amendments of 1965, 1966, 1967 and 1969: urged states to set standards for clean air; established cooperative planning with states to set regulations to limit particulate pollution.

Mental Retardation Facilities and Community Mental Health Centers Construction Act of 1963 (amendment to the PHS Act): funded research on mental retardation; amendments funded drug abuse education programs.

Amendments to Title V of the Social Security Act in 1963, 1965, and 1967: added special project grants for maternity and infant care for low-income mothers and infants; comprehensive services for low-income children and youth; added special project grants for child dental services.

Economic Opportunity Act of 1964 (Antipoverty Program): OEO neighborhood health centers were established through community action provisions; included many preventive services such as family planning and well-baby care.

Federal Water Pollution Control Act of 1965 and amendments: switched enforcement responsibilities for water control from the Department of Interior to DHEW and required states to set standards for water quality; the act and amendments set and strengthened standards to prevent illness induced by water pollution.

Grants to the States for Medical Assistance Programs — Title XIX of the Social Security Act of 1965 (Medicaid) and amendments: created a federal-state matching program with voluntary state participation to partially replace the Kerr-Mills program. Participating states had to provide five basic services and could include optional preventive services; 1967 amendments required that states provide health screening services for Medicaid eligible children; later amendments required family planning services.

Comprehensive Health Planning and Public Health Service Amendments of 1966 (Partnership for Health): provided discretionary funds to state health departments which could be used for preventive purposes.

Water Quality Improvement Act of 1970: increased restrictions on thermal pollution from nuclear power plants.

Clean Air Act Amendments of 1970 and 1977: established ambient air quality standards, strengthened automobile pollution standards, and set emission standards for high-pollution plants.

Communicable Disease Control Amendments of 1970 (amendments to the PHS Act): reestablished categorical grant programs to control communicable diseases such as tuberculosis, venereal disease, measles, rubella.

Occupational Safety and Health Act of 1970 (OSHA) and amendments: established strong standard-setting authority in the secretary of Labor to set a minimum level of protection for workers against specified hazards; attempted to prevent occupational and work-related diseases.

Family Planning Services and Population Research Act of 1970 (amendment to the PHS Act): authorized monies for family planning programs and services, except abortion.

National Sickle Cell Anemia Control Act and National Cooley's Anemia Control Act of 1972 (amendments to the PHS): authorized grants and contracts for screening, counseling, and information related to these diseases.

Environmental Pesticide Control Act of 1972: required registration of pesticides and gave EPA authority to ban use of hazardous pesticides.

Health Maintenance Organization Act of 1973 (amendment to the PHS Act) and amendments in 1976, 1978, and 1981: provided grants and contracts to determine the feasibility of and plan HMOs; provided grant contracts and loan guarantees for initial development and loans guarantees for initial operating costs; originally required to offer family planning, infertility services, preventive dental and eye care for children; amendments removed dental care but added well-child care from birth and periodic health exams for adults.

Safe Drinking Water Act of 1974: set standards for allowable levels of pollutants and chemicals in public drinking water systems.

National Health Planning and Resources Development Act of 1974; an amendment to the Public Health Services Act (PL-93-641): created a system of local and state planning agencies to examine the total array of health care services and facilities in a community from preventive through long-term care.

Toxic Substances Control Act of 1976: regulates chemical substances impacting on health and the environment; provides grants to the states; banned manufacture and use of PCBs.

Resource Conservation Recovery Act of 1976: develops management plans for safe disposal of discarded materials; regulates the management of hazardous wastes.

Clean Water Act of 1977: created best (conventional) technology standards for water quality by 1984.

Title IV of the Health Services and Centers Amendments of 1978: deals with interests in disease prevention and health promotion; requires the secretary of DHSS to submit a national disease prevention profile to Congress every three years.

Comprehensive Environmental Response, Compensation and Liability Act of 1980: established a federal superfund to clean up chemical dumps and toxic wastes.

Omnibus Budget Reconciliation Act of 1981: increased preventive adolescent pregnancy-related services; decreased funding for other preventive programs by consolidation of categorical programs into block grants funded at a 25 percent reduction.

APPENDIX 9

Selected Federal Legislation with Acute Care, Recovery and Cure Components

Merchant Marine Seaman Act of 1798: provided care for sick seamen.

Merchant Marine Hospitals Act of 1870: continued acute care for sick seamen.

Biologics Control Act of 1902: regulated biological products used in acute care.

Food and Drug Act of 1906 (Wiley): controlled drugs used in acute care for impurities.

Vocational Educational Act of 1917 (Smith-Hughes Act): provided federal funds for licensed practical nursing (LPN) programs.

Maternity and Infancy Act of 1921 (Sheppard-Towner Act): provided grants to states to provide maternal and child health services.

Veterans Act of 1924 and amendments: extended medical care to veterans not only for treatment of disabilities associated with military service but also for other conditions requiring hospitalization.

Ransdell Act of 1930: created the National Institute of Health from the Hygienic Laboratory which conducted research on better ways to treat diseases.

Title V of the Social Security Act of 1935: provided grants to states for maternal and child health and child welfare services and for services to crippled children.

National Cancer Act of 1937: created the National Cancer Institute and authorized research in NIH laboratories, grants to nongovernment scientists, and fellowships to train scientists and clinicians.

Federal Food, Drug, and Cosmetic Act of 1938 and amendments: strengthened the Food and Drug Act of 1906.

Venereal Disease Control Act of 1938: made venereal disease services more available; treated active cases of syphilis and gonorrhea.

Public Health Service Act of 1944: facilitated provision of acute care by aiding the establishment of state and local health departments; continued marine hospitals and their services; extended medical services to penal and correctional institutions.

Hospital Survey and Construction Act of 1946 (Hill-Burton Amendment to the PHS): provided monies for construction and modernization of acute care hospitals.

Mental Health Act of 1946 (amendment to PHS Act): included mental health problems in the grant-in-aid programs in the PHS Act, and established the National Institute of Mental Health.

Mental Health Study Act of 1955 (amendment to the PHS Act): authorized grants to facilitate a research program into methods and resources for care of the mentally ill.

Health Amendments Act of 1956 (amendment to the PHS Act): added special project grants dealing with problems of state mental hospitals.

Social Security Amendments of 1960 (Kerr-Mills Act): established a program of medical assistance for the aged which gave payments to states for medical care for medically indigent persons 65 and over; state participation was optional, with only 25 states participating.

Health Services Act of 1962 for Agricultural Migratory Workers (amendment to the PHS Act): established a program of grants for family clinics and other health services for migrant workers.

Amendments to Title V of the Social Security Act in 1963, 1965, and 1967: added special project grants for maternity and infant care for low-income mothers and infants; comprehensive services for low-income children and youth; added special project grants for child dental services.

Mental Retardation Facilities and Community Mental Health Centers Construction Act of 1963 (amendment to the PHS Act): added mental retardation services into previous grant and facilities

construction programs. The 1965 amendments provided personnel grants to staff community mental health centers. The 1968
amendments added grants to construct and staff alcoholism programs. The 1970 amendments extended alcoholic and narcotic
addition services and included drug abuse and drug dependence;
added child mental health services. The 1970 and 1975 amendments included developmental disabilities and other neurological
handicapping conditions.

Economic Opportunity Act of 1964 (Antipoverty Program): OEO
neighborhood health centers were established through community action provisions, provided fairly comprehensive range
of acute care services.

Heart Disease, Cancer, and Stroke Amendments of 1965 to the
Public Health Service Act (Regional Medical Program): established regional cooperative programs among medical schools,
hospitals, and other research institutions; developed programs
of research, training and continuing education in those three
disease categories.

Health Insurance for the Aged — Title XVIII of the Social Security
Act (Medicare) and amendments: established a program of
national health insurance for the elderly. Part A provides basic
protection against the costs of hospital and selected post-hospital
services. Part B is a voluntary program financed by premium
payments from enrollees with matching federal revenues and
provides supplemental medical insurance benefits. Amendments
added patients who receive cash payments under the disability
provisions of the Social Security Act and later patients who
required hemodialysis or renal transplants were included as
disabled for Medicare.

Grants to the States for Medical Assistance Programs — Title XIX
of the Social Security Act (Medicaid) and amendments: created
a federal-state matching program with voluntary state participation to partially replace the Kerr-Mills program. Participating
states had to provide five basic services: inpatient and outpatient,
other laboratory and x-ray, physician, and skilled nursing home
services. States could include a number of other optional services; required and optional services changed with amendments.

Comprehensive Health Planning and Public Health Service Amendments of 1966 (Partnership for Health): provided discretionary
funds to state health departments which could be used for
acute care.

National Sickle Cell Anemia Control Act and National Cooley's Anemia Control Act of 1972 (amendments to the PHS): authorized grants and contracts for screening, treatment, counseling, and information related to these diseases.

Health Maintenance Organization Act of 1973 (amendment to the PHS Act) and amendments in 1976, 1978, and 1981: provided grants and contracts to determine the feasibility of and plan HMOs; provided grants, contracts and loan guarantees for initial development and loans guarantees for initial operating costs. Required to include basic inpatient and outpatient services, short-term mental health, medical treatment for alcohol and drug abuse, laboratory and x-ray services, and home health services.

Emergency Medical Services Systems Act of 1973 (amendment to the PHS Act): established grants and contracts for the development and improvement of area emergency medical systems and for related planning.

National Health Planning and Resources Development Act of 1974; an amendment to the Public Health Services Act (PL-93-641): created a system of local and state planning agencies to examine the total array of health care services and facilities in a community from preventive through long-term care.

Omnibus Budget Reconciliation Act of 1981: reduced funding for acute care services by consolidating categorical programs into block grants funded at 25 percent reduction; reduced number of Medicaid eligibles and federal Medicaid funds; eliminated some acute care services (alcohol detoxification, occupational therapy to qualify for home health services) in Medicare; closed Public Health Service hospitals.

Tax Equity and Fiscal Responsibility Act of 1982: one major emphasis was to modify payment structures for hospitals for Medicare.

APPENDIX 10

Selected Federal Legislation with Long-term Care and Preservation of Life Components

Veterans Act of 1924 and amendments: extended medical care to veterans not only for treatment of disabilities associated with military service but also for other conditions requiring hospitalization or long-term care.

Hospital Survey and Construction Act of 1946 (Hill-Burton Amendment to the PHS): through 1954 and 1961 amendments, provided funds for construction of nursing homes.

Health Amendments Act of 1956 (amendment to the PHS Act): added special project grants dealing with problems of state mental hospitals.

Health Insurance for the Aged — Title XVIII of the Social Security Act (Medicare) and amendments: established a program of national health insurance for the elderly; provided limited nursing home care of up to 100 days originally only following a period of hospitalization.

Grants to the States for Medical Assistance Programs — Title XIX of the Social Security Act (Medicaid) and amendments: created a federal-state matching program with voluntary state participation to partially replace the Kerr-Mills program. Participating states had to provide five basic services including skilled nursing services; states could offer intermediate care as an optional service.

National Health Planning and Resources Development Act of 1974; an amendment to the Public Health Services Act (PL-93-641): created a system of local and state planning agencies to examine the total array of health care services and facilities in a community from preventive through long-term care.

Omnibus Budget Reconciliation Act of 1981: made technical reimbursement changes in payments to nursing homes; reduced numbers of Medicaid eligibles.

Tax Equity and Fiscal Responsibility Act of 1982: extended to limited categories of services for hospice care; included some technical reimbursement changes for nursing homes.

BIBLIOGRAPHY

Acton, J. 1975. "Non-Monetary Factors in the Demand for Medical Services: Some Empirical Evidence." *Journal of Political Economy*. 83:595-614.

Aday, Lu Anne, Ronald Andersen, and Gretchen Fleming. 1980. *Health Care in the U.S.: Equitable for Whom?* Beverly Hills, Calif.: Sage.

Aday, Lu Anne, and Ronald Andersen. 1975. *Development of Indices of Access to Medical Care*. Ann Arbor, Mich.: Health Administration Press.

Aiken, Linda H., Robert J. Blendon, and David E. Rogers. 1981a. "The Shortage of Hospital Nurses: A New Perspective." *American Journal of Nursing*. 81:1612-18.

——. 1981b. "The Shortage of Hospital Nurses: A New Perspective." *Annals of Internal Medicine*. 95:365-72.

Allison, R. F. 1976. "Administrative Responses to Prospective Reimbursement." *Topics in Health Care Financing*. 3:97-111.

Andersen, Ronald. 1968. *Behavioral Model of Families' Use of Health Services*. Research Series 25. Chicago: Center for Health Administration Studies, University of Chicago.

Andersen, Ronald, Joanna Lion, and Odin W. Anderson. 1975. *Two Decades of Health Services: Social Survey Trends in Use and Expenditure*. Cambridge, Mass.: Ballinger.

Andersen, Ronald, and John Newman. 1972. "Societal and Individual Determinants of Medical Care Utilization in the United States." *Milbank Memorial Fund Quarterly – Health and Society*. 51:95-124.

Andrews, Richard N. L. 1976. *Environmental Policy and Administrative Change*. Lexington, Mass.: Lexington Books.

Arrow, Kenneth. 1963. "Uncertainty and the Welfare Economics of Medical Care." *American Economic Review*. 53:941-73.

Baker, F. D. 1976. "Prospective Rate Setting in Washington State." *Topics in Health Care Financing*. 3:57-81.

Bane, Frank (Chairman of the Surgeon General's Consultant Group on Medical Education). 1959. *Physicians for a Growing America*. Washington, D.C.: U.S. Government Printing Office.

Banta, David H., Anne Kesselman Burns, and Clyde J. Behney. 1983. "Policy Implications of the Diffusion and Control of Medical Technology." *Annals of the American Academy of Political and Social Science*. 468:165-81.

Beck, R. G. 1974. "The Effects of Copayment on the Poor." *Journal of Human Resources*. 9:129-42.

Berki, S. E. 1983a. "The Design of Case-Based Hospital Payment Systems." *Medical Care*. 21:1-13.

———. 1983b. "Health Care Policy: Lessons from the Past and Issues of the Future." *Annals of the American Academy of Political and Social Science*. 468:231-46.

Berkman, L. F., and S. L. Syme. 1979. "Social Networks, Host Resistance, and Mortality — A Nine Year Follow-Up Study of Alameda County Residents." *American Journal of Epidemiology*. 109:186-204.

Bice, Thomas W. 1980. "Health Services Planning and Regulation." *Introduction to Health Services*, edited by Stephen J. Williams and Paul R. Torrens. New York: John Wiley and Sons.

"Billion-Dollar Election." 1982. *Newsweek*. November 8, 1982, pp. 30-32.

Blanpain, J., L. Delesie, and H. Nys. 1978. *National Health Insurance and Health Resources: The European Experience*. Cambridge Mass.: Harvard University Press.

Blumberg, Mark S. 1979. "Provider Price Changes for Improved Health Care Use." *Health Handbook*, edited by George K. Chacko. Amsterdam: North Holland.

Boskin, Michael J., and Aaron Wildavsky. 1982. "The Worst of Times/the Best of Times in Budgeting." *The Federal Budget: Economics and Politics*, edited by Michael J. Boskin and Aaron Wildavsky. San Francisco: Institute for Contemporary Studies.

Boulding, Kenneth E. 1973. "The Concept of Need for Health Services." *Economic Aspects of Health Care*. New York: Prodist.

Broida, J., M. Lerner, and F. N. Lohrenz. 1975. "Impact of Membership in an Enrolled Prepaid Population on Utilization of Health Services in a Group Practice." *New England Journal of Medicine*. 292:780-83.

Brown, D., and H. Lapan. 1979. "The Supply of Physicians' Services." *Economic Inquiry*. 17:269-79.

Brown, Lawrence D. 1983. "The Prospects for Prospective Payment." *Journal of Health Politics, Policy, and Law*. 7:987-95.

Bunker, J. P., 1970. "A Comparison of Operations and Surgeons in U.S. and in England and Wales." *New England Journal of Medicine*. 282:135-44.

Bunker, J., and B. Brown. 1974. "The Physician-Patient as an Informed Consumer of Surgical Services." *New England Journal of Medicine*. 290:1051-55.

Burch, J. 1972. "Recent Bereavement in Relation to Suicide." *Journal of Psychosomatic Medicine*. 16:361-66.

Burney, I. L., G. J. Scheiber, M. O. Blaxell, and J. R. Gabel. 1978. "Geographic Variations in Physicians' Fees: Payments to Physicians Under Medicare and Medicaid." *Journal of the American Medical Association*. 240:1368-71.

Burns, James MacGregor, J. W. Peltason, and Thomas E. Cronin. 1981. *Government by the People*. 11th ed. Englewood Cliffs, N.J.: Prentice-Hall.

Campbell, Angus, Philip E. Converse, Warren E. Miller, and Donald E. Stokes. 1960. *The American Voter*. New York: John Wiley and Sons.

Center for Disease Control. 1978. *Data from the U.S. Immunization Survey*. Washington, D.C.: Government Printing Office.

Chambers, W. N., and M. F. Reiser. 1953. "Emotional Stress in the Precipitation of Congestive Heart Failure." *Psychosomatic Medicine*. 15:38-60.

Chelf, Carl P. 1981. *Public Policymaking in America: Difficult Choices, Limited Solutions*. Santa Monica, Calif.: Goodyear.

Chen, E., and S. Cobb. 1960. "Family Structure in Relation to Health and Disease." *Journal of Chronic Diseases*. 12: 544-67.

Chiswick, B. 1976. "Hospital Utilization: An Analysis of SMSA Differences in Occupancy Rates, Admission Rates, and Bed Rates." *Explorations in Economic Research*. 3:326-78.

Cobb, Sydney. 1976. "Social Support as a Moderator of Life Stress." *Psychosomatic Medicine*. 38:300-14.

———. 1974. "Physiological Changes in Men Whose Jobs Were Abolished." *Journal of Psychosomatic Research*. 18:245-58.

Competition and Consumer Choice: National Health Care Legislative Proposals. 1981. Washington, D.C.: Blue Cross/Blue Shield Association.

Congressional Budget Office. 1981. *Medicaid: Choices for 1982 and Beyond*. Washington, D.C.: U.S. Congress.

Cooper, B. S., and D. P. Rice. 1976. "The Economic Cost of Illness Revisited." *Social Security Bulletin*. 39:21-36.

Council on Wage and Price Stability. 1976. *The Complex Puzzle of Rising Health Care Costs*. Washington, D.C.: Executive Office of the President.

Cowgill, Donald O. 1974. "The Aging of Populations and Societies." *Annals of the American Academy of Political and Social Science*. 415:1-18.

Cromwell, Jerry, and James Kanak. 1982. "The Effects of Prospective Reimbursement Programs on Hospital Adoption and Service Sharing." *Health Care Financing Review*. 4:67-88.

Dahl, Robert A., and Charles E. Lindblom. 1953. *Politics, Economics, and Welfare*. New York: Harper.

Davis, Karen. 1973. "Hospital Costs and Medicare Program." *Social Security Bulletin*. 36:1-9.

Davis, Karen, Marsha Gold, and Diane Makuc. 1981. "Access to Health Care for the Poor: Does the Gap Remain?" *Annual Review of Public Health*. 2:150-82.

Davis, Karen, and Cathy Schoen. 1978. *Health and the War on Poverty: A Ten Year Appraisal*. Washington, D.C.: Brookings Institution.

Davis, Karen, and R. Reynolds. 1976. "The Impact of Medicare and Medicaid on Access to Medical Care." *The Role of Health Insurance in the Health*

Services Sector, edited by R. M. Rosett. New York: National Bureau of Economic Research.

Davis, Karen, and Louise Russell. 1972. "The Substitution of Hospital Outpatient Care for Inpatient Care." *Review of Economics and Statistics.* 54:109-20.

Demkovich, Linda E. 1981. "The Nurse Shortage: Do We Need to Train More or Just Put Them to Work." *National Journal.* 9:837-40.

Detsky, Allan S. 1978. *The Economic Foundations of National Health Policy.* Cambridge, Mass.: Ballinger.

Dodd, Lawrence C., and Richard L. Schott. 1979. *Congress and the Administrative State.* New York: John Wiley and Sons.

Dodd, Lawrence C., and Bruce I. Oppenheimer, eds. 1977. *Congress Reconsidered.* New York: Praeger.

Donabedian, Avedis B. 1969. "An Evaluation of Prepaid Group Practice." *Inquiry.* 6:3-27.

Donovan, L. 1980. "Survey of Nursing Incomes. Part 2. What Increases Income Most?" *RN.* 43:27-30.

Dowling, W. L. 1976. "Prospective Rate Setting: Concept and Practice." *Topics in Health Care Financing.* 3:7-37.

_____. 1974. "Prospective Reimbursement of Hospitals." *Inquiry.* 11:163-80.

Downs, Anthony. 1967. *Inside Bureaucracy.* Boston: Little, Brown.

_____. 1957. *An Economic Theory of Democracy.* New York: Harper & Row.

Drew, Elizabeth. 1982a. "Politics and Money – Part I." *The New Yorker*, December 6, 1982, pp. 54-149.

_____. 1982b. "Politics and Money – Part II." *The New Yorker*, December 13, 1982, pp. 57-111.

Dubos, Rene. 1959. *The Mirage of Health.* New York: Harper & Row.

Dutton, Diana. 1980. "Children's Health Care: The Myth of Equal Access."

Vol. 4, *Background Papers, Better Health for Our Children: A National Strategy, the Report of the Select Panel for the Promotion of Child Health.* Washington, D.C.: U.S. Department of Health and Human Services.

Eastaugh, Steven R. 1981. *Medical Economics and Health Care Finance.* Boston: Auburn House.

Egbert, L. D., G. E. Battib, C. E. Welch, and M. K. Bartlett. 1964. "Reduction of Post-Operative Pain by Encouragement and Instruction of Patients." *New England Journal of Medicine.* 270:825-27.

Ensminger, B. 1976. "The Eight Billion Dollar Hospital Bed Overrun." *Public Citizens Health Research Group Report.*

Enterline, P. E., V. Salter, A. D. McDonald, and J. C. McDonald. 1973. "The Distribution of Medical Services Before and After 'Free' Medical Care — The Quebec Experience." *New England Journal of Medicine.* 289:1174-78.

Enthoven, Alain C. 1980. *Health Plan: The Only Practical Solution to the Soaring Costs of Medical Care.* Reading, Mass.: Addison-Wesley.

——. 1978a. "Consumer Choice Health Plan: Inflation and Inequity in Health Care Today: Alternatives for Cost Control and an Analysis of Proposals for National Health Insurance." *New England Journal of Medicine.* 298: 650-58.

——. 1978b. "Consumer Choice Health Plan: A National Health Insurance Proposal Based on Regulated Competition in the Private Sector." *New England Journal of Medicine.* 298:709-20.

Evans, R. 1974. "Supplier Induced Demand: Some Empirical Evidence and Implications." *The Economics of Health and Medical Care,* edited by M. Perlman. New York: John Wiley and Sons.

Facts About Nursing, 1972-1973. 1973. Kansas City, Missouri: American Nurses Association.

Falk, I. S. 1983. "Some Lessons from the Fifty Years Since the CCMC Final Report, 1932." *Journal of Public Health Policy.* 4:135-61.

Feder, Judith, Jack Hadley, and John Holahan. 1981. *Insuring the Nation's Health: Market Competition, Catastrophic and Comprehensive Approaches.* Washington, D.C.: The Urban Institute.

Fein, Rashi. 1980. "Social and Economic Attitudes Shaping American Health Policy." *Milbank Memorial Fund Quarterly/Health and Society*. 58:349-85.

———. 1971. Testimony. Hearings Before the Subcommittee on Health of the Committee on Labor and Public Welfare. U.S. Senate, February 22 and 23. 92nd Cong., 1st sess., pt 1. Washington, D.C.: U.S. Government Printing Office.

———. 1967. *The Doctor Shortage: An Economic Diagnosis*. Washington, D.C.: Brookings Institution.

Feldstein, Martin. 1977. "Quality Change and the Demand for Hospital Care." *Econometrica*. 45:1681-1702.

———. 1973. "The Welfare Loss of Excess Health Insurance." *Journal of Political Economy*. 81:251-80.

———. 1971. "Hospital Cost Inflation: A Study of Nonprofit Price Dynamics." *American Economic Review*. 61:853-72.

———. 1970. "The Rising Price of Physicians' Services." *Review of Economics and Statistics*. 52:121-33.

Feldstein, Paul J. 1973. "Research on the Demand for Health Services." *Economic Aspects of Health Care*. New York: Prodist.

Feldstein, Paul J., and Glenn A. Melnick. 1982. "Political Contributions by Health PACs to the 96th Congress." *Inquiry*. 19:283-94.

Feldstein, Paul J., and Ruth Severson. 1964. "The Demand for Medical Care." *Report of the Commission on the Cost of Medical Care*. Chicago: American Medical Association.

Fenno, Richard F. 1973. *Congressmen in Committees*. Boston: Little, Brown.

Fesler, James W. 1980. *Public Administration: Theory and Practice*. Englewood Cliffs, N.J.: Prentice-Hall.

Flexner, Abraham. 1910. *Medical Education in the United States and Canada*. Report to the Carnegie Foundation for the Advancement of Teaching. New York: Carnegie Foundation Bulletin No. 4.

Friedman, Milton. 1962. *Capitalism and Freedom*. Chicago: The University of Chicago Press.

Fuchs, Victor. 1978. "The Supply of Surgeons and the Demand for Surgical Operations." *Journal of Human Resources*. 13 (supplement):35-56.

———. 1974. *Who Shall Live? Health, Economics and Social Choice*. New York: Basic Books.

Fuchs, Victor, and M. Kramer. 1973. *Determinants of Expenditures for Physicians Services in the United States, 1948-1968*. Paper Series, National Bureau of Economic Research.

Fuchs, Victor, ed. 1972. *Essays In the Economics of Health and Medical Care*. New York: National Bureau of Economic Research.

Gianfrancesco, Frank D. 1980. "Hospital Specialization and Bed Occupancy Rates." *Inquiry*. 17:260-67.

Gaus, C. R., and F. J. Hellinger. 1976. "Results of Prospective Reimbursement." *Topics in Health Care Financing*. 3:83-96.

Gibson, Robert M. 1980. "National Health Expenditures, 1979." *Health Care Financing Review* 2:1-36.

Gibson, Robert M., and Daniel R. Waldo. 1981. "National Health Expenditures, 1980." *Health Care Financing Review* 3:1-54.

Ginsberg, Eli. 1980. "The Competitive Solution: Two Views." *New England Journal of Medicine*. 303:1112-15.

GMENAC. 1980. *Graduate Medical Education National Advisory Committee Report to the Secretary DHSS*. 1: 1 (September):1-123.

Gornick, M. 1976. "Ten Years of Medicare." *Social Security Bulletin*. 4:3-21.

Griffiths, A., and Z. Bankowski. 1980. *Economics and Health Policy*. Geneva, Switzerland: Council for International Organizations of Medical Sciences and the Sandoz Institute for Health and Socio-Economic Studies.

Haber, L. D. 1966. "The Epidemiology of Disability: II. The Measurement of Functional Capacity Limitations." In *Social Security Survey of the Disabled, 1966*, U.S. Department of Health, Education, and Welfare, Social Security Administration. Washington, D.C.: U.S. Government Printing Office.

Hadley, Jack. 1982. *More Medical Care, Better Health? An Economic Analysis of Mortality Rates*. Washington, D.C.: Urban Institute Press.

Hale, George E., and Marian Lief Palley. 1981. *The Politics of Federal Grants.* Washington, D.C.: Congressional Quarterly Press.

Harris, L., and Associates Incorporated. 1978. *Health Maintenance.* Newport Beach: Pacific Mutual Life Insurance Co.

Health Care Financing Administration. 1982. *Health Care Financing Trends, March 1982.* Health Care Financing Administration (HCFA) Publication No. 03140.

Health PAC. 1971. *The American Health Empire: Power, Profits, and Politics.* New York: Vintage.

Hellinger, Fred J. 1978. "An Empirical Analysis of Several Prospective Reimbursement Systems." *Hospital Cost Containment: Selected Notes for Future Policy*, edited by M. Zubkoff, I. E. Raskin, and R. S. Hamft. New York: Prodist.

____. 1976. "Prospective Reimbursement through Budget Review: New Jersey, Rhode Island, and Western Pennsylvania." *Inquiry.* 13:309-320.

Hill, D. B., and J. E. Veney. 1970. "Kansas Blue Cross/Blue Shield Outpatient Benefits Experiment." *Medical Care.* 8:143-58.

Hochban, Jacquelyn, Bert Ellenbogen, Jan Benson, and Roger M. Olson. 1981. "The Hill-Burton Program and Changes in Health Services Delivery." *Inquiry.* 18:61-69.

Holahan, J., J. Hadley, W. Scanlon, and R. Lee. 1978. *Physician Pricing in California.* Washington, D.C.: Urban Institute Working Paper, Report 998-10.

Holden, Constance. 1981. "EPA Hard Hit by Budget Cuts." *Science.* 214: 306-7.

Horn, Susan D., Bette Chachich, and Cathy Clopton. 1983a. "Measuring Severity of Illness: A Reliability Study." *Medical Care.* 21:705-14.

Horn, Susan D., Phoebe D. Sharkey, and Dennis A. Bertram. 1983b. "Measuring Severity of Illness: Homogeneous Case Mix Groups." *Medical Care.* 21: 14-30.

Hornbrook, Mark, and John Rafferty. 1982. "The Economics of Hospital Reimbursement." *Advances in Health Economics and Health Services Research.* 3:79-115.

"Hospital Expenses Continue Decline in September 1982." 1983. *Hospitals.* January 16:59.

Iglehart, John K. 1983. "Medicare Begins Prospective Payment of Hospitals." *New England Journal of Medicine.* 308:1428-32.

———. 1982. "New Jersey's Experiment with DRG-Based Hospital Reimbursement." *New England Journal of Medicine.* 307:1655-60.

Institute of Medicine. 1976a. *Controlling the Supply of Hospital Beds.* Washington, D.C.: National Academy of Sciences.

———. 1976b. *Medicare-Medicaid Reimbursement Policies: Part 3, Volume 3.* Washington, D.C.: National Academy of Sciences.

Jacobs, Philip. 1980. *The Economics of Health and Medical Care: An Introduction.* Baltimore: University Park Press.

Johnson, D. 1980. "Multihospital System Survey." *Modern Healthcare.* 15:57-64.

Kane, R. L., J. M. Kasteler, R. M. Gray, eds. 1976. *The Health Gap: Medical Services and the Poor.* New York: Springer.

Kasper, Judith A., and Gerald Barrish. 1982. *Usual Sources of Medical Care and Their Characteristics.* National Health Care Expenditures Study Data Preview 12. Hyattsville, Md.: National Center for Health Services Research.

Kasper, Judith A., Daniel C. Walden, and Gail R. Wilensky. 1980. *Who Are the Uninsured?* National Health Care Expenditures Study Data Preview 1. Hyattsville, Md.: National Center for Health Services Research.

Keefe, William J., and Morris S. Ogul. 1977. *The American Legislative Process: Congress and the States.* 4th ed. Englewood Cliffs, N.J.: Prentice-Hall.

Kelly, T., and G. Schieber. 1972. *Factors Affecting Medical Services Utilization.* Washington, D.C.: Urban Institute.

Kitagawa, E. M., and P. M. Hauser. 1973. *Differential Mortality in the United States: A Study in Socioeconomic Epidemiology.* Cambridge, Mass.: Harvard University Press.

Klarman, Herbert E., and Helen H. Jaszi, eds. 1970. *Empirical Studies in Health Economics.* Baltimore, Md.: Johns Hopkins University Press.

Klaw, Spencer. 1975. *The Great American Medical Show*. New York: Viking Press.

Kleinman, Joel C. 1980. *NHIS Results by Income and Insurance*. Hyattsville, Md.: National Center for Health Statistics.

Kleinman, Joel C., Marsha Gold, and Diane Makuc. 1981. "Use of Ambulatory Medical Care by the Poor: Another Look at Equity." *Medical Care*. 19: 1011-29.

Kronenfeld, Jennie J. 1978. "Provider Variables and the Utilization of Ambulatory Care." *Journal of Health and Social Behavior*. 19:68-76.

Kronenfeld, Jennie J., Edgar D. Charles, John B. Wayne, Albert Oberman, Nicholas Kouchoukos, William J. Rogers, John A. Mantle, Charles E. Rackley, and Richard O. Russell. 1979. "Unstable Angina Pectoris: An Examination of Modes and Costs of Therapy." *Circulation*. 60: Part 2, I-11 – I-22.

Kukla, Steven F., and Henry J. Bachofer. 1983. "Building Up Reporting Systems." *Hospitals*. 57 (July 16):77-80.

Kutner, Nancy G. 1982. "Cost-Benefit Issues in U.S. National Health Legislation: The Case of the End-Stage Renal Disease Program." *Social Problems* 30:51-64.

LaLonde, M. 1975. *A New Perspective on the Health of Canadians*. Ottawa, Canada: Information Canada.

Lave, L. B., and E. P. Seskin. 1977. *Air Pollution and Human Health*. Baltimore, Md.: Johns Hopkins University Press.

Law, Sylvia A. 1976. *Blue Cross: What Went Wrong?* 2nd ed. New Haven, Conn.: Yale University Press.

Lee, Philip R., and Carroll L. Estes. 1983. "New Federalism and Health Policy." *Annals of the American Academy of Political and Social Science*. 468:88-102.

Lee, Philip R., Lauren LeRoy, Janice Stalcup, and John Beck. 1976. *Primary Care in a Specialized World*. Cambridge, Mass.: Ballinger.

Lee, Roger, and Lewis Jones. 1933. *The Fundamentals of Good Medical Care*. Chicago: University of Chicago Press.

Lerner, M., and R. N. Stutz. 1977. "Have We Narrowed the Gaps Between the Poor and the Non-Poor? Part II: Narrowing the Gaps, 1959-1961 to 1969-1971." *Medical Care*. 15:620-35.

Lewis, C. 1969. "Variations in the Incidence of Surgery." *New England Journal of Medicine*. 281:800.

Lewis, C. E., and H. Keairnes. 1970. "Controlling Costs of Medical Care by Expanding Insurance Coverage." *New England Journal of Medicine*. 282: 1405-12.

Lindblom, Charles E. 1977. *Politics and Markets: The World's Political-Economic Systems*. New York: Basic Books.

Link, C. R., S. H. Long, and R. F. Settle. 1980. "Medicare and Utilization of Health Care Services by the Elderly: New Evidence." Syracuse, N.Y.: Maxwell School.

Long, Michael J. 1981. "The Role of Consumer Location in the Demand for Inpatient Care." *Inquiry*. 18:266-73.

Lowrie, Edmund G., and C. L. Hampers. 1981. "The Success of Medicare's End-Stage Renal Disease Program." *New England Journal of Medicine* 305:434-38.

Luce, B. R., and S. O. Schweitzer. 1978. "Smoking and Alcohol Abuse, a Comparison of Their Economic Consequences." *New England Journal of Medicine*. 298:561-71.

Luft, Harold. 1978a. "How Do HMOs Achieve Their 'Savings'?" *New England Journal of Medicine*. 298:1136-43.

____ . 1978b. "Why Do HMOs Seem to Provide More Health Maintenance Services?" *Milbank Memorial Fund Quarterly/Health and Society*. 56:140-68.

Lynch, Thomas D. 1979. *Public Budgeting in America*. Englewood Cliffs, N.J.: Prentice-Hall.

Macridis, Roy C. 1983. *Contemporary Political Ideologies: Movements and Regimes*. 2nd ed. Boston: Little, Brown.

Madans, J., and J. C. Kleinman. 1980. *Utilization of Ambulatory Medical and Dental Services Among the Poor and Nonpoor*. Hyattsville, Md.: National Center for Health Statistics.

Manning, Willard G., Jr., Joseph P. Newhouse, and John E. Ware, Jr. 1982. "The Status of Health in Demand Estimation: Beyond Excellent, Good, Fair, and Poor." *Economic Aspects of Health*, edited by Victor Fuchs. Chicago: University of Chicago Press.

Marmer, Ted R. 1977. "Rethinking National Health Insurance." *Public Interest*. 46:73-94.

Mather, H. G. 1974. "Intensive Care." *British Medical Journal*. 2:322.

May, J. 1975. "Utilization of Health Services." *Equity in Health Services*, edited by Ronald Andersen, Jo Anna Kravits, and Odin Anderson. Cambridge, Mass.: Ballinger.

McClure, Walter. 1983. "The Competition Strategy for Medical Care." *Annals of the American Academy of Political and Social Science*. 468:30-47.

____. 1982. "Toward Development and Application of a Qualitative Theory of Hospital Utilization." *Inquiry*. 19:117-35.

____. 1981. "Structure and Incentive Problems in Economic Regulation of Medical Care." *Milbank Memorial Fund Quarterly: Health and Society*. 59:107-44.

McKeown, Thomas. 1979. *The Role of Medicine: Dream, Mirage or Nemesis*. 2nd ed. Princeton, N.J.: Princeton University Press.

McKinlay, Sonja M., and John B. McKinley. 1977. "The Questionable Contribution of Medical Measures to the Decline of Mortality in the U.S. in the Twentieth Century." *Milbank Memorial Fund Quarterly, Health and Society* 55:405-28.

Mechanic, David, and Linda H. Aiken. 1982. "A Cooperative Agenda for Medicine and Nursing." *New England Journal of Medicine*. 307:747-50.

Mills, R., R. B. Fetter, D. C. Riedell, and R. F. Averill. 1976. "AUTOGRP: An Interactive Computer System for the Analysis of Health Care Data." *Medical Care*. 14:603-15.

Monsa, G. N., Jr. 1970. "Marginal Revenue and the Demand for Physicians' Services." *Empirical Studies in Health Economics*, edited by H. E. Klarman. Baltimore, Md.: Johns Hopkins University Press.

Mundth, E. D., and W. G. Austin. 1975. "Surgical Measures For Coronary Heart Disease, Patients 1-3." *New England Journal of Medicine* 2:13-19.

Musgrave, Richard, and Peggy B. Musgrave. 1976. *Public Finance in Theory and Action*. New York: McGraw-Hill.

Mushkin, Selma J. 1974. *Consumer Incentives for Health Care*. New York: Prodist.

The Nation's Nurses: 1972 Inventory of Registered Nurses. 1974. Publication No. D/43. Kansas City, Missouri: American Nurses Association.

National Center for Health Statistics (NCHS). 1982 *Health United States, 1982*. Washington, D.C.: U.S. Government Printing Office.

National Center for Health Statistics (NCHS). 1981. *Health United States, 1981*. Washington, D.C.: U.S. Government Printing Office.

National Center for Health Statistics (NCHS). 1980. *Health United States, 1980*. Washington, D.C.: U.S. Government Printing Office.

National Center for Health Statistics (NCHS). 1979a. *Health United States, 1979*. Washington, D.C.: U.S. Government Printing Office.

National Center for Health Statistics (NCHS). 1979b. *Physician Visits: Volume and Interval Since Last Visit, United States, 1975*. Vital and Health Statistics Series 10, no. 128. DHEW Publication No. (PHS) 79-1556.

National Center for Health Statistics (NCHS). 1972. *Physician Visits: Volume and Interval Since Last Visit, United States, 1969*. Vital and Health Statistics Series 10, no. 75. DHEW Publication No. (HSM) 72-1064.

National Institute on Alcohol Abuse and Alcoholism. 1978. *Third Special Report to the U.S. Congress on Alcohol and Health*. DHEW Pub. No. (ADM) 78-569. Washington, D.C.: U.S. Government Printing Office.

National Institutes of Health. 1981. *NIH Almanac, 1981*. Washington, D.C.: U.S. Department of Health and Human Services.

Newhouse, J. P. 1978. "Insurance Benefits, Out-of-Pocket Payments, and the Demand for Medical Care: A Review of the Literature." *Health and Medical Care Services Review*. 1:3-15.

_____ . 1974. "A Design for a Health Insurance Experiment." *Inquiry*. 11:5-27.

_____ . 1970. "A Model of Physician Pricing." *Southern Economic Journal*. 37: 174-83.

Newhouse, J. P., W. G. Manning, C. N. Morris, L. L. Orr, N. Duan, E. B. Keeler, A. Leibowitz, K. H. Marquis, M. S. Marquis, C. E. Phelps, and R. H. Brook. 1982. *Some Interim Results from a Controlled Trial of Cost Sharing in Health Insurance*. Santa Monica, Calif.: RAND Publication Series R-2847-HHS.

Newhouse, J. P., and M. S. Marquis. 1978. "The Norms Hypothesis and the Demand for Medical Care." *Journal of Human Resources*. 13 (supplement): 159-82.

Newhouse, J. P., and C. E. Phelps. 1976. "New Estimates of Price and Income Elasticities of Medical Care Services." *The Role of Health Insurance in the Health Services Sector*, edited by R. Rossett. New York: Watson Academic.

_____. 1974. "Price and Income Elasticities for Medical Care Services." *The Economics of Health and Medical Care*, edited by M. Perlman. New York: John Wiley and Sons.

Newhouse, J. P., C. E. Phelps, and W. B. Schwartz. 1974. "Policy Options and the Impact of National Health Insurance." *New England Journal of Medicine*. 290:1345-59.

"Nursing and Nurse Education: Public Policies and Private Actions." 1983. Washington, D.C.: National Academy Press.

Patrick, D. L., J. W. Bush, and M. N. Chen. 1973. "Toward An Operational Definition of Health." *Journal of Health and Social Behavior* 14:6-23.

Pauley, Mark V. 1974. "Economic Aspects of Consumer Use." *Consumer Incentives for Health Care*, edited by Selma J. Mushkin. New York: Prodist.

Pauley, M., and Redisch, M. 1973. "The Not-for-Profit Hospital as a Physicians Cooperative." *American Economic Review*. 63:87-99.

Pearson, David A. 1976. "The Concept of Regionalized Personal Health Services in the United States, 1920-1975." *The Regionalization of Personal Health Services*, edited by Ernest W. Saward. New York: Prodist.

Perkoff, G. T., L. Kahn, and P. J. Haas. 1976. "The Effects of an Experimental Prepaid Group Practice on Medical Care Utilization and Cost." *Medical Care*. 14:432-49.

Peters, B. Guy. 1982. *American Public Policy: Process and Performance*. New York: Franklin Watts.

Phelps, C. E., and J. P. Newhouse. 1974. "Coinsurance, the Price of Time, and the Demand for Medical Services." *Review of Economics and Statistics*. 56:334-42.

——. 1972. "Effects of Coinsurance: A Multivariate Analysis." *Social Security Bulletin*. 35:20-28.

President's Commission for the Study of Ethical Problems in Medicine and Biomedical and Behavioral Research. 1983. Vol. 1, *Securing Access to Health Care: The Ethical Implications of Differences in the Availability of Health Services*. Washington, D.C.: U.S. Government Printing Office.

President's Commission on the Health Needs of the Nation. 1953. Vols. 1 and 2, *Building America's Health*. Washington, D.C.: U.S. Government Printing Office.

Raffel, Marshall W. 1980. *The U.S. Health System: Origins and Functions*. New York: John Wiley and Sons.

Rafferty, John. 1974. *Health Manpower and Productivity*. Lexington, Mass.: D. C. Heath.

Reinhardt, Uwe E. 1981. "The GMENAC Forecast: An Alternative View." *American Journal of Public Health*. 71:1149-57.

——. 1975. *Physician Productivity and the Demand for Health Manpower*. Cambridge, Mass.: Ballinger.

Reiser, Stanley J. 1978. *Medicine and the Reign of Technology*. Cambridge, Mass.: Cambridge University Press.

Renne, K. S. 1974. "Measurement of Social Health in a General Population Survey." *Social Science Research*. 3:25-44.

Reynolds, W. J., W. A. Rushing, and D. L. Miles. 1974. "The Validation of a Function Status Index." *Journal of Health and Social Behavior*. 15:271-88.

Ripley, Randall. 1983. *Congress: Process and Policy*. New York: W. W. Norton Co.

Ro, K. K., and R. Auster. 1969. "An Output Approach to Incentive Reimbursement for Hospitals." *Health Services Research*. 4:177-87.

Roemer, M. I., C. E. Hopkins, L. Carr, and F. Gartside. 1975. "Copayments for Ambulatory Care: Penny-wise and Pound-foolish." *Medical Care*. 13:457-66.

Rosenthal, Gerald. 1964. *The Demand for Medical Care Facilities*. Chicago: American Hospital Association.

Rosett, R. M., and L. Huang. 1973. "The Effect of Health Insurance on the Demand for Medical Care." *Journal of Political Economy*. 81:281-305.

Rossiter, Louis F. 1982. *Dental Services: Use, Expenditures, and Sources of Payment*. National Health Care Expenditure Study, Data Preview 8. Hyattsville, Md.: National Center for Health Services Research.

Rourke, Frances E. 1976. *Bureaucracy, Politics, and Public Policy*. 2nd ed. Boston: Little, Brown.

Samuelson, Paul A. 1973. *Economics*. 9th ed. New York: McGraw-Hill.

Saward, E. W., and M. R. Greenlick. 1972. "Health Policy and the HMO." *Milbank Memorial Fund Quarterly*. 50:147-76.

Scheffler, Richard M., and Louis F. Rossiter, eds. 1982. *Advances in Health Economics and Health Services Research*. Greenwich, Conn.: Aijai Press.

Schick, Allen. 1981. *Reconciliation and the Congressional Budget Process*. Washington, D.C.: American Enterprise Institute for Public Policy Research.

Schlenger, William E. 1976. "A New Framework for Health." *Inquiry*. 13:207-14.

Scitovsky, Anne A., and Nelda McCall. 1977. "Coinsurance and the Demand for Physician Services: Four Years Later." *Social Security Bulletin*. 40: 19-27.

Scitovsky, Anne A., and Nelda M. Snyder. 1972. "Effect of Coinsurance on the Use of Physician Services." *Social Security Bulletin*. 35:3-19.

Shapiro, S., J. J. Williams, and A. S. Yerby. 1967. "Patterns of Medical Use by the Indigent Aged Under Two Systems of Medical Care." *American Journal of Public Health*. 57:784-90.

Shyrock, Richard. 1947. *American Medical Research*. New York: Commonwealth Fund.

Sloan, Frank, 1976a. "A Micro Analysis of Physicians' Hours of Work Decisions." *Economics of Health and Medical Care*, edited by M. Perlman. New York: John Wiley and Sons.

_____ . 1976b. "Physician Fee Inflation: Evidence from the Late 1960's." *The Role of Health Insurance in the Health Services Sector*, edited by R. Rosett. New York: Watson Academic.

Sloan, Frank, J. Cromwell, and J. Mitchell. 1978. *Private Physicians and Public Programs*. Lexington, Mass.: Lexington Books.

Starfield, Barbara. 1982. "Child Health and Socioeconomic Status." *American Journal of Public Health*. 72:532-34.

Starr, Paul. 1982. *The Social Transformation of American Medicine*. New York: Basic Books.

"State Rate Controls: Documentation of the Bureaucracy's Imperfect Plan." 1978 (Dec. 11-13). *Federation of American Hospitals Review*.

Stevens, Rosemary. 1971. *American Medicine and The Public Interest*. New Haven, Conn.: Yale University Press.

Strickland, Stephen. 1978. *Research and the Health of Americans: Improving the Policy Process*. Lexington, Mass.: Lexington Books.

_____ . 1972. *Politics, Science, and Dread Disease: A Short History of United States Medical Research Policy*. Cambridge, Mass.: Harvard University Press.

Surgeon General's Report on Health Promotion and Disease Prevention. 1979a. *Healthy People*. Washington, D.C.: U.S. Government Printing Office.

_____ . 1979b. *Healthy People: Background Papers*. Washington, D.C.: U.S. Government Printing Office.

Taylor, Amy K. 1983. *Inpatient Hospital Services: Use, Expenditures, and Sources of Payment*. National Health Care Expenditures Study Data Preview 15. Hyattsville, Md.: National Center for Health Services Research.

Taylor, Amy K., and Walter R. Lawson. 1981. *Employer and Employee Expenditures for Private Health Insurance*. National Health Care Expenditures Study Data Preview 7. Hyattsville, Md.: National Center for Health Services Research.

Theriault, K. 1978. *The AUTOGRP Reference Manual*. Working Paper No. W-857. New Haven, Conn.: Yale University Center for Health Studies.

Thompson, Frank J. 1981. *Health Policy and the Bureaucracy: Politics and Implementation.* Cambridge, Mass.: MIT Press.

Thompson, John D., Richard F. Averill, and Robert B. Fetter. 1979. "Planning, Budgeting, and Controlling — One Look at the Future: Case Mix Cost Accounting." *Health Services Research.* 14:111-25.

Torrens, Paul R. 1978. *The American Health Care System: Issues and Problems.* St. Louis: C. V. Mosby.

U.S. Census Bureau. 1982. *Statistical Abstract, 1981.* Washington, D.C.: U.S. Census Bureau.

U.S. Department of Health, Education, and Welfare. 1977. *Health of the Disadvantaged: Chartbook.* Publication No. (HRA) 77-628. Washington, D.C.: U.S. Government Printing Office.

U.S. Department of Health and Human Services. 1981. *Supply and Characteristics of Selected Health Personnel.* Publication No. (HRA) 81-20. Washington, D.C.: U.S. Government Printing Office.

Usher, Robert. 1977. *Changing Mortality Rates with Perinatal Intensive Care and Regionalization.* Seminars in Parinatology. 1:309-19.

Vahovich, S. 1977. "Physicians' Supply Decisions by Specialty: TSLS Model." *Industrial Relations.* 16:51-60.

Vayda, Eugene. 1973. "A Comparison of Surgical Rates." *New England Journal of Medicine.* 289:1224.

Vladeck, Bruce C. 1980. *Unloving Care: The Nursing Home Tragedy.* New York: Basic Books.

Vladeck, Bruce C., and James P. Firman. 1983. "The Aging of the Population and Health Services." *Annals of the American Academy of Political and Social Science.* 468:132-48.

Walden, Daniel C. 1982. *Eyeglasses and Contact Lenses: Purchases, Expenditures, and Sources of Payment.* National Health Care Expenditures Study, Data Preview 11. Hyattsville, Md.: National Center for Health Services Research.

Wallace, Helen, Edwin M. Gold, and Allan C. Oglesby. 1982. *Maternal and Child Health Practices: Problems, Resources and Methods of Delivery.* 2nd ed. New York: John Wiley and Sons.

Ward, Richard A. 1975. *The Economics of Health Resources*. Reading, Mass.: Addison-Wesley.

Warren, Kenneth F. 1982. *Administrative Law in the American Political System*. St. Paul, Minn.: West.

Weber, Max. 1958. *The Protestant Ethic and the Spirit of Capitalism*, translated by Talcott Parsons. New York: Charles Scribner and Sons.

Weidenbaum, M. L. 1978. *The Costs of Government Regulation Business*. Washington, D.C.: Subcommittee on Economic Growth and Stabilization of the Joint Economic Committee, U.S. Congress.

Weisman, Carol S. 1982. "Recruit from Within: Hospital Nurse Retention in the 1980's." *Journal of Nursing Administration*. 12:24-31.

Weisman, Carol S., Cheryl S. Alexander, and Gary A. Chase. 1981. "Determinants of Hospital Staff Nurse Turnover." *Medical Care*. 19:431-43.

Wennberg, J., et al. 1975. "Evaluating the Level of Hospital Performance." *Journal of the Maine Medical Association*. 66:298-306.

Wildavsky, Aaron. 1979. *The Politics of the Budgetary Process*. 3rd ed. Boston: Little, Brown.

_____. 1977. "Doing Better and Feeling Worse: the Political Pathology of Health Policy." *Doing Better and Feeling Worse: Health in the U.S.*, edited by John H. Knolls. New York: W. W. Norton.

Wilensky, Gail R., and Marc L. Berk. 1982. "Health Care, the Poor, and the Role of Medicaid." *Health Affairs*. 1:93-100.

Williams, R. G. A., M. Johnston, L. A. Willis, and A. E. Bennett. 1976. "Disability: A Model and Measurement Technique." *Journal of Epidemiology and Community Health*. 30:71-78.

Williamson, John W. 1978. *Assessing and Improving Health Care Outcomes: The Health Accounting Approach to Quality Assurance*. Cambridge, Mass.: Ballinger.

Wilson, Florence A., and Duncan Neuhauser. 1982. *Health Services in the United States*. 2nd ed. Cambridge, Mass.: Ballinger.

Wolinsky, Frederic D. 1978. "Assessing the Effects of Predisposing, Enabling, and Illness Morbidity Characteristics on Health Services Utilization." *Journal of Health and Social Behavior*. 19:384-96.

World Health Organization. 1958. *The First Ten Years of the World Health Organization*. Geneva: World Health Organization.

Worthington, P. N. 1976. "Prospective Reimbursement of Hospitals to Promote Efficiency: New Jersey." *Inquiry*. 13:302-8.

Yankelovich, Skelly, and White. 1979. *The General Mills American Family Report, 1978-1979, Family Health in an Era of Stress*. Minneapolis: General Mills Inc.

Yelin, Edward H., Jane S. Kramer, and Wallace V. Epstein. 1983. "Is Health Care Use Equivalent Across Social Groups: A Diagnosis-Based Study." *American Journal of Public Health*. 73:563-71.

Yett, Donald D. 1970a. "Causes and Consequences of Salary Differentials in Nursing." *Inquiry*. 7:78-99.

____. 1970b. "The Chronic 'Shortage' of Nurses: A Public Policy Dilemma." *Empirical Studies in Health Economics: Proceedings of the Second Conference on the Economics of Health*, edited by Herbert E. Klarman. Baltimore, Md.: Johns Hopkins University Press.

SUBJECT INDEX

267

AUTHOR INDEX

ABOUT THE AUTHORS

JENNIE JACOBS KRONENFELD

Jennie Jacobs Kronenfeld is an associate professor at the University of South Carolina, Columbia, S.C. She teaches in the Department of Health Administration, School of Public Health. Until 1980, she was on the faculty at the University of Alabama in Birmingham.

Dr. Kronenfeld has published widely in the areas of public health and medical sociology. Her articles have appeared in the *Journal of Health and Social Behavior, Social Science and Medicine*, and the *American Journal of Public Health*. She has coauthored *Social and Economic Impacts of Coronary Artery Disease*.

Dr. Kronenfeld holds a B.A. in history and sociology from the University of North Carolina, Chapel Hill; and an M.A. and Ph.D. in sociology from Brown University, Providence, Rhode Island.

MARCIA LYNN WHICKER

Marcia Lynn Whicker is an associate professor at the University of South Carolina, teaching in the Department of Government and International Studies. Prior to 1978, she was on the faculties at Temple University in Philadelphia, and Wayne State University in Detroit.

Dr. Whicker has published in the areas of public administration and public policy. Her articles have appeared in *Journal of Policy Studies, American Sociological Review*, and *Legislative Studies Quarterly*. She coedited *Perspectives on Taxing and Spending Limits in the United States*.

Dr. Whicker holds a B.A. in political science and economics from the University of North Carolina, Chapel Hill; an M.P.A. in public administration from the University of Tennessee, Knoxville; and an M.S. in economics and an M.A. and Ph.D. in political science from the University of Kentucky, Lexington.